RAND McNALLY

Atlas of World Geography

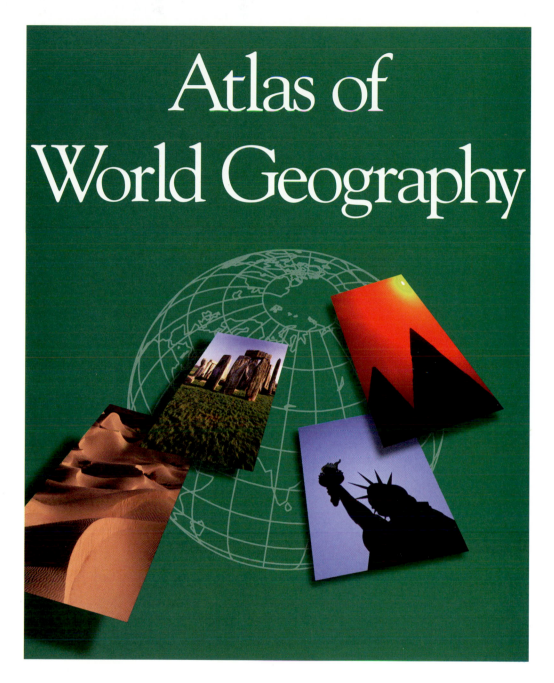

Saunders College Publishing
Special Edition

Executive Editor
Jon M. Leverenz

Editors
Brett R. Gover
Ann T. Natunewicz

Art Direction
John C. Nelson

Design
Donna M. McGrath

Cover Design
Brian C. Doherty

Design Production
DePinto Graphic Design

Cartographic Direction
V. Patrick Healy

Cartographic Staff
Robert K. Argersinger
Lynn Jasmer
Patty A. Porter
James A. Purvis
L. Charlene Smith
Stephen F. Steiner
James Wooden
David C. Zapenski

Research
Susan K. Hudson

Continental Thematic Maps
Thomas F. Vitacco
Marzee L. Eckhoff
Gwynn A. Lloyd
Robert L. Merrill
David R. Simmons
Ashley James Snyder
Barbara Benstead-Strassheim
Dara L. Thompson

Photo Research
Feldman and Associates, Inc.

Photograph Credits:

Comstock: front cover (r)

FPG International: © Jim Cummins, front cover (b); © Mark Scott, front cover (t)

H. Armstrong Roberts: © R. Kord, 7, 11 (b); © Zefa, 100; © M. Schneiders, 108; © Smith/Zefa, 150 (b)

© Randall Hyman: 101

© Wolfgang Kaehler: 135

Odyssey Chicago: © R. Frerck, 152

Tony Stone Images: © K. Wood, 9 (t); © Mark Segal, 68; © David Frazier, 69; © Jacques Jangoux, 98 (t); © John Warden, 98 (b); © Owen Franken, 110; © John Lamb, 122 (t); © Yann Layma, 134; © Paul Chelsey, 153

Information Credits:

Volcano data, pages 9, 12, and 16: Tom Simkin, Smithsonian Institution Global Volcanism Program

Earthquake data, page 17: Paula Dunbar, National Geophysical Data Center, National Oceanic and Atmospheric Administration

Australia information, page 18: Australian Tourist Commission

Much of the information on the destruction of the Amazonian rain forest, page 101, was provided by Fred Engel of the Center for Earth and Planetary Science, National Air and Space Museum, Smithsonian Institution, Washington, D.C.

Atlas of World Geography

Published and printed in the United States of America

ISBN: 0-528-17790-0

Table of Contents

4

Using the Atlas

Maps and Atlases

Today, satellite images (Figure 1) and aerial photography show us the face of the Earth in precise detail. It is hard to imagine how difficult it once was to ascertain what our planet looked like—even small parts of it. Yet from earliest history we have evidence of humans trying to depict the world through maps and charts.

Figure 1

Twenty-five hundred years ago, on a tiny clay tablet the size of a hand, the Babylonians inscribed the earth as a flat disk (Figure 2) with Babylon at the center. The section of the Cantino map of 1502 (Figure 3) is an example of a portolan chart used by mariners to chart the newly discovered Americas. Handsome and useful maps have been produced by many cultures. The Mexican map (Figure 4) drawn in 1583 marks hills with wavy lines and roads with footprints between parallel lines. The methods and materials used to create these maps were dependent upon the technology available, and their accuracy suffered considerably. The maps in this atlas show the detail and accuracy that cartographers are now able to achieve. They benefit from our ever-increasing technology, including satellite imagery and computer-assisted cartography.

Figure 2

In 1589, Gerardus Mercator used the word "atlas" to describe a collection of maps. Atlases have become a unique and indispensable reference for graphically defining the world and answering the question "Where?" Only on a map can the countries, cities, roads, rivers, and lakes covering a vast area be simultaneously viewed in their relative locations. Routes between places can be traced, trips planned,

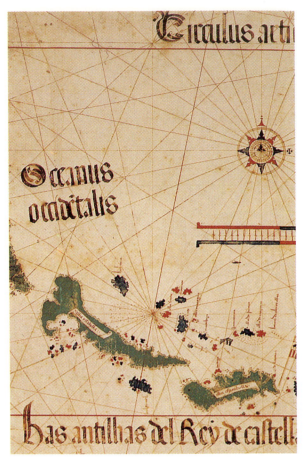
Figure 3

Figure 4

boundaries of neighboring states and countries examined, distances between places measured, the meandering of rivers and streams and the sizes of lakes visualized, and remote places imagined.

Getting the Information

An atlas can be used for many purposes, from planning a trip to finding hot spots in the news and supplementing world knowledge. To realize the potential of an atlas, the user must be able to:

1) Find places on the maps
2) Measure distances
3) Determine directions
4) Understand map symbols

Finding Places

One of the most common and important tasks facilitated by an atlas is finding the location of a place in the world. A river's name in a book, a city mentioned in the news, or a potential vacation spot may prompt your need to know where the place is located. The illustrations and text below explain how to find Lagos, Nigeria.

1) Look up the place-name in the index at the back of the atlas. Lagos, Nigeria can be found in the map on page 128, and it can be located on the map by its latitude and longitude, expressed in degrees: 7 North Latitude, 3 East Longitude (Figure 5).

La Fayette, In., U.S. 40N	87W	**90**
Lafayette, La., U.S. 30N	92W	**95**
Laghouat, Alg. 34N	3 E	**128**
Lagos, Nig. 7N	3 E	**128**
La Grande, Or., U.S. 45N	118W	**82**
LaGrange, Ga., U.S. 33N	85W	**92**
Lahore, Pak. 32N	74 E	**143**
Lahti, Fin. 61N	26 E	**116**

Figure 5

2) Turn to the map of Northern Africa on page 128. Note that the latitude appears in the right and left margins of the map, and the longitude in the upper and lower margins.

3) To find Lagos on the map, place your left index finger on the left margin at 7 degrees (between 5 and 10); and your right index finger in the top margin at 3 degrees East (between 0 and 5). Move your left finger across the map and your right finger down the map. Your fingers will meet in the area in which Lagos is located (Figure 6).

Figure 6

Figure 7

Measuring Distances

In planning trips, determining the distances between two places is essential, and an atlas can help in travel preparation. For instance, to determine the approximate distance between Paris, France and Amsterdam, Netherlands, follow these three steps:

1) Lay a slip of paper on the map on page 117 so that its edge touches the two cities. Adjust the paper so only one corner touches Paris. Mark the paper directly at the spot where Amsterdam is located (Figure 7).

2) Place the paper along the scale of miles beneath the map. Position the corner at 0 and line up the edge of the paper along the scale. The pencil mark on the paper indicates Amsterdam is between 250 and 300 miles from Paris (Figure 8).

3) To find the exact distance, make a second pencil mark at the 250-mile point of the scale. Then slide the paper to the left so that this second mark is lined up with 0 on the scale (Figure 9). The Amsterdam mark now falls at the third 10-mile point on the scale. This means that the Paris and Amsterdam are approximately 250 plus 30—or 280—miles apart.

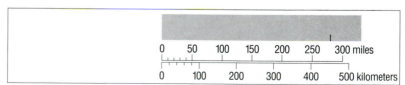

Figure 8

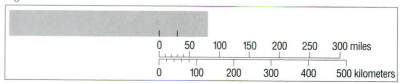

Figure 9

Determining Directions

Most of the maps in the atlas are drawn so that when oriented for normal reading, north is at the top of the map, south is at the bottom, west is at the left, and east is at the right. Most maps have a series of lines drawn across them—the lines of latitude and longitude. Lines of latitude, or parallels of latitude, are drawn east and west. Lines of longitude, or meridians of longitude, are drawn north and south (Figure 10, at bottom of page).

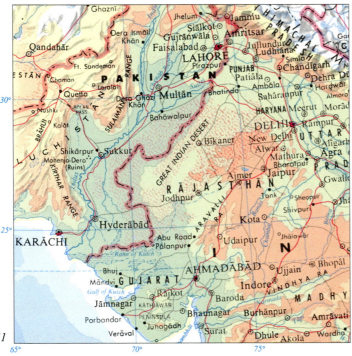

Figure 11

Parallels and meridians appear as either curved or straight lines. For example, in the section of the map of Southwestern Asia (Figure 11), from page 143, the parallels of latitude appear as curved lines. The meridians of longitude are curved vertical lines.

Latitude and longitude lines help locate places on maps. Parallels of latitude are numbered in degrees north and south of the Equator. Meridians of longitude are numbered in degrees east and west of a line called the Prime Meridian, running through Greenwich, England, near London. Any place on Earth can be located by the latitude and longitude lines running through it.

To determine directions or locations on the map, you must use the parallels and meridians. For example, suppose you want to know which is farther north, Karachi, Pakistan or Delhi, India. The map in Figure 11 shows that Karachi is south of the 25° parallel of latitude and that Delhi is north of it. Therefore Delhi is farther north than Karachi. By looking at the meridians of longitude, you can determine which city is farther east. Karachi is approximately 2° east of the 65° meridian, and Delhi is about 2° east of the 75° meridian. Delhi is farther east than Karachi.

Understanding Map Symbols

In a very real sense, every map is a symbol representing the world or part of it. It is a reduced representation of the Earth: each of the world's features —cities, rivers, etc.—is represented by a symbol. Map symbols may take the form of points, such as dots or squares (often used for cities, capital cities, or points of interest) or lines (roads, railroads, rivers). Symbols may also occupy an area, showing extent of coverage (terrain, forests, deserts). They seldom look like the feature they represent and therefore must be identified and interpreted. For instance, some of the maps in this atlas define political units by a colored line depicting their boundaries. Neither the colors nor the boundary lines are actually found on the surface of the Earth, but because countries and states are such important political components of the world, strong symbols are used to represent them. The Legend on page 51 of this atlas identifies the symbols used on the maps.

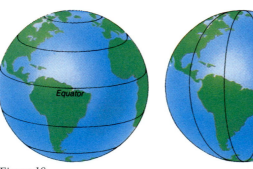

Figure 10

The Answer Section

Questions and Answers

World Superlatives, Facts, and Rankings

Questions and Answers

North America

Q What is the difference between "Central America" and "Middle America"?

A The term "Central America" refers to the North American countries which lie south of Mexico and north of Colombia: Belize, Guatemala, Honduras, El Salvador, Nicaragua, Costa Rica, and Panama. The Caribbean islands are not considered part of Central America. "Middle America" is comprised of Central America as well as Mexico and all of the Caribbean islands.

Q What is the largest U.S. city east of Reno, Nevada and west of Chicago?

Los Angeles, California

A Surprisingly, the answer is Los Angeles. Although Los Angeles is located on the Pacific Coast, it actually lies slightly farther east than Reno. The coast, which forms the western edge of the U.S., curves dramatically eastward below Cape Mendocino in northern California. San Diego, at the southern end of California's coast, is approximately as far east as the eastern borders of Washington and Oregon. *(Refer to map on pages 74-75.)*

Q Which is the southernmost U.S. state? The northernmost? The westernmost? The easternmost?

A Hawaii is the southernmost state; Alaska is both the westernmost and the northernmost. The question of which state is the easternmost is a bit problematic. Generally, Maine is considered to be the easternmost, since it extends farther east than any other state along the Atlantic seaboard. However, Alaska is technically the easternmost state, since the Aleutian Islands cross the 180° longitude line which divides the globe into eastern and western hemispheres. These islands sit at the eastern edge of the eastern hemisphere.

Q How many national flags have flown over Texas?

A Six. Spain (1682-1821), France (1685-1686), Mexico (1821-1836), the Republic of Texas (1836-1845), the United States (1845-1861), the Confederate States of America (from 1861 until the state was re-admitted to the Union in 1870), and the United States again (1870 through the present). Texas is the only U.S. state to have existed as an independent country.

Q What is the oldest city in the United States to be founded by Europeans?

A St. Augustine, Florida. Spanish explorer Juan Ponce de León, searching for the Fountain of Youth, landed nearby and claimed the area for Spain in 1513. The French established a colony on the site in 1564, but it was destroyed in 1565 by the Spanish, who then founded the present city. The oldest U.S. state capital is Santa Fe, New Mexico, which was founded in 1609, also by the Spanish.

Q What is Papiamento?

A Papiamento is a language which blends Dutch, Spanish, Portuguese, English, and Indian words. It is the principal language of Aruba and other islands in the Dutch Caribbean, and is spoken by an estimated 200,000 people.

Q If you were on a ship sailing from the Atlantic Ocean to the Pacific Ocean, in which direction would you be traveling as you passed through the Panama Canal?

A Southeast. The Pacific lies west of the Atlantic, and it would seem that a ship passing through the canal from the Atlantic would be sailing west. However, because of the twisting shape of the Isthmus of Panama, the canal's Pacific end lies south and east of its Atlantic end. *(Refer to inset map on page 96.)*

Q Into what body of water does the Colorado River empty?

A Currently, it doesn't empty into any body of water. Until recently, the river flowed into the Gulf of California. As the populations of water-poor Arizona and California have soared, more and more water has been drawn from the river for farms, industry, and homes. Today the Colorado is barely a trickle when it crosses the border into Mexico, and it disappears in the desert before it reaches the Gulf of California.

Q What is Canada's smallest province? Its largest?

A Prince Edward Island is Canada's smallest province, at 2,185 square miles (5,660 sq km). Canada's largest province is Quebec, which covers 594,860 square miles (1,540,680 sq km). The Northwest Territories represent the country's largest administrative division, spreading over an area of 1,322,910 square miles (3,426,320 sq km). If the Northwest Territories were an independent country, it would be larger than all but six of the world's countries: Russia, Canada, China, Brazil, the United States, and Australia.

Q What is the Continental Divide?

A An imaginary line running down the backbone of North America. Except for those which empty into the Great Basin and other basins, rivers to the west of this line flow into the Pacific Ocean, including its bays and gulfs; rivers to the east flow into the Atlantic or Arctic oceans, including their bays and gulfs. From northwest Canada south to New Mexico, the Divide runs along the crest of the Rocky Mountains, and in northern Mexico it follows the ridge of the Sierra Madre Occidental. All continents except frozen Antarctica have "divides."

Q Is Niagara Falls the highest waterfall in the world?

A Not even close. Niagara Falls' maximum drop of 167 feet (51 m) is surpassed by at least 22 waterfalls in North America alone. The highest waterfall in the world is Angel Falls in Venezuela, which spills 3,212 feet (979 m) from a flat mountain plateau. However, Niagara Falls ranks first in a different category: more than 210,000 cubic feet of water cascade over its edge each second, an amount nearly double that of any other waterfall.

Niagara Falls actually consists of two separate waterfalls: American Falls, at left, and Canadian (Horseshoe) Falls.

Q **What did ships do before the Panama Canal was built?**

A Before the canal opened, ships traveling between New York and San Francisco would sail 13,000 miles (21,000 km) around the entire continent of South America. When the canal opened in 1914, this journey was shortened to 5,200 miles (8,400 km). However, the canal is now too narrow for many of today's largest ocean-going vessels, so they must once again sail around South America to reach their destination. A project to widen the canal began in 1992.

Gatun Lake, Panama Canal

Q **What is the largest inland body of water in Central America?**

A Lake Nicaragua, which has a surface area of 3,150 square miles (8,158 sq km). Its only outlet is the San Juan River, which flows into the Caribbean Sea. Lying in a lowland region called the Nicaragua Depression, the lake was once part of the sea but became separated when the land began to rise. The freshwater lake is home to many species of fish usually found only in salt water, including sharks, tuna, and swordfish.

Q **Why does Minnesota have so many lakes?**

A During the height of the most recent Ice Age, glaciers moved southward from the Arctic regions to cover Canada and much of the northern U.S., including Minnesota. As they advanced, the glaciers scoured the landscape, gouging out countless depressions. When the Earth's climate grew warmer, the glaciers began to melt and retreat, and the depressions filled with meltwater to become lakes. Although Minnesota bills itself as the "Land of 10,000 Lakes," it actually has more than 15,000 lakes. Other areas of the world which experienced extreme glaciation, including parts of Europe and Siberia, also contain many lakes.

Q **What is the most popular U.S. national park?**

A Great Smoky Mountains National Park. Covering over 521,500 acres (211,200 hectares) in eastern Tennessee, the park receives approximately 9.1 million visitors each year. Arizona's Grand Canyon National Park has the second-highest visitor count: it receives around 4.6 million people annually.

Q **What two U.S. states share borders with the most other states?**

A Missouri and Tennessee, which each border eight other states. Missouri borders Iowa, Illinois, Kentucky, Tennessee, Arkansas, Oklahoma, Kansas, and Nebraska. Tennessee borders Kentucky, Virginia, North Carolina, Georgia, Alabama, Mississippi, Arkansas, and Missouri.

Q **How many U.S. states border only one other state?**

A One: Maine, which borders only New Hampshire. Two states, Alaska and Hawaii, border no others.

Q **What is the one place in North America where you can see both the Atlantic Ocean and the Pacific Ocean?**

A Irazú, a volcano in central Costa Rica. From its summit, both the Atlantic and Pacific oceans can be seen on a clear day.

Q **Where is the Yucatan Peninsula?**

A This thumb of land juts off of southeastern Mexico, separating the Gulf of Mexico from the Caribbean Sea. Yucatan was the center of the Maya civilization from about the first century B.C. through the tenth century A.D. Extensive Mayan ruins can be found at Chichén Itzá, Kabah, Mayapán, Tulum, and Uxmal. Near the town of Chicxulub at the northern tip of the peninsula, there is evidence of an enormous crater which is thought to be the point of impact of a meteorite 65 million years ago. The impact would have sent so much dust into the atmosphere that the sun's rays would have been blocked for months or perhaps years, lowering temperatures globally and possibly causing the extinction of the dinosaurs.

Q **What is the oldest capital city in the Americas?**

A Mexico City. The city originated as Tenochtitlán, the capital of the Aztecs, founded in the mid-1300s. By the early 1500s, the city had a population of perhaps 150,000, which was not only greater than any other city in the Americas but also greater than any European city at the time. In 1521, after a three-month siege, Spanish invaders under Hernán Cortés captured Tenochtitlán, razed the entire city, and founded Mexico City upon its ruins.

Q **What is the most densely populated country in North America?**

A El Salvador, which has a density of 650 people per square mile (251 per sq km). The U.S. ranks eighth, with 69 people per square mile (27 per sq km). Canada, the continent's largest country, is by far the least densely populated: it averages only 7.3 people per square mile (2.8 per sq km).

Q **What is the largest island in Caribbean Sea?**

A Cuba, the world's 15th-largest island. It has a land area of 42,800 square miles (110,800 sq km). The second-largest Caribbean island is Hispaniola, which covers 29,400 square miles (76,200 sq km) and contains the countries of Haiti and the Dominican Republic. Jamaica, measuring 4,200 square miles (11,000 sq km), is the third-largest Caribbean island.

Q **How many U.S. states have volcanoes that have been active in this century?**

A Four. Alaska has the most: 34 of its volcanoes, most of which are located on the Alaska Peninsula and the Aleutian Islands, have erupted since 1900. The other states with documented eruptions in this century are: Hawaii (3), Washington (1), and California (1).

Caldera and lava lake of Kilauea, on the island of Hawaii

Q **What is the only Caribbean island with large oil reserves?**

A Trinidad. The island's economy is based on oil, which accounts for about 80% of its exports. As a result of oil wealth, Trinidadians enjoy a higher standard of living than the people of most other Caribbean countries.

Q **Which U.S. state has the highest average elevation?**

A Colorado, with an average elevation of 6,800 feet (2,074 m) above sea level. However, the four highest peaks in the U.S. are found not in Colorado but in Alaska.

Questions and Answers

South America

Q What is Latin America?

A The term "Latin America" designates the parts of North and South America which were settled by Spanish and Portuguese colonists and still retain a Hispanic character. These include Mexico, Cuba, Puerto Rico, the Dominican Republic, some of the smaller islands in the West Indies, all of Central America except for Belize, and all of South America except for Guyana, Suriname, and French Guiana.

Q If you flew due south from Chicago, which South American country would you fly over first?

A You wouldn't fly over any South American countries. A straight line drawn south from Chicago passes through the Gulf of Mexico, Central America, and the Pacific Ocean. Point Parinas, Peru, the westernmost point of mainland South America, is about 500 miles (800 km) east of this line. The Galapagos Islands, which belong to Ecuador, lie about 75 miles (120 km) west of the line.

Q What percentage of the world's coffee beans come from South America?

A South America currently produces approximately 45% of the world's coffee beans. Brazil leads the continent, producing just under one-quarter of the world total. Another 16% are grown in Colombia. Coffee plants require hot, moist climates, and they yield the most flavorful beans when cultivated at elevations between 3,000 and 6,000 feet (900 and 1800 m). South America's principal coffee-growing regions are found in the Brazilian and Guiana Highlands, and in the valleys and foothills of the Andes.

Q What scientist made the Galapagos Islands famous?

A Charles Darwin, who visited the islands during his 1831-1836 expedition on the H.M.S. *Beagle.* Darwin's observations of how various animal species had adapted to life on the islands contributed to his ground-breaking theory of evolution, which he presented in the 1859 book *On the Origin of Species.*

Giant Galapagos turtle

Q Where are the Falkland Islands?

A In the Atlantic Ocean, about 275 miles (440 km) off the east coast of Argentina. The Falklands are a dependency of the United Kingdom, and nearly all of the residents are English-speakers of British descent. Argentina, which has asserted claims to the Falklands since 1816, invaded and occupied the islands in 1982. The U.K. sent a large task force that defeated the Argentineans in a war lasting less than a month.

Q What South American country is the longest when measured from north to south?

A Brazil. The country measures 2,725 miles (4,395 km) north to south, which is the approximate distance from New York City to Reno, Nevada. The second-longest country is Chile, with a length of 2,647 miles (4,270 km). In contrast to its great length, Chile measures only 235 miles (380 km) east to west at its widest point.

Q What was discovered in Venezuela's Lake Maracaibo in 1914?

A Oil. Maracaibo sits above one of the world's largest oil fields, and today the lake's surface is a thicket of oil derricks. Wealth from oil exportation has helped to make Venezuela one of the richest countries in Latin America.

Q What is Patagonia?

A Patagonia is a wind-swept plateau region occupying the southern third of South America, east of the Andes. The plateau receives little precipitation, and its only vegetation is scrubby grasses and thorny desert shrubs. The name "Patagonia" probably comes from the Grand Patagon, a dog-headed monster in a European romance called *Primaleon of Greece*. In 1592, the crew members of the ship *Desire* were attacked by a war-party of Tehuelche Indians wearing dog masks.

Q What South American city is the world's highest national capital?

A La Paz, Bolivia. The city sprawls across the floor of a deep canyon high in the Andes, at an elevation of 12,000 feet (19,350 km)—approximately the same height as the summit of Japan's Mt. Fuji. The canyon walls protect the city from the bitterly cold winds that whip across the surrounding plateau. Visitors from lower elevations often suffer from altitude sickness for several days until their bodies adjust to the thin, oxygen-poor air.

Q What is the southernmost city in the world?

A Ushuaia, Argentina, on the island of Tierra del Fuego. This city of 29,452 people lies at 54°48' south latitude, less than 700 miles (1,100 km) from Antarctica. The world's southernmost city with a population greater than 100,000 is Punta Arenas, Chile, located 150 miles (240 km) northwest of Ushuaia.

Q How many South American countries are named for famous people or cities?

A Three. Bolivia was named for Simón Bolívar, the revolutionary who helped to liberate much of northern South America from Spanish rule. Colombia takes its name from the explorer Christopher Columbus, who "discovered" South America in 1498 and sailed along the coast of present-day Colombia in 1502. The name "Venezuela" is Spanish for "Little Venice." When European explorers reached Lake Maracaibo in 1499, they found villages built on pilings over the shallow waters, which reminded them of Venice, Italy.

Q Why is South America sometimes referred to as "the hollow continent"?

A South America earned this nickname because most of its people live on or near the coasts; the interior is sparsely populated. Sixteen of the 20 largest metropolitan areas lie within 200 miles (320 km) of the coast. The continent's uneven population distribution has both a historical and a geographical explanation. Beginning in the 16th century, European colonists settled in the coastal regions from which raw materials were shipped back to Europe. The Amazon rain forest—hot, humid, and nearly impenetrable in places—has discouraged settlement of the northern half of the continent, and the Andes present a formidable barrier to eastward expansion from the Pacific coast. *(Refer to population map on page 99.)*

Q How many of South America's 20 longest rivers empty into the Pacific Ocean?

A None. South America's continental divide runs along the crest of the Andes at the continent's western edge. In most places the divide lies within 200 miles (320 km) of the Pacific coast. Rivers originating west of the divide have only a short distance to travel before reaching the Pacific. Rivers flowing east from the divide have nearly the whole expanse of the continent to cross before emptying into the Atlantic.

Q What South American city was the capital of the Inca empire?

A Cusco, Peru. The city was built by the Incas in the fourteenth century and served as their capital for 200 years until it was destroyed by Francisco Pizarro in 1533. Today, Cusco thrives as a major tourist attraction. Many of its houses and buildings are constructed on foundations of stone first cut by the Incas. Lying about 50 miles (80 km) northwest of Cusco is Machu Picchu, a well-preserved mountaintop Inca city, which was rediscovered in 1911.

Cathedral and rooftops in Cusco

Q What stretch of ocean off the South American coast is considered one of the most treacherous to ships?

A The Drake Passage. Approximately 500 miles (1,800 km) wide, this strait separates Cape Horn—at the southern tip of South America—from the South Shetland Islands which lie just north of Antarctica. First traversed in 1615, the passage was part of a major trade route between the Atlantic and Pacific oceans until 1914, when the Panama Canal opened. Frigid temperatures, rough waters, and high winds make the passage treacherous for all vessels but especially for the sailing ships of centuries past. Because the passage is so perilous, many ships avoid it by cutting through the Strait of Magellan to the north. However, this strait has its own dangers: it is narrow and twisting, and has been the site of numerous major shipwrecks.

Q Where is the Land of Fire?

A At the southern tip of South America. Tierra del Fuego, Spanish for "Land of Fire," is a group of islands lying south of the Strait of Magellan. When Portuguese explorer Ferdinand Magellan arrived in 1520, he named the islands after observing the native inhabitants carrying torches. The largest island, also called Tierra del Fuego, accounts for two-thirds of the land area of the island group. The eastern third of the islands belong to Argentina, and the rest belong to Chile.

Q What are the Nazca Lines?

A The Nazca Lines are gigantic drawings that were etched into Peru's desert floor by the Nazca people between 500 B.C. and A.D. 500. Scattered across 200 square miles (520 sq km), they form the world's largest display of art. The drawings fall into two categories: animal motifs and geometric patterns of crisscrossing straight lines. They were made by scraping away the top layer of red gravel to reveal the yellow sand below it. Archaeologists still disagree about the purpose of the Nazca Lines, but some theories hold that the lines formed ancient highways or were used as a giant calendar.

Q What is "El Niño"?

A El Niño is a seasonal ocean current that flows south along the Pacific coast of South America. The current takes its name—which is Spanish for "the Child"—from its usual arrival during the Christmas season. In normal years, when El Niño reaches northern Peru, southeasterly trade winds push its warm surface waters westward across the Pacific, away from the coast. Every four or five years, these trade winds weaken, allowing El Niño to travel farther south along the coast, raising local water temperatures by several degrees. This warmer water kills plankton and fish, crippling the fishing industry. Increased evaporation leads to excessive rainfall over parts of South America. The change in El Niño's normal flow pattern affects other ocean currents which often leads to dramatic climatic changes around the world.

Q How many of the Earth's species are found in the Amazon rain forest?

A Most of the Amazon basin has not been fully explored, and therefore most of its plant and animal species have not yet been catalogued. However, scientists estimate that the Amazon rain forest, which covers less than 5% of the Earth's total land area, contains almost one-half of the planet's animal and plant species. One in ten of the most common medicines we use today comes from rain forest plants, and scientists believe that cures for many diseases, such as cancer, might be derived from plant species not yet discovered.

Q Where in South America could you find places in which no rainfall has ever been recorded?

A The Atacama Desert in northern Chile. This barren land of sand, rocks, borax lakes and saline deposits is one of the driest regions in the world. In parts of the desert, no rainfall has ever been recorded, and the city of Arica, at the northern edge, endured more than 14 consecutive years of drought from October 1903 through January 1918.

Q What South American possession lies farthest from the mainland?

A Easter Island, situated 2,300 miles (3,700 km) west of Chile in the Pacific Ocean. This small volcanic island was discovered on Easter Sunday in 1722, and was annexed by Chile in 1888. Although it belongs to Chile, geographically Easter Island is considered to be part of Oceania, not South America. It is best known for its strange monuments: scattered over the island are more than 600 huge stone faces, the earliest dating back more than 1,500 years.

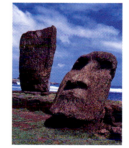

Ancient statues, Easter Island

Q Where are the pampas?

A These flat, grassy plains—which are much like the prairies of North America—are found in the temperate regions of southern South America, east of the Andes. The largest such plain, known simply as the Pampa, covers much of central and northern Argentina, and extends into Uruguay. Since the 1550s, when European colonists introduced cattle to the Pampa, livestock raising has been a thriving industry. For many people, gauchos, or Argentinean cowboys, are the enduring symbol of the Pampa, although in the last century farming has superseded cattle ranching in economic importance.

Questions and Answers

Europe

Q Where is the Black Forest?

A In southwestern Germany, between the Rhine and Neckar rivers. The Black Forest, or *Schwarzwald* in German, is a mountainous region that takes its name from the dark coniferous trees that cover its slopes. Its fertile valleys provide good pastureland and produce grapes for wine, and its trees supply the lumber and woodworking industries, as well as toy and cuckoo clock manufacturers. The region's scenic beauty, winter sports facilities, and mineral springs attract many tourists each year.

Q How many national capitals are located on the Danube River?

A Four. The capital cities of Bratislava (Slovakia), Budapest (Hungary), Belgrade (Yugoslavia), and Vienna (Austria) are all found along the banks of the Danube. Five other capitals are located on tributaries of the Danube: Bucharest (Romania), Sofia (Bulgaria), Ljubljana (Slovenia), Zagreb (Croatia), and Sarajevo (Bosnia & Herzegovina).

Old Town of Zagreb, Croatia

Q What is killing the forests of Northern Europe?

A Acid rain. In the atmosphere, airborne pollutants—especially sulfur and nitrogen dioxides from automobile and industrial emissions—adhere to water droplets, and then fall back to Earth as acidified rain, snow, or hail. This precipitation poisons plant and animal life, erodes buildings, and contaminates soil and drinking water. As a result of acid rain, as many as one-half of the trees in Germany's Black Forest and Switzerland's central alpine region are dead or dying. At least 4,000 lakes in Sweden are so acidic that no fish survive in them. To combat acid rain, the countries of the European Union recently agreed to significantly reduce nitrogen oxide and sulfur dioxide emissions.

Q What independent countries were once part of the U.S.S.R.?

A When the Union of Soviet Socialist Republics (U.S.S.R.) broke up in 1991, its 15 republics all became independent countries: Armenia, Azerbaijan, Belarus, Estonia, Georgia, Kazakhstan, Krygyzstan, Latvia, Lithuania, Moldova, Russia, Tajikistan, Turkmenistan, Ukraine, and Uzbekistan.

Q How many times has the name of St. Petersburg, Russia, changed in this century?

A Three times. St. Petersburg was founded in 1703 by Peter the Great. In 1914, its name was changed to Petrograd, Russian for "Peter's City," and then in 1924 it was changed again, this time to Leningrad, in honor of Vladimir Lenin, the founder of Russian Communism. In 1991, following the collapse of Communist rule, the city name was changed back to St. Petersburg. Older citizens joke about being born in St. Petersburg, attending school in Petrograd, working in Leningrad, and growing old in St. Petersburg—all while living in the same place.

Q What independent countries were once part of Yugoslavia?

A Prior to 1991, Yugoslavia was comprised of six republics: Bosnia and Herzegovina, Croatia, Macedonia, Montenegro, Serbia, and Slovenia. In 1991-92, four of the six republics—Croatia, Slovenia, Macedonia, and Bosnia and Herzegovina—declared their independence. Yugoslavia now comprises only two republics, Serbia and Montenegro.

Q What is the Chunnel?

A "Chunnel" is a nickname for the English Channel Tunnel, which connects England and France via rail under the English Channel. There are actually three separate tunnels: two for trains and a parallel service tunnel. The tunnels run for 31 miles between Coquelles, France, and Folkestone, England, at an average depth of 150 feet (46 m) below the seafloor. Work on the tunnels began in 1987, and the first trains crossed under the Channel in 1994.

Q Where is "Europe's Grand Canyon"?

A Along the Verdon River in the Provence region of southeastern France. The Verdon has carved a deep, narrow gorge, known as the Grand Cañon du Verdon, through the limestone plateau between the town of Castellane and the artificial Lac de Ste-Croix. The gorge stretches for 13 miles (21 km) and reaches a depth of 3,170 feet (965 m). It is considered one of the natural wonders of Europe.

Q What is the only volcano on the European mainland that has erupted in the 20th century?

A Mt. Vesuvius (Vesuvio), located in southern Italy nine miles (15 km) east of Naples. It has been active through much of the century, with significant eruptions in 1906, 1929, and 1944. Two thousand years ago, most Romans did not recognize Vesuvius as a volcano, and numerous farming communities thrived on the fertile land around its base. Then, in August of A.D. 79, the volcano exploded in a mighty eruption, burying the cities of Pompeii, Herculaneum, and Stabiae under cinders, ash, and mud, and killing more than 3,500 people.

Q How many European countries fall partially within the Arctic Circle?

A Four: Finland, Norway, Russia, and Sweden. Technically, a fifth country could be added to this list: Iceland's mainland ends just short of the Arctic Circle, but one of the country's islands, Grimsey, straddles the line, its northern half sitting within the Circle.

The historic Henningsvaer Port in the Lofoten Islands of Norway, north of the Arctic Circle

Q Where is Waterloo, site of Napoleon's famous defeat?

A Today, Waterloo is a suburb of Brussels, Belgium, although at the time of the battle—June 18, 1815—it lay 12 miles (19 km) away from the city, which was then much smaller. At Waterloo, the troops of French emperor Napoleon I were defeated by British forces under the command of the Duke of Wellington and Prussian forces led by Gebhard Blücher. The French defeat ended the Napoleonic Wars, which had begun in 1803.

Q Is Venice, Italy, really sinking?

A Yes, although at a much slower rate than earlier in the century. The city, which dates back to the 4th century A.D., is built on 118 small islands in a lagoon at the top of the Adriatic Sea. Its buildings sit on foundations of wooden pilings driven deep into the underlying sand, silt and clay. Originally the buildings were safely above high tide level, but over the course of 15 centuries, natural compaction of the sub-soil caused the city to sink more than 30 inches (76 cm). Earlier this century, groundwater was

Gondola and canal, Venice

pumped out of the subsoil to satisfy water needs on the mainland. This proved disastrous for Venice: the city quickly sank another five inches (13 cm) at a time when the sea level was rising by four inches (10 cm). The pumping was stopped, and Venice's sinking has slowed to its earlier "natural" rate. Unfortunately, the foundations of many buildings have been severely damaged by high water.

Q Which independent European countries are smaller than Rhode Island, the smallest U.S. state?

A Seven independent European countries cover a smaller area than Rhode Island's 1,545 square miles (4,002 sq km): Vatican City, Monaco, San Marino, Liechtenstein, Malta, Andorra, and Luxembourg.

Q How many official languages are recognized in Switzerland?

A Four: German, French, Italian, and Romansch. German is the most widely spoken language: 65% of the Swiss speak a dialect known as *Schwyzerdütsch*, or Swiss German. French is spoken by 18% of the population, Italian by 10%, and Romansch by only 1%.

Q Why is Ukraine called "the breadbasket of Europe"?

A Ukraine's topography—flat plains, or "steppes," cover most of the country—and extremely fertile soils combine to make it one of the world's most outstanding agricultural areas. In 1994, the country produced almost 36 million tons (33 metric tons) of grain. Major crops include wheat, rye, barley, corn, potatoes, sunflower seeds, sugar beets, and cotton. Ukraine also has thriving dairy and livestock industries, as well as many food-processing plants.

Q If the Caspian Sea is a *sea*, then how can it be the world's largest *lake*?

A Actually, it is both a sea *and* a lake. The word "sea" is used most often to designate specific regions of the oceans that are more or less surrounded by land; however, it can also apply to inland bodies of water, especially if they are large and/or salty. The Caspian Sea is both large and salty, so it is called a sea. "Lake" is a general term for inland bodies of water of substantial size. The Caspian Sea lies inland and has a surface area of 143,240 square miles (370,990 sq km), so it is also considered to be a lake. Other "sea-lakes" in the world include the Aral Sea, the Dead Sea, the Sea of Galilee, and California's Salton Sea.

Q Where is Transylvania?

A In northwestern Romania. The region is bounded by the Carpathian Mountains in the north and east, the Transylvanian Alps in the south, and by Romania's borders with Hungary and Yugoslavia in the west. A high plateau, averaging 1,000 to 1,600 feet (300 to 500 m) in elevation, covers much of Transylvania. In Bram Stoker's 1897 novel *Dracula*, Transylvania is the home of the blood-sucking Count. Stoker based the story on local vampire legends, many of which persist today: in some parts of eastern Europe, peasants still wear garlic necklaces and hang garlic wreaths from their doors to ward off vampire spirits.

Q What countries contain parts of the Carpathian Mountains?

A Five: the Czech Republic, Slovakia, Poland, Ukraine, and Romania. Curving for more than 900 miles (1,450 km) along the north and east sides of the Danube plain in central and eastern Europe, the Carpathians roughly form a half-circle connecting the Alps and the Balkans. The mountain system consists of two main parts: the Northern Carpathians, which include the Beskid and the Tatra ranges, and the Southern Carpathians, also called the Transylvanian Alps. The Carpathians' highest peak is Gerlachovský štít in Slovakia, which rises to 8,711 feet (2,655 m).

Q Where is Lapland?

A In northern Scandinavia. Lapland is home to the Lapps, a nomadic people who have traditionally engaged in hunting, fishing, and reindeer-herding. When the Finns arrived in the southern part of present-day Finland 2,000 years ago, they found the Lapps already settled there. Over the years, the Lapps have been pushed north, and their territory has expanded to cover parts of northern Norway, Sweden, Finland, and northwestern Russia. Today, there are approximately 42,000 Lapps, most of whom work in a variety of farming, construction, and service fields. The Finnish government has made many efforts to protect the Lapps' language, called Sami, and culture.

Q What European country has a shorter coastline than any other maritime country in the world?

A Monaco, whose Mediterranean coastline is a mere three-and-a-half miles (5.6 km) long. Another European country, Bosnia and Herzegovina, ranks second in this category: its coast on the Adriatic Sea between Croatia and Yugoslavia is only 13 miles (21 km) long. In third place is Slovenia, whose Adriatic coast is 29 miles (47 km) long.

Harbor and coastline, Monaco

Q What European city is the largest city in the world north of the Arctic Circle?

A Murmansk, Russia, a city of 472,900 people located on the Kola Gulf of the Barents Sea. Although Murmansk lies approximately 150 miles north of the Arctic Circle, its harbor remains ice-free throughout the year due to the moderating effect of a warm ocean current called the North Atlantic Drift. While there are thousands of cities and towns north of the Arctic Circle, there are none at all south of the Antarctic Circle at the opposite end of the world.

Questions and Answers

Africa

Q What is the East African Rift System?

A This term refers to a series of rift valleys running through East Africa from Mozambique to the southern end of the Red Sea. These valleys are part of the Great Rift Valley, a 4,000-mile (6,430-km)-long depression that also includes the Red Sea, the Dead Sea, and the rest of the Jordan Valley. The East African Rift System marks the line along which geological forces are splitting East Africa off from the rest of the continent. Eventually, everything east of the Rift System—including all or part of present-day Mozambique, Tanzania, Rwanda, Burundi, Uganda, Kenya, Ethiopia, Djibouti, and Somalia—will be a huge island off of Africa's eastern coast. Madagascar was attached to the African mainland before similar forces split it off into an island 175 million years ago.

Q What is the Serengeti?

A Located in northern Tanzania, east of Lake Victoria and west of Kilimanjaro, the Serengeti is a vast plain of grassland, acacia bushes, forest, and rocky outcrops.

Giraffes on the Serengeti

Serengeti National Park, established in 1951, covers an area of the plain about the size of Connecticut. The park is home to one of the last great concentrations of African wildlife, including antelope, buffalo, cheetahs, elephants, gazelles, giraffes, hyenas, leopards, lions, black rhinoceroses, wildebeests and zebras. Tourists from all over the world visit the park to observe the wildlife and to witness the large-scale animal migrations that occur in May and June.

Q How has the Aswan High Dam affected the Nile Valley ?

A Before the dam was built in 1971, floodwaters inundated the Nile Valley each fall, depositing fresh, fertile silt across the valley floor. This annual replenishment of the soil helped agriculture to thrive in the valley for thousands of years. The dam ended the annual floods, and now much of the Nile's water-borne silt settles to the bottom of Lake Nassar, the enormous artificial lake behind the dam. Water evaporating from the lake's surface has increased the regional humidity, which has accelerated the decay of many of the valley's great tombs and monuments. On the positive side, the dam supplies more than 25% of Egypt's hydro-electric power, and desert irrigation projects using water from Lake Nassar have created 900,000 new acres of arable land.

Q What is remarkable about the delta of the Okavango River?

A It is the largest inland delta in the world. The Okavango originates in the mountains of central Angola and flows 1,000 miles (1,600 km) to the northwest corner of Botswana, where it spills over the Gomare fault and fans out into a swampy delta covering 4,000 square miles (10,350 sq km). Meandering through a myriad of shallow channels, the waters of the Okavango quickly evaporate. The small amount that eventually emerges from the southeastern end of the delta represents less than 5% of the river's pre-delta flow.

Q What African country was previously known as Upper Volta?

A Burkina Faso. The Volta River's three upper branches —the Volta Blanche (White Volta), Volta Rouge (Red Volta), and Volta Noire (Black Volta)—all originate within the country, hence the earlier name. Burkina Faso, the Mossi-dialect name adopted in 1984, translates roughly as "Country of Honest Men."

Q What are the most important crops grown in Africa?

A Africa is the world's leading producer of cocoa beans (55% of the world total) and cassava roots (45% of the world total). It is also a major producer of grain and millet sorghum (27%), coffee (20%), peanuts (20%), palm oil (14%), tea (12%), and olive oil (12%).

Woman in sorghum fields, Bema

Q What object found along the banks of the Orange River in 1867 changed the course of South African history?

A A 21-carat diamond. The discovery of this gem near Hopetown precipitated a huge diamond rush, and thousands of people from all over the continent and the world raced to southern Africa. The town of Kimberley, site of the famous open mine known as the Big Hole, became the diamond capital of the world. Between 1871 and 1914, more than 14 million carats of diamonds were removed from the mine, which eventually reached a depth of 4,000 feet (1,220 m) and a width of one mile (1.6 km).

Q What is Cabinda?

A A coastal province of Angola that lies north of the Congo River and is separated from the rest of the country by a 19-mile (31-km)-wide corridor belonging to Zaire. Most of Cabinda's 2,807 square miles (7,270 sq km) are covered by tropical forest. Offshore lie rich oil fields which produce one million barrels annually.

Q What African country was founded in 1847 by freed American slaves?

A Liberia, whose name comes from the Latin word *liber*, meaning "free." It is the only country in sub-Saharan Africa that has never been ruled by a colonial power. Liberia's capital city, Monrovia, was named for James Monroe, the fifth U.S. president.

Q What two African countries border only a single other country?

A Lesotho and Gambia. Lesotho is surrounded entirely by South Africa. Gambia is bordered in the north, east, and south by Senegal; to its west lies the Atlantic Ocean.

Q What is the Ngorongoro Crater?

A Located in northern Tanzania, Ngorongoro is the crater of a volcano that has been extinct for several million years. It has a diameter of 9 miles (14.5 km) and its walls rise about 2,000 feet (610 m) above its floor. The crater supports an abundance of wildlife, including wildebeests, elephants, rhinoceroses, hippopotamuses, lions, leopards, and flamingoes. In 1956 Ngorongoro was established as a conservation area, but its ecological balance is threatened by growing numbers of tourists and the large cattle herds of the nomadic Masai people.

Q Why is it difficult to say how large Lake Chad is?

A The lake's size fluctuates dramatically throughout the year. Numerous rivers and streams flow into Lake Chad, but it has no outlet. During the summer rainy season, floodwaters swell the lake to 10,000 square miles (25,900 sq km) and occasionally to twice that size. Even at its maximum size the lake is extremely shallow; its greatest depth is only 25 feet (8 m). By the end of the following spring, evaporation has shrunk the lake by 60%, to about 4,000 square miles (10,360 sq km). In recent decades, Lake Chad's cyclical fluctuations have been greatly affected by recurring droughts, which have reduced the flow of water into the lake and accelerated evaporation. Its volume has dropped by 80% since 1970.

Q What is significant about the location of Khartoum, Sudan?

A Khartoum, the capital of Sudan, is located at the point where the White Nile and Blue Nile rivers meet to form the Nile. Capitalizing on its strategic location, the city has become Sudan's commercial center and transportation hub. It is built on a curving strip of land that resembles the trunk of an elephant: the name "Khartoum" comes from the Arabic *Ras-al-hartum*, which means "end of the elephant's trunk."

Q What is Africa's newest country?

A Eritrea, which officially became independent in 1993. An Italian colony from 1890 to 1941, Eritrea was captured by the British during World War II. In 1952, the United Nations awarded Eritrea to Ethiopia under the condition that it be ruled as a self-governing territory. Ethiopia violated this agreement by annexing Eritrea in 1962, touching off a civil war which lasted more than 30 years. Eritrea formally declared its independence in May 1993, two years after defeating Ethiopia's Marxist regime.

Q What is the Sahel?

A The Sahel is a semiarid region that separates the Sahara Desert from the tropical savanna and rain forests of central Africa. It stretches halfway across the continent, from Mauritania in the west to Chad in the east, in a band averaging more than 1,000 miles (1,600 km) in width. Most of the Sahel is semiarid savanna, with low grasses in the north and tall grasses in the south. Annual precipitation varies from 4 inches to 24 inches (100 to 600 mm). The 8-month dry season makes farming difficult, and the region has experienced several severe droughts in this century.

Woman returning from well in the Sahel

Q In what country would you find Africa's northernmost point?

A Tunisia. The northernmost point is Cape Ben Sekka, which lies just north of the continent's northernmost town, Bechater. Parts of five European countries—Greece, Italy, Malta, Portugal, and Spain—lie farther south than Cape Ben Sekka. From the tip of the cape, Africa stretches southward approximately 5,000 miles (8,000 km) to its southernmost point, Cape Agulhas in South Africa.

Q How has the Sahara Desert changed in the last 5,000 years?

A Scientists believe that 5,000 years ago the climate of the Sahara was more temperate and far less arid than it is today. Much of the region was grassland. Around 3000 B.C. global climate patterns began to shift, and the region entered an arid period which continues today. The desert currently covers 3,500,000 square miles (9,100,000 sq km), an area nearly as large as the United States, and its size is increasing. In recent decades, recurring droughts and overgrazing in the Sahel region have contributed to the Sahara's southward expansion.

Q What is the traditional mode of transportation in the Sahara Desert?

A The camel, or more specifically, the one-humped dromedary, which was domesticated at least 3,000 years ago. Dromedaries are extremely well-suited to desert conditions. They have the ability to store water in their hump, and can tolerate water losses equal to one-fourth of their body weight. Their heavy-lidded eyes and closeable nostrils offer protection in sandstorms. Today, as the Saharan road system expands, truck convoys are replacing camel caravans, although trucks require frequent refueling, often overheat in the desert sun, and grind to a halt when sand clogs their engines.

Camel eating leaves

Q Which African country can boast the greatest known deposits, variety, and output of minerals in the world?

A South Africa. It has the world's largest known deposits of chromite, gold, manganese, platinum, and vanadium. The country leads the world in production of gold, chromite, vanadium, and the platinum group metals: platinum, palladium, iridium, rhodium, and ruthenium. It is also one of the leading producers of manganese, antimony, and gem and industrial diamonds.

Q Where is the Horn of Africa?

A This term refers to the horn-shaped area of eastern Africa that juts into the Indian Ocean. Somalia and Ethiopia occupy most of the horn. The cape of Gees Gwardafuy and the city of Caluula sit at the northeastern tip of the horn, marking the entrance to the Gulf of Aden, which connects the Arabian Sea and the Red Sea.

Q What is the Valley of the Kings?

A This narrow valley, across the Nile River from the city of Luxor, contains the tombs of the pharaohs who ruled Egypt during the New Kingdom period, 1550 B.C. to 1200 B.C. The tombs are carved deep into the sandstone walls of the valley; most have five to fifteen rooms. Among the pharaohs buried in the valley are Ramses II, Ramses VI, and Seti I. Upon their death, the pharaohs were mummified and then entombed with all of the material things that they might need in the afterlife, including gold, jeweled ornaments, furniture, clothing, and food. Most of the tombs were soon looted by robbers, who removed all items of value. However, in 1922 the tomb of Tutankhamen—"King Tut"—was discovered with most of its riches untouched.

Questions and Answers

Asia

Q What natural features form the physical boundary between Europe and Asia?

A Europe and Asia share the same huge landmass, which is known as Eurasia. The imaginary line dividing this landmass into two continents runs through the Ural Mountains, the Ural River, the Caspian Sea, the Caucasus mountains, the Black Sea, the Bosporus strait, the Sea of Marmara, and the Dardanelles strait.

Q How many countries lie partially within Europe and partially within Asia?

A Four: Azerbaijan, which is traversed by the Caucasus Mountains; Kazakhstan, whose far western lands lie west of the Ural River; Russia, which is split by the Ural Mountains, and Turkey, which includes a small area on the northwestern side of the Sea of Marmara.

Q Why was the Great Wall of China built?

A To defend China against invasion by the Huns and other enemies. Defensive walls were built in China

The Great Wall winding through a hilly region in northern China

as early as the 6th century B.C. In 214 B.C., under Emperor Shih Huang-ti, the existing walls were connected to form a single continuous wall with watchtowers. This wall was extended during the Han Dynasty (202 B.C. – A.D. 220) and the Sui Dynasty (A.D. 581 – 618). Seven hundred years later the wall had mostly crumbled, and in the late 1400s, under the Ming Emperors, it was completely rebuilt. The portions of the wall that remain today are those that were constructed during this most recent period.

Q How has the Aral Sea changed in recent decades?

A It has shrunk by about 40% since 1960. The sea once covered nearly 25,000 square miles (64,720 sq km) and was the fourth-largest inland body of water in the world. Today it covers only about 13,000 square miles (33,600 sq km), and the former port city of Muynak lies 30 miles (48 km) inland. The sea's shrinkage can be blamed on cotton farming in the surrounding desert. Soviet-era efforts to establish a profitable cotton industry led to the creation of an extensive network of irrigation canals. These huge canals drain large amounts of water from the Syr Darya and Amu Darya, the only two rivers that empty into the sea.

Q What is the Ring of Fire?

A "Ring of Fire" designates the narrow band of active volcanoes encircling the Pacific Ocean basin. Of the approximately 1,500 volcanoes in the world that have been active within the last 10,000 years, more than two-thirds are part of the Ring. Over half of the Ring's active volcanoes are found in its Asian portion, which passes through Russia's Kamchatka Peninsula, the Kuril Islands, Japan, and the Philippines. The Ring of Fire's most recent major volcanic event was the 1991 eruption of Pinatubo on the Philippine island of Luzon, which prompted the evacuation of 250,000 people.

Q What part of Asia is called Indochina?

A "Indochina" refers to the southeastern Asian peninsula situated south of China and east of India. Countries located on the peninsula are Cambodia, Laos, Myanmar (Burma), Thailand, Vietnam, and the western portion of Malaysia. The eastern part of the Indochinese peninsula, including Cambodia, Laos, and Vietnam, was formerly known as French Indochina because of France's strong colonial presence there.

Q The Khyber Pass links which two countries?

A Afghanistan and Pakistan. Approximately 33 miles (53 km) long and reaching a maximum elevation of about 3,500 feet (1,067 m), the pass cuts through the Safed Koh mountains just south of the Kabul River, connecting the high plateau of Afghanistan with the Indus Valley. It has been used for centuries as a caravan route and as an invasion route into India. Today it is also traversed by a paved highway and, in Pakistan, by a railroad. In the 1980s several million refugees fleeing Afghanistan's civil war crossed into Pakistan via the pass.

Q What Persian Gulf country is a federation of seven Arab sheikdoms?

A United Arab Emirates, formed in 1971 through the unification of the sheikdoms of Abu Dhabi, Ajman, Dubai, Fujeirah, Sharjah, and Umm al-Qawain. Ras al-Khaimah joined the federation in 1972. Underdeveloped a few decades ago, the U.A.E. has been transformed by oil wealth into a modern and affluent country.

Q What Asian country contains, or is bordered by, six of the world's ten highest mountains?

A Nepal. Within Nepal or along its borders with China and India are found the following peaks: Mt. Everest (highest in the world), Kanchenjunga (3rd), Makalu (4th), Dhawalāgiri (5th), Annapurna (7th), and Xixabangma Feng (9th). Nanda Devi (10th) lies only 50 miles (80 km) northwest of Nepal's western border.

Q Where is the Empty Quarter?

A This hostile desert is found in the southern third of the Arabian Peninsula. Called *Ar Rub' Al-Khālī*, or "the Empty Quarter" in Arabic, it covers 250,000 square miles (647,000 sq km) and is the world's largest continuous sand body. Few people live in the Empty Quarter, and much of the region has never been explored.

Q What Asian volcanic eruption has been called the loudest natural explosion in recorded history?

A The 1883 eruption of Krakatau (Krakatoa), an island volcano between Sumatra and Java. Krakatau exploded three times on August 26 and 27, 1883, shooting tremendous amounts of gas and ash 50 miles (80 km) into the atmosphere. The explosions were so violent that they were heard nearly 3,000 miles (4,653 km) away on Rodrigues Island in the western Indian Ocean. Krakatau collapsed into itself, and when the explosions were over most of the island was submerged under 900 feet of water. Tsunamis up to 130 feet (40 m) high slammed the coasts of Sumatra and Java, washing away hundreds of villages and killing more than 36,000 people.

Q **At their closest point, how far apart are Asia and North America?**

A At the narrowest point of the Bering Strait, Asia and North America are separated by only 56 miles (90 km). Russia's Big Diomede (Ratmanov) Island and the United States' Little Diomede Island, which lie in the middle of the strait, are only 2.5 miles (4 km) apart.

Q **Where is the Fertile Crescent?**

A This term refers to a crescent-shaped area of fertile land in the Middle East which begins in the south with Egypt's Nile Valley, runs north along the eastern coast of the Mediterranean Sea, then turns southeast through Mesopotamia, the land between the Tigris and Euphrates rivers, and ends at the head of the Persian Gulf. The Fertile Crescent was the birthplace of some of the world's oldest civilizations, including the Sumerians, Babylonians, and Assyrians.

Q **What country was Pakistan part of before it became independent?**

A India. Conflicts between Hindus and Muslims in British India led to the creation of Pakistan as a separate Muslim state in 1947. Originally, Pakistan included the two main centers of Muslim population, which lay in northwest and east India. The two areas, West Pakistan and East Pakistan, were separated by 1,000 miles (1,600 km). In 1971, East Pakistan declared its independence and changed its name to Bangladesh. The name "Pakistan" comes from the Urdu words *pakh*, meaning "pure," and *stan*, meaning "land."

Q **What was Sri Lanka called before 1972?**

A Ceylon, which is the name the British had given to the island when they claimed it in 1796. The island became independent in 1948, and in 1972 was renamed Sri Lanka, which in the Sinhala language means "Resplendent Land."

The Taj Mahal

Q **What is India's most famous tomb?**

A The Taj Mahal, located in the city of Agra. Often described as one of the world's most beautiful buildings, it was built by the Mogul emperor Shah Jahan to honor the memory of his wife, Mumtaz-i-Mahal. Construction began in 1631 and was completed in 1648.

Q **What two seas are linked by the Suez Canal?**

A The Red Sea and the Mediterranean Sea. Before the 101-mile (163-km) canal was built in the mid-1800s, ships traveling between Europe and the Far East had to sail all the way around the southern tip of Africa. Depending on the origin and destination of the ship, the canal could shorten its trip dramatically. For example, a ship sailing from London to Bombay would have to travel almost 11,000 miles (17,700 km) around the African continent. Using the Suez Canal, the trip could be shortened to 6,300 miles (10,140 km), a distance reduction of over 40%.

Q **Which independent Asian country has the highest population density?**

A The tiny republic of Singapore, with 11,874 people per square mile (4,593 per sq km). Singapore's 2,921,000 people occupy an island measuring only 26 miles east-to-west and 14 miles north-to-south. If non-independent entities are included, the Portuguese dependency of Macau has the continent's highest density, with 57,571 people per square mile (22,000 per sq km).

Q **How long is Japan, from north to south?**

A The islands of Japan stretch approximately 1,900 miles (3,060 km) from Hokkaido in the north to the Sakishima Archipelago in the south. This is approximately equal to the distance between New York City and Denver.

Landscape on Hokkaido, Japan's northernmost island

Q **What region is known as the "Roof of the World"?**

A Tibet, the high plateau region which lies north of the Himalayas. Covering 471,000 square miles (1,220,000 sq km), and with an average elevation of 15,000 feet (4,600 m), the Tibetan Plateau is the largest and highest plateau in the world. Much of Tibet is uninhabited; the region's fewer than two million people are concentrated in the valleys of the Brahmaputra (Yarlung) River and its tributaries.

Q **Which Asian country leads the world in number of earthquake-related deaths recorded in this century?**

A China, where 48 deadly earthquakes have killed an estimated 967,420 people since 1900. During the same period Iran has lost 147,293 people in 57 earthquakes, and in Japan 32 earthquakes have killed 123,462 people.

Q **What cities mark the endpoints of the Trans-Siberian Railway?**

A The longest railway line in the world, the Trans-Siberian Railway stretches 5,764 miles (9,297 km) between Moscow in the west and the Pacific Coast port city of Nakhodka (near Vladivostok) in the east. The eight-day journey between the two cities includes stops in 92 Russian cities and towns.

Q **How many people live on the Indonesian island of Java?**

A Java is home to approximately 118 million people. It is the world's most populous island, although it is only the 13th-largest in area. By contrast, the island of Cuba is four-fifths the size of Java, but its population is only one-eleventh as large.

Q **What was the name of Ho Chi Minh City, Vietnam, prior to 1975?**

A Saigon. When the city fell to North Vietnamese forces in 1975, it was renamed for Ho Chi Minh, founder of the Indochina Communist Party and president of North Vietnam from 1945 until his death in 1969.

Questions and Answers

Oceania (including Australia and New Zealand)

Q What is Oceania?

A The name "Oceania" refers to the scattered islands of a vast area of the Pacific Ocean, from Palau in the west to Easter Island in the east, and from the Midway Islands in the north to New Zealand in the south. The three main island groups of Oceania are Melanesia, Micronesia, and Polynesia. The continent of Australia and the islands of New Zealand are sometimes considered part of Oceania.

Q What is the Outback?

A This nickname refers to Australia's vast, largely uninhabited interior. Over the years, the Outback's harsh beauty and its remoteness from the rest of Australia have made it popular with adventurous explorers and travelers. Through depictions in literature, art, and film, the region has become an integral part of Australia's identity. However, it is difficult to characterize the Outback, for its boundaries are undefined and its landscape varies from hot deserts to lush wilderness.

Eucalyptus tree in the Outback, Northern Territory

Q Why is Australia sometimes referred to as "the Land Down Under"?

A This nickname originated with the British, who began colonizing Australia in the late 1700s. Because of its extreme southern location in relation to Britain, Australia was considered "Down." The "Under" part of the phrase refers to the continent's position "under" the Eurasian landmass. But while people from the Northern Hemisphere think of Australia as "Down Under," Australians do not.

Q How much of Australia is arid or semiarid?

A More than two-thirds of the continent is considered to be arid or semiarid. The arid areas comprise several large deserts, including the Great Victoria Desert, the Gibson Desert, the Great Sandy Desert, and the Simpson Desert.

Q What distinction does Wellington, New Zealand have among national capitals of independent countries?

A Located at 41°18' south latitude, Wellington is the world's southernmost national capital. In second place is Canberra, Australia, which lies at 35°17' south latitude.

Q What is unusual about how the island of Nauru was formed?

A Nauru, the world's smallest republic, began as a coral atoll. Over the millennia, accumulated bird droppings filled in the central lagoon and created an 8-square-mile (21-sq-km) island whose highest point rises 210 feet (64 m) above sea level. The droppings are a rich source of phosphate, which is used in making fertilizers. Phosphate mining has long been Nauru's economic mainstay, but the resource will soon be exhausted.

Q What are the principal islands of New Zealand?

A Two islands, North Island and South Island, account for more than 98% of New Zealand's total land area. The country also includes Stewart Island, the Chatham Islands, the Antipodes Islands, the Auckland Islands, and hundreds of tiny islets.

Q What is Ayers Rock?

A Ayers Rock, now called by its Aboriginal name, Uluru, is a huge, red, oval-shaped rock outcropping that rises 2,831 feet (863 m) above the plains of central Australia. One of the largest monoliths in the world, Uluru is actually the summit of a massive sandstone hill, most of which is hidden underground. Aborigines consider Uluru sacred and incorporate numerous places around it into their ceremonial life.

Q What is the ratio of sheep to humans in Australia and New Zealand?

A Because both countries are major wool, mutton, and lamb producers, Australia and New Zealand each have a high ratio of sheep to humans. In Australia, there are 132 million sheep, or seven sheep for each human in the country. In New Zealand, the ratio is even greater: the country's 50 million sheep translate into 14 sheep for each human.

Q How many of Oceania's countries have become independent since 1975?

A Eight. Papua New Guinea became independent in 1975, the Solomon Islands and Tuvalu in 1978, Kiribati in 1979, Vanuatu in 1980, the Marshall Islands and the Federated States of Micronesia in 1986, and Palau (Belau) in 1994.

Q What is the Great Barrier Reef?

A This vast coral reef system is the longest in the world, stretching 1,181 miles (1,900 km) along Australia's northeast coast. It is composed of reefs, shoals, and hundreds of islands. Popular with divers, the Great Barrier Reef is home to a myriad of aquatic creatures.

Q On what island is Robert Louis Stevenson buried?

A Stevenson, author of *Dr. Jekyll and Mr. Hyde*, *Kidnapped*, and *Treasure Island*, is buried on the island of Upolu in Western Samoa. Born in Edinburgh, Scotland in 1850, Stevenson sailed to the South Pacific in 1888 and settled permanently in Samoa in 1890. He died there in 1894.

Q Where does Sydney rank among Australia's most populous cities?

A Measured by actual city population, Sydney is not even ranked in the top hundred: only 13,501 people live within its tiny city limits. Brisbane is Australia's largest city, with 751,115 people. The Sydney metropolitan area, however, is by far the largest in Australia, with 3,538,749 people.

Harbor and skyline of Sydney

Q What is Australia's only island state?

A Tasmania, which lies about 150 miles (240 km) south of the Australian mainland. Measuring 26,200 square miles (67,800 sq km) in area, it is the smallest of Australia's six states and accounts for less than 1% of the country's area. Originally part of New South Wales, Tasmania became a separate colony in 1825 and a state in 1901. Hobart, its capital, is home to 45% of the state's population.

World

Q Which country has the most time zones?

A Russia, with ten. The United States and Canada are tied for second place with six times zones each. Interestingly, China, the world's third largest country, has only one time zone, although the sun rises and sets almost four hours earlier at the country's eastern edge than at its western edge. Many other countries, including Nepal, Norway, and Algeria, have also adopted a single time zone to simplify daily life. (Refer to World Time Zones map on pages 64-65.)

Q Through how many continents does the International Dateline pass?

A Only one: Antarctica. The Dateline runs through the Pacific Ocean, between the North and South poles. Its jagged course approximately follows the 180° longitude line, although in places it veers as much as 750 miles (1,200 km) east or west of this line.

Q Which of the world's rivers flows through, or along the border of, the most countries?

A The Danube. The second-longest river in Europe (after the Volga), the Danube originates in southwestern Germany and flows through or borders eight countries: Germany, Austria, Slovakia, Hungary, Croatia, Yugoslavia, Romania, and Bulgaria. The Danube's drainage basin spreads over a total of 15 countries.

Q What is the longest mountain system in the world?

A The Andes, which stretch for almost 4,500 miles (7,200 km) along the western edge of South America from Venezuela in the north to Tierra del Fuego in the south. The second-longest system is the Rocky Mountains, the major mountain system of North America. The Rockies extend for 2,500 miles (4,000 km) from northern Canada south to northern New Mexico.

Q What are Pangaea and Panthalassa?

A Scientists believe that all of the landmasses of the world were once joined together in a single supercontinent. Given the name Pangaea, Greek for "all land," this supercontinent was surrounded by a vast universal ocean called Panthalassa, meaning "all seas." Between 225 and 190 million years ago, shifting of the Earth's crustal plates caused Pangaea to break up into northern and southern landmasses, referred to as Laurasia and Gondwanaland. As the plates continued to move, these two landmasses eventually split up into the six landmasses that exist today.

Q What is the one man-made structure that can be seen from space, with an unaided eye?

A The Great Wall of China. To astronauts orbiting hundreds of miles above the Earth, the 4,000-mile (6,500-km)-long Great Wall—the largest structure ever built by human hands—appears as nothing more than a fine line meandering across the hills and plains of northern China. It was once thought that the wall would be visible from the moon, but during a 1969 lunar mission, astronaut Alan Bean found this to be untrue.

Q Which continent has the highest population density?

A Asia, which has a density of 198 people per square mile (76 per square km). Excluding Antarctica, which is uninhabited, the lowest continental density is found in Australia, where there are only 6 people per square mile (2.4 per sq km).

Q Which continent has the most countries?

A Africa, which has 53 independent countries and eight dependencies: Ascension, British Indian Ocean Territory, Mayotte, Reunion, St. Helena, Spanish North Africa, Tristan da Cunha, and Western Sahara. Asia ranks second, with 47 independent countries, one internally self-governing country (Bhutan), and one dependency (Macau). Antarctica has no countries, and the entire continent of Australia is covered by the country of the same name.

Q What country borders the most other countries?

A The People's Republic of China is the most "neighborly" country in the world, for it shares its borders with 15 countries or dependencies: Kazakhstan, Kyrgyzstan, Tajikistan, Afghanistan, Pakistan, India, Nepal, Bhutan, Myanmar, Laos, Vietnam, Macau, North Korea, Russia, and Mongolia. Russia is in second place, bordering 14 countries: Finland, Norway, Estonia, Latvia, Belarus, Lithuania, Poland, Ukraine, Georgia, Azerbaijan, Kazakhstan, China, Mongolia, and North Korea. However, Macau will soon drop from China's list. Currently administered by the Portugal, the territory will revert to Chinese control in 1999.

Q What were the Seven Wonders of the Ancient World?

A The Colossus of Rhodes (in modern-day Greece), the Hanging Gardens of Babylon (Iraq), the Pyramids and Sphinx of Egypt, the Temple of Artemis at Ephesus (Turkey), the Statue of Zeus at Olympia (Greece), the Mausoleum at Halicarnassus (Turkey), and the Pharos of Alexandria (Egypt). Of these seven wonders, only the Pyramids and Sphinx remain standing today.

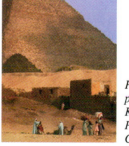

People and pyramids at Khufu, Giza Plateau, Cairo

Q Where would you be if you were at 0° latitude, 0° longitude?

A The point where 0° latitude, the Equator, intersects 0° longitude, the Prime Meridian, is located in the Atlantic Ocean off the western coast of Africa, 380 miles (610 km) south of Ghana and 670 miles (1,080 km) west of Gabon.

Q What are the official languages of the United Nations?

A There are more than 2,000 known languages in the world, but official business of the United Nations is conducted in only the following six, which are among the most widely spoken: Mandarin Chinese, English, Arabic, Spanish, Russian, and French.

The Universe and Solar System

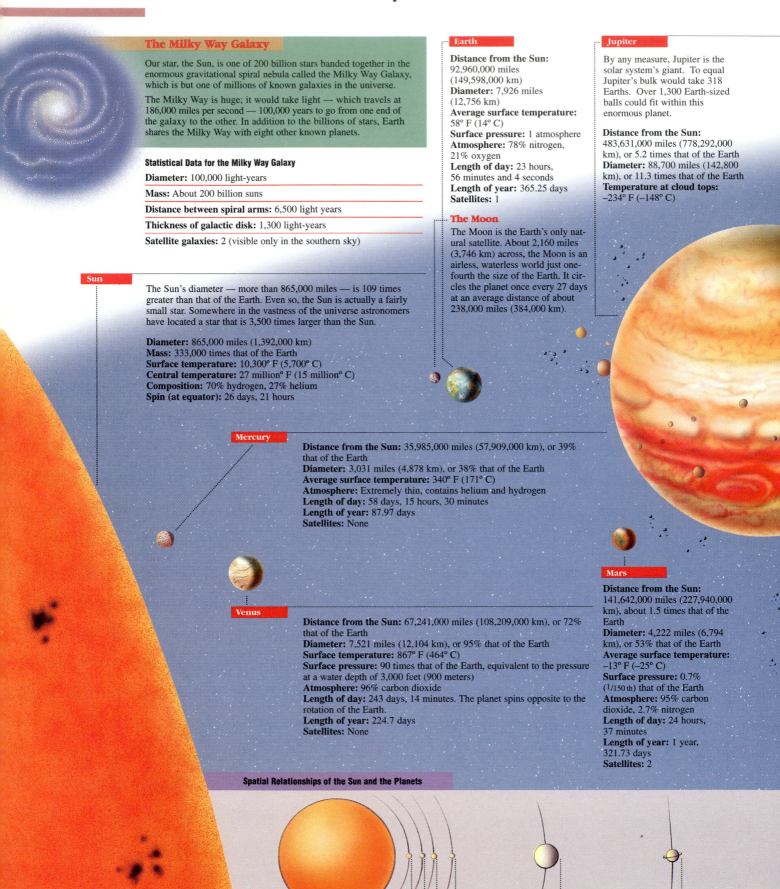

The Milky Way Galaxy

Our star, the Sun, is one of 200 billion stars banded together in the enormous gravitational spiral nebula called the Milky Way Galaxy, which is but one of millions of known galaxies in the universe.

The Milky Way is huge; it would take light — which travels at 186,000 miles per second — 100,000 years to go from one end of the galaxy to the other. In addition to the billions of stars, Earth shares the Milky Way with eight other known planets.

Statistical Data for the Milky Way Galaxy

Diameter: 100,000 light-years

Mass: About 200 billion suns

Distance between spiral arms: 6,500 light years

Thickness of galactic disk: 1,300 light-years

Satellite galaxies: 2 (visible only in the southern sky)

Sun

The Sun's diameter — more than 865,000 miles — is 109 times greater than that of the Earth. Even so, the Sun is actually a fairly small star. Somewhere in the vastness of the universe astronomers have located a star that is 3,500 times larger than the Sun.

Diameter: 865,000 miles (1,392,000 km)
Mass: 333,000 times that of the Earth
Surface temperature: 10,300° F (5,700° C)
Central temperature: 27 million° F (15 million° C)
Composition: 70% hydrogen, 27% helium
Spin (at equator): 26 days, 21 hours

Mercury

Distance from the Sun: 35,985,000 miles (57,909,000 km), or 39% that of the Earth
Diameter: 3,031 miles (4,878 km), or 38% that of the Earth
Average surface temperature: 340° F (171° C)
Atmosphere: Extremely thin, contains helium and hydrogen
Length of day: 58 days, 15 hours, 30 minutes
Length of year: 87.97 days
Satellites: None

Venus

Distance from the Sun: 67,241,000 miles (108,209,000 km), or 72% that of the Earth
Diameter: 7,521 miles (12,104 km), or 95% that of the Earth
Surface temperature: 867° F (464° C)
Surface pressure: 90 times that of the Earth, equivalent to the pressure at a water depth of 3,000 feet (900 meters)
Atmosphere: 96% carbon dioxide
Length of day: 243 days, 14 minutes. The planet spins opposite to the rotation of the Earth.
Length of year: 224.7 days
Satellites: None

Earth

Distance from the Sun: 92,960,000 miles (149,598,000 km)
Diameter: 7,926 miles (12,756 km)
Average surface temperature: 58° F (14° C)
Surface pressure: 1 atmosphere
Atmosphere: 78% nitrogen, 21% oxygen
Length of day: 23 hours, 56 minutes and 4 seconds
Length of year: 365.25 days
Satellites: 1

The Moon

The Moon is the Earth's only natural satellite. About 2,160 miles (3,746 km) across, the Moon is an airless, waterless world just one-fourth the size of the Earth. It circles the planet once every 27 days at an average distance of about 238,000 miles (384,000 km).

Jupiter

By any measure, Jupiter is the solar system's giant. To equal Jupiter's bulk would take 318 Earths. Over 1,300 Earth-sized balls could fit within this enormous planet.

Distance from the Sun: 483,631,000 miles (778,292,000 km), or 5.2 times that of the Earth
Diameter: 88,700 miles (142,800 km), or 11.3 times that of the Earth
Temperature at cloud tops: –234° F (–148° C)

Mars

Distance from the Sun: 141,642,000 miles (227,940,000 km), about 1.5 times that of the Earth
Diameter: 4,222 miles (6,794 km), or 53% that of the Earth
Average surface temperature: –13° F (–25° C)
Surface pressure: 0.7% (1/150 th) that of the Earth
Atmosphere: 95% carbon dioxide, 2.7% nitrogen
Length of day: 24 hours, 37 minutes
Length of year: 1 year, 321.73 days
Satellites: 2

Spatial Relationships of the Sun and the Planets

Sun Mercury Venus Earth Mars Jupiter Saturn

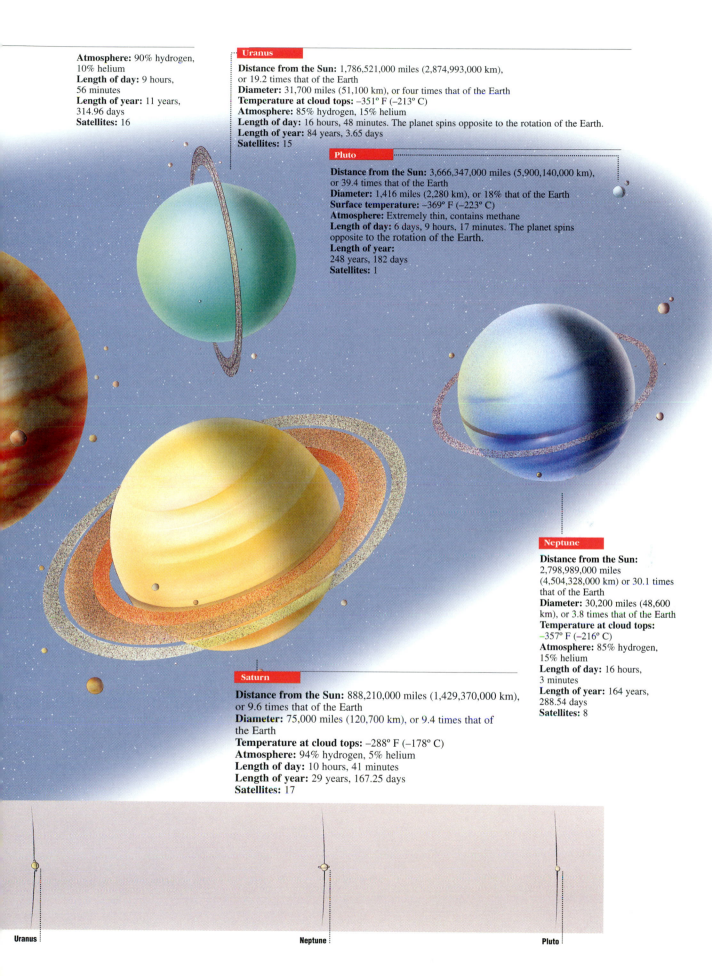

Atmosphere: 90% hydrogen, 10% helium
Length of day: 9 hours, 56 minutes
Length of year: 11 years, 314.96 days
Satellites: 16

Uranus

Distance from the Sun: 1,786,521,000 miles (2,874,993,000 km), or 19.2 times that of the Earth
Diameter: 31,700 miles (51,100 km), or four times that of the Earth
Temperature at cloud tops: –351° F (–213° C)
Atmosphere: 85% hydrogen, 15% helium
Length of day: 16 hours, 48 minutes. The planet spins opposite to the rotation of the Earth.
Length of year: 84 years, 3.65 days
Satellites: 15

Pluto

Distance from the Sun: 3,666,347,000 miles (5,900,140,000 km), or 39.4 times that of the Earth
Diameter: 1,416 miles (2,280 km), or 18% that of the Earth
Surface temperature: –369° F (–223° C)
Atmosphere: Extremely thin, contains methane
Length of day: 6 days, 9 hours, 17 minutes. The planet spins opposite to the rotation of the Earth.
Length of year: 248 years, 182 days
Satellites: 1

Neptune

Distance from the Sun: 2,798,989,000 miles (4,504,328,000 km) or 30.1 times that of the Earth
Diameter: 30,200 miles (48,600 km), or 3.8 times that of the Earth
Temperature at cloud tops: –357° F (–216° C)
Atmosphere: 85% hydrogen, 15% helium
Length of day: 16 hours, 3 minutes
Length of year: 164 years, 288.54 days
Satellites: 8

Saturn

Distance from the Sun: 888,210,000 miles (1,429,370,000 km), or 9.6 times that of the Earth
Diameter: 75,000 miles (120,700 km), or 9.4 times that of the Earth
Temperature at cloud tops: –288° F (–178° C)
Atmosphere: 94% hydrogen, 5% helium
Length of day: 10 hours, 41 minutes
Length of year: 29 years, 167.25 days
Satellites: 17

Uranus   Neptune   Pluto

The Earth

History of the Earth

Estimated age of the Earth:
At least 4.6 billion (4,600,000,000) years.

Formation of the Earth:
It is generally thought that the Earth was formed from a cloud of gas and dust (A) revolving around the early Sun. Gravitational forces pulled the cloud's particles together into an ever denser mass (B), with heavier particles sinking to the center. Heat from radioactive elements caused the materials of the embryonic Earth to melt and gradually settle into core and mantle layers. As the surface cooled, a crust formed. Volcanic activity released vast amounts of steam, carbon dioxide and other gases from the Earth's interior. The steam condensed into water to form the oceans, and the gases, prevented by gravity from escaping, formed the beginnings of the atmosphere (C).

The calm appearance of our planet today (D) belies the intense heat of its interior and the violent tectonic forces which are constantly reshaping its surface.

A

B

C

D

Periods in Earth's history

Earth's history is divided into different **eras**, which are subdivided into **periods**.

The most recent periods are themselves subdivided into **epochs**. The main divisions and subdivisions are shown below.

	Began	Ended	
	(million years ago)		
Precambrian Era			
Archean Period	3,800	2,500	Start of life
Proterozoic Period	2,500	590	Life in the seas
Paleozoic Era			
Cambrian Period	590	500	Sea life
Ordovician Period	505	438	First fishes
Silurian Period	438	408	First land plants
Devonian Period	408	360	Amphibians
Carboniferous Period	360	286	First reptiles
Permian Period	286	248	Spread of reptiles
Mesozoic Era			
Triassic Period	248	213	Reptiles and early mammals
Jurassic Period	213	144	Dinosaurs
Cretaceous Period	144	65	Dinosaurs, dying out at the end
Cenozoic Era			
Tertiary Period			
Paleocene	65	55	Large mammals
Eocene	55	38	Primates begin
Oligocene	38	25	Development of primates
Miocene	25	5	Modern-type animals
Pliocene	5	2	Australopithecus ape, ancestor to the human race
Quaternary Period			
Pleistocene	2	0.01	Ice ages; true humans
Holocene	0.01	Present	Modern humans

Source: *Atlas of the Universe* by Patrick Moore, Reed International Books Limited, 1994.

Internal Structure of the Earth

In its simplest form, the Earth is composed of a crust, a mantle with an upper and lower layer, and a core, which has an inner region.

Temperatures in the Earth increase with depth, as is observed in a deep mine shaft or bore-hole, but the prediction of temperatures within the Earth is made difficult by the fact that different rocks conduct heat at different rates: rock salt, for example, has 10 times the heat conductivity of coal. Also, estimates have to take into account the abundance of heat-generating atoms in a rock. Radioactive atoms are concentrated toward the Earth's surface, so the planet has, in effect, a thermal blanket to keep it warm. The temperature at the center of the Earth is believed to be approximately 5,400° F (3,000° C).

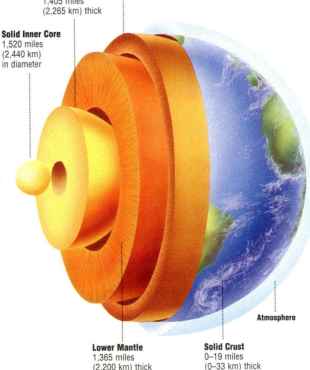

Upper Mantle
415 miles
(667 km) thick

Molten Outer Core
1,405 miles
(2,265 km) thick

Solid Inner Core
1,520 miles
(2,440 km)
in diameter

Atmosphere

Lower Mantle
1,365 miles
(2,200 km) thick

Solid Crust
0–19 miles
(0–33 km) thick

Chemical composition of the Earth:

The chemical composition of the Earth varies from crust to core. The upper crust of continents, called sial, is mainly granite, rich in aluminum and silicon. Oceanic crust, or sima, is largely basalt, made of magnesium and silicon. The mantle is composed of rocks that are rich in magnesium and iron silicates, whereas the core, it is believed, is made of iron and nickel oxides.

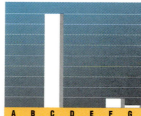

- ···· Sial
- ···· Sima
- ···· Upper Mantle
- ···· Lower Mantle
- ···· Outer Core
- ···· Inner Core

A. Silicon
B. Aluminum
C. Iron
D. Calcium
E. Magnesium
F. Nickel
G. Other

Sial (upper crust of continents)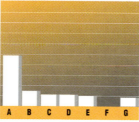

Sima (oceanic crust)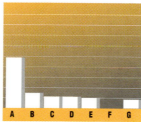

Mantle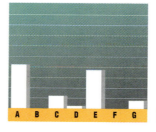

Core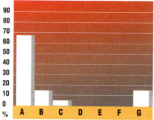

Measurements of the Earth

Equatorial circumference of the Earth: 24,901.45 miles (40,066.43 km)

Polar circumference of the Earth: 24,855.33 miles (39,992.22 km)

Equatorial diameter of the Earth: 7,926.38 miles (12,753.54 km)

Polar diameter of the Earth: 7,899.80 miles (12,710.77 km)

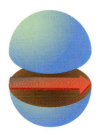

Equatorial radius of the Earth: 3,963.19 miles (6,376.77 km)

Polar radius of the Earth: 3,949.90 miles (6,355.38 km)

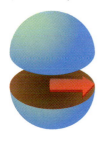

Estimated weight of the Earth:

6,600,000,000,000,000,000,000 tons, or 6,600 billion billion tons (5,940 billion billion metric tons)

Total surface area of the Earth: 197,000,000 square miles (510,230,000 sq km)

Total land area of the Earth (including inland water and Antarctica): 57,900,000 square miles (150,100,000 sq km)

Total ocean area of the Earth: 139,200,000 square miles (360,528,000 sq km), or 70% of the Earth's surface area

Total area of the Earth's surface covered with water (oceans and all inland water): 147,750,000 square miles (382,672,500 sq km), or 75% of the Earth's surface area

Types of water: 97% of the Earth's water is salt water; 3% is fresh water

Life on Earth

Number of plant species on Earth: About 350,000

Number of animal species on Earth: More than one million

Estimated total human population of the Earth: 5,628,000,000

Movements of the Earth

Mean distance of the Earth from the Sun: About 93 million miles (149.6 million km)

Period in which the Earth makes one complete orbit around the Sun: 365 days, 5 hours, 48 minutes, and 46 seconds

Speed of the Earth as it orbits the Sun: 66,700 miles (107,320 km) per hour

Period in which the Earth makes one complete rotation on its axis: 23 hours, 56 minutes and 4 seconds

Equatorial speed at which the Earth rotates on its axis: More than 1,000 miles (1,600 km) per hour

The Shape of the Earth

Comparing the Earth's equatorial and polar dimensions reveals that our planet is actually not a perfect sphere but rather an oblate spheroid, flattened at the poles and bulging at the equator. This is the result of a combination of gravitational and centrifugal forces.

An even more precise term for the Earth's shape is "geoid" — the actual shape of sea level, which is lumpy, with variations away from spheroid of up to 260 feet (80 m). This lumpiness reflects major variations in density in the Earth's outer layers.

The Seasons
(Northern Hemisphere)

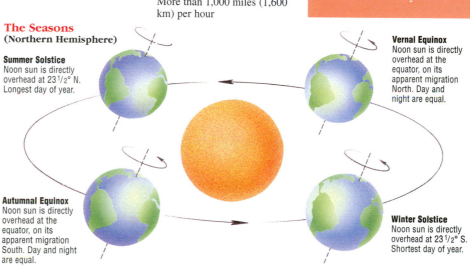

Summer Solstice
Noon sun is directly overhead at 23 1/2° N. Longest day of year.

Autumnal Equinox
Noon sun is directly overhead at the equator, on its apparent migration South. Day and night are equal.

Vernal Equinox
Noon sun is directly overhead at the equator, on its apparent migration North. Day and night are equal.

Winter Solstice
Noon sun is directly overhead at 23 1/2° S. Shortest day of year.

Continents and Islands

The word "continents" designates the largest continuous masses of land in the world.

For reasons that are mainly historical, seven continents are generally recognized: Africa, Antarctica, Asia, Australia, Europe, North America, and South America. Since Asia and Europe actually share the same land mass, they are sometimes identified as a single continent, Eurasia.

The lands of the central and south Pacific, including Australia, New Zealand, Micronesia, Melanesia, and Polynesia, are sometimes grouped together as Oceania.

The Continents

Africa

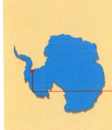

Area in square miles (sq km):
11,700,000 (30,300,000)
Estimated population (Jan. 1, 1995):
697,600,000
Population per square mile (sq km):
60 (23)
Mean elevation in feet (meters):
1,900 (580)
Highest elevation in feet (meters):
Kilimanjaro, Tanzania, 19,340 (5,895)
Lowest elevation in feet (meters):
Lac Assal, Djibouti, 515 (157) below sea level

Antarctica

Area in square miles (sq km):
5,400,000 (14,000,000)
Estimated population (Jan. 1, 1995):
Uninhabited
Population per square mile (sq km):
0 (0)
Mean elevation in feet (meters):
6,000 (1,830)
Highest elevation in feet (meters):
Vinson Massif, 16,066 (4,897)
Lowest elevation in feet (meters):
Deep Lake, 184 (56) below sea level

Asia

Area in square miles (sq km):
17,300,000 (44,900,000)
Estimated population (Jan. 1, 1995):
3,422,700,000
Population per square mile (sq km):
198 (76)
Mean elevation in feet (meters):
3,000 (910)
Highest elevation in feet (meters):
Mt. Everest, China (Nepal)–Tibet, 29,028 (8,848)
Lowest elevation in feet (meters):
Dead Sea, Israel–Jordan, 1,339 (408) below sea level

Australia

Area in square miles (sq km):
2,966,155 (7,682,300)
Estimated population (Jan. 1, 1995):
18,205,000
Population per square mile (sq km):
6.1 (2.4)
Mean elevation in feet (meters):
1,000 (305)
Highest elevation in feet (meters):
Mt. Kosciusko, New South Wales, 7,310 (2,228)
Lake Eyre, South Australia, 52 (16) below sea level

Europe

Area in square miles (sq km):
3,800,000 (9,900,000)
Estimated population (Jan. 1, 1995):
712,100,000
Population per square mile (sq km):
187 (72)
Mean elevation in feet (meters):
980 (300)
Highest elevation in feet (meters):
Gora El'brus, Russia, 18,510 (5,642)
Lowest elevation in feet (meters):
Caspian Sea, Asia-Europe, 92 (28) below sea level

North America

Area in square miles (sq km):
9,500,000 (24,700,000)
Estimated population (Jan. 1, 1995):
453,300,000
Population per square mile (sq km):
48 (18)
Mean elevation in feet (meters):
2,000 (610)
Highest elevation in feet (meters):
Mt. McKinley, Alaska, U.S., 20,320 (6,194)
Lowest elevation in feet (meters):
Death Valley, California, U.S., 282 (84) below sea level

Oceania (incl. Australia)

Area in square miles (sq km):
3,300,000 (8,500,000)
Estimated population (Jan. 1, 1995):
28,400,000
Population per square mile (sq km):
8.6 (3.3)
Mean elevation in feet (meters):
0 (0)
Highest elevation in feet (meters):
Mt. Wilhelm, Papua New Guinea, 14,793 (4,509)
Lowest elevation in feet (meters):
Lake Eyre, South Australia, 52 (16) below sea level

South America

Area in square miles (sq km):
6,900,000 (17,800,000)
Estimated population (Jan. 1, 1995):
313,900,000
Population per square mile (sq km):
45 (18)
Mean elevation in feet (meters):
1,800 (550)
Highest elevation in feet (meters):
Cerro Aconcagua, Argentina, 22,831 (6,959)
Lowest elevation in feet (meters):
Salinas Chicas, Argentina, 138 (42) below sea level

World

Area in square miles (sq km):
57,900,000 (150,100,000)
Estimated population (Jan. 1, 1995):
5,628,000,000
Population per square mile (sq km):
97 (37)
Mean elevation in feet (meters):
0 (0)
Highest elevation in feet (meters):
Mt. Everest, China–Nepal, 29,028 (8,848)
Lowest elevation in feet (meters):
Dead Sea, Israel–Jordan, 1,339 (408) below sea level

Largest Islands

Rank	Name	Area square miles	square km
1	Greenland, North America	840,000	2,175,600
2	New Guinea, Asia-Oceania	309,000	800,000
3	Borneo (Kalimantan), Asia	287,300	744,100
4	Madagascar, Africa	226,500	587,000
5	Baffin Island, Canada	195,928	507,451
6	Sumatra (Sumatera), Indonesia	182,860	473,606
7	Honshū, Japan	89,176	230,966
8	Great Britain, United Kingdom	88,795	229,978
9	Victoria Island, Canada	83,897	217,291
10	Ellesmere Island, Canada	75,767	196,236
11	Celebes (Sulawesi), Indonesia	73,057	189,216
12	South Island, New Zealand	57,708	149,463
13	Java (Jawa), Indonesia	51,038	132,187
14	North Island, New Zealand	44,332	114,821
15	Cuba, North America	42,800	110,800
16	Newfoundland, Canada	42,031	108,860
17	Luzon, Philippines	40,420	104,688
18	Iceland, Europe	39,800	103,000
19	Mindanao, Philippines	36,537	94,630
20	Ireland, Europe	32,600	84,400
21	Hokkaidō, Japan	32,245	83,515
22	Sakhalin, Russia	29,500	76,400
23	Hispaniola, North America	29,400	76,200
24	Banks Island, Canada	27,038	70,028
25	Tasmania, Australia	26,200	67,800
26	Sri Lanka, Asia	24,900	64,600
27	Devon Island, Canada	21,331	55,247
28	Berkner Island, Antarctica	20,005	51,829
29	Alexander Island, Antarctica	19,165	49,652
30	Tierra del Fuego, South America	18,600	48,200
31	Novaya Zemlya, north island, Russia	18,436	47,764
32	Kyūshū, Japan	17,129	44,363
33	Melville Island, Canada	16,274	42,149
34	Southampton Island, Canada	15,913	41,214
35	Axel Heiberg, Canada	15,498	40,151
36	Spitsbergen, Norway	15,260	39,523
37	New Britain, Papua New Guinea	14,093	36,500
38	Taiwan, Asia	13,900	36,000
39	Hainan Dao, China	13,100	34,000
40	Prince of Wales Island, Canada	12,872	33,339
41	Novaya Zemlya, south island, Russia	12,633	32,730
42	Vancouver Island, Canada	12,079	31,285
43	Sicily, Italy	9,926	25,709
44	Somerset Island, Canada	9,570	24,786
45	Sardinia, Italy	9,301	24,090
46	Bathurst Island, Canada	7,600	19,684
47	Shikoku, Japan	7,258	18,799
48	Ceram (Seram), Indonesia	7,191	18,625
49	North East Land, Norway	6,350	16,446
50	New Caledonia, Oceania	6,252	16,192
51	Prince Patrick Island, Canada	5,986	15,509
52	Timor, Indonesia	5,743	14,874
53	Sumbawa, Indonesia	5,549	14,377
54	Ostrov Oktyabr'skoy Revolyutsii, Russia	5,511	14,279
55	Flores, Indonesia	5,502	14,250
56	Samar, Philippines	5,100	13,080
57	King William Island, Canada	4,961	12,853
58	Negros, Philippines	4,907	12,710
59	Thurston Island, Antarctica	4,854	12,576
60	Palawan, Philippines	4,550	11,785

Islands, Islands, Everywhere

Four islands — Hokkaidō, Honshū, Kyūshū, and Shikoku —
constitute 98% of Japan's total land area, but the country is actually
comprised of more than 3,000 islands. Similarly, two islands —
Great Britain and Ireland — make up 93% of the total land area of
the British Isles, but the island group also includes more than 5,000
smaller islands.

Greenland
New Guinea
Borneo
Madagascar
Baffin Island
Sumatra
Honshū
Great Britain
Victoria Island
Ellesmere Island

Major World Island Groups

Aleutian Islands (Pacific Ocean)
Alexander Archipelago (Pacific Ocean)
Azores (Atlantic Ocean)
Bahamas (Atlantic Ocean)
Balearic Islands (Mediterranean Sea)
Bismarck Archipelago (Pacific Ocean)
British Isles (Atlantic Ocean)
Cape Verde Islands (Atlantic Ocean)
Dodecanese (Mediterranean Sea)
Faeroe Islands (Atlantic Ocean)
Falkland Islands (Atlantic Ocean)
Fiji Islands (Pacific Ocean)
Galapagos Islands (Pacific Ocean)
Greater Sunda Islands (Indian/Pacific Oceans)
Hawaiian Islands (Pacific Ocean)
Ionian Islands (Mediterranean Sea)
Islas Canarias (Atlantic Ocean)
Japan (Pacific Ocean)
Kikládhes (Mediterranean Sea)
Kuril Islands (Pacific Ocean)
Lesser Sunda Islands (Indian Ocean)
Moluccas (Pacific Ocean)
Nansei Shotō (Pacific Ocean)
New Hebrides (Atlantic Ocean)
New Siberian Islands (Arctic Ocean)
Novaya Zemlya (Arctic Ocean)
Philippine Islands (Pacific Ocean)
Severnaya Zemlya (Arctic Ocean)
Solomon Islands (Pacific Ocean)
Spitsbergen (Arctic Ocean)
West Indies (Atlantic Ocean)

Contrasting Population Densities

Some islands are among
the most densely populated
places on Earth, while
others are among the least
densely populated. This
fact is dramatically
illustrated by
the following
comparison of
five islands:

Manhattan, N.Y., U.S., (pop. 1,488,000) — 67,636/sq mile (26,105/sq km)

Singapore Island, Singapore (pop. 2,921,000) — 11,874/sq mile (4,593/sq km)

Long Island, N.Y., U.S. (pop. 6,863,000) — 4,984/sq mile (1,925/sq km)

Population per square mile (sq km)

Baffin Island, Canada (pop. 8,800) — 0.04/sq mile (0.02/sq km)

Greenland (pop. 57,000) — 0.07/sq mile (0.03/sq km)

Mountains, Volcanoes, and Earthquakes

The Tallest Mountain in the World

With its peak reaching 29,028 feet (8,848 m) above sea level, Mt. Everest ranks as the *highest* mountain in the world, but not the *tallest*. That title goes to Mauna Kea, one of the five volcanic mountains that make up the island of Hawaii. From its base on the floor of the Pacific Ocean, Mauna Kea rises 33,476 feet (10,210 m)—more than six miles—although only the top 13,796 feet (4,205 m) are above sea level.

Seafloor Atop Mt. Everest

When Sir Edmund Percival Hillary and Tenzing Norgay reached the summit of Mt. Everest in 1953, they probably did not realize they were standing on the seafloor.

The Himalayan mountain system was formed through the process of plate tectonics. Ocean once separated India and Asia, but 180 million years ago the Indo-Australian crustal plate, on which India sits, began a northward migration and eventually collided with the Eurasian plate. The seafloor between the two landmasses crumpled and was slowly thrust upward. Rock layers that once lay at the bottom of the ocean now crown the peaks of the highest mountains in the world.

Principal Mountain Systems and Ranges of the World

Alaska Range (North America)
Alps (Europe)
Altai (Asia)
Andes (South America)
Appennino (Europe)
Atlas Mountains (Africa)
Appalachian Mountains (North America)
Brooks Range (North America)
Carpathian Mountains (Europe)
Cascade Range (North America)
Caucasus (Europe/Asia)
Coast Mountains (North America)
Coast Ranges (North America)
Great Dividing Range (Australia)
Greater Khingan Range (Asia)
Himalayas (Asia)
Hindu Kush (Asia)
Karakoram Range (Asia)
Kunlun Shan (Asia)
Madre Occidental, Sierra (North America)
Madre Oriental, Sierra (North America)
Nevada, Sierra (North America)
Pamirs (Asia)
Pyrenees (Europe)
Rocky Mountains (North America)
Sayan Khrebet (Asia)
Southern Alps (New Zealand)
Tien Shan (Asia)
Urals (Europe)
Zagros Mountains (Asia)

Principal Mountains of the World

Δ = Highest mountain in range, region, country, or state named

Location	Feet	Meters
Africa		
Kilimanjaro, Δ Tanzania (Δ Africa)	19,340	5,895
Kirinyaga (Mount Kenya), Δ Kenya	17,058	5,199
Margherita Peak, Δ Uganda-Δ Zaire	16,763	5,109
Ras Dashen Terara, Δ Ethiopia	15,158	4,620
Meru, Mount, Tanzania	14,978	4,565
Karisimbi, Volcan, Δ Rwanda-Zaire	14,787	4,507
Elgon, Mount, Kenya-Uganda	14,178	4,321
Toubkal, Jebel, Δ Morocco (Δ Atlas Mts.)	13,665	4,165
Cameroon Mountain, Δ Cameroon	13,451	4,100
Antarctica		
Vinson Massif, Δ Antarctica	16,066	4,897
Kirkpatrick, Mount	14,856	4,528
Markham, Mount	14,049	4,282
Jackson, Mount	13,747	4,190
Sidley, Mount	13,717	4,181
Wade, Mount	13,396	4,083
Asia		
Everest, Mount, Δ China-Δ Nepal (Δ Tibet; Δ Himalayas; Δ Asia; Δ World)	29,028	8,848
K2 (Qogir Feng), China-Δ Pakistan (Δ Kashmir; Δ Karakoram Range)	28,250	8,611
Kanchenjunga, Δ India-Nepal	28,208	8,598
Makalu, China-Nepal	27,825	8,481
Dhawalāgiri, Nepal	26,810	8,172
Nanga Parbat, Pakistan	26,660	8,126
Annapurna, Nepal	26,504	8,078
Gasherbrum, China-Pakistan	26,470	8,068
Xixabangma Feng, China	26,286	8,012
Nanda Devi, India	25,645	7,817
Kamet, China-India	25,447	7,756
Namjagbarwa Feng, China	25,446	7,756
Muztag, China (Δ Kunlun Shan)	25,338	7,723
Tirich Mir, Pakistan (Δ Hindu Kush)	25,230	7,690
Gongga Shan, China	24,790	7,556
Kula Kangri, Δ Bhutan	24,784	7,554
Kommunizma, Pik, Δ Tajikistan (Δ Pamir)	24,590	7,495
Nowshak, Δ Afghanistan-Pakistan	24,557	7,485
Pobedy, Pik, China-Russia	24,406	7,439
Chomo Lhari, Bhutan-China	23,997	7,314
Muztag, China	23,891	7,282
Lenina, Pik, Δ Kyrgyzstan-Tajikistan	23,406	7,134
Api, Nepal	23,399	7,132
Kangrinboqê Feng, China	22,028	6,714
Hkakabo Razi, Δ Myanmar	19,296	5,881
Damavand, Qolleh-ye, Δ Iran	18,386	5,604
Agri Dagi (Mount Ararat), Δ Turkey	16,854	5,137
Fuladi, Kuh-e, Afghanistan	16,847	5,135
Jaya, Puncak, Δ Indonesia (Δ New Guinea)	16,503	5,030
Klyuchevskaya, Vulkan, Russia (Δ Poluostrov Kamchatka)	15,584	4,750
Trikora, Puncak, Indonesia	15,584	4,750
Belukha, Gora, Kazakhstan-Russia	14,783	4,506
Turgen, Mount, Mongolia	14,311	4,362
Kinabalu, Gunong, Δ Malaysia (Δ Borneo)	13,455	4,101
Yü Shan, Δ Taiwan	13,114	3,997
Erciyes Dagi, Turkey	12,851	3,917
Kerinci, Gunung, Indonesia (Δ Sumatra)	12,467	3,800
Fuji San, Δ Japan (Δ Honshu)	12,388	3,776
Rinjani, Gunung, Indonesia (Δ Lombok)	12,224	3,726
Semeru, Gunung, Indonesia (Δ Java)	12,060	3,676
Hadūr Shu'ayb, Jabal an-, Δ Yemen (Δ Arabian Peninsula)	12,008	3,660
Australia / Oceania		
Wilhelm, Mt., Δ Papua New Guinea	14,793	4,509
Giluwe, Mt., Papua New Guinea	14,330	4,368
Bangeta, Mt., Papua New Guinea	13,520	4,121
Victoria, Mt., Papua New Guinea (Δ Owen Stanley Range)	13,238	4,035
Cook, Mt., Δ New Zealand (Δ South Island)	12,316	3,754
Europe		
El'brus, Gora, Δ Russia (Δ Caucasus; Δ Europe)	18,510	5,642
Dykhtau, Mt., Russia	17,073	5,204
Blanc, Mont (Monte Bianco) Δ France-Δ Italy (Δ Alps)	15,771	4,807
Dufourspitze, Italy-Δ Switzerland	15,203	4,634
Weisshorn, Switzerland	14,783	4,506
Matterhorn, Italy-Switzerland	14,692	4,478
Finsteraarhorn, Switzerland	14,022	4,274
Jungfrau, Switzerland	13,642	4,158
Écrins, Barre des, France	13,458	4,102
Viso, Monte, Italy (Δ Cottian Alps)	12,602	3,841
Grossglockner, Δ Austria	12,461	3,798
Teide, Pico de, Δ Spain (Δ Canary Is.)	12,188	3,715
North America		
McKinley, Mt., Δ Alaska (Δ United States; Δ North America)	20,320	6,194
Logan, Mt., Δ Canada (Δ Yukon; Δ St. Elias Mts.)	19,551	5,959
Orizaba, Pico de, Δ Mexico	18,406	5,610
St. Elias, Mt., Alaska-Canada	18,008	5,489
Popocatépetl, Volcán, Mexico	17,930	5,465
Foraker, Mt., Alaska	17,400	5,304
Iztaccíhuatl, Mexico	17,159	5,230
Lucania, Mt., Canada	17,147	5,226
Fairweather, Mt., Alaska-Canada (Δ British Columbia)	15,300	4,663
Whitney, Mt., Δ California	14,494	4,418
Elbert, Mt., Δ Colorado (Δ Rocky Mts.)	14,433	4,399
Massive, Mt., Colorado	14,421	4,396
Harvard, Mt., Colorado	14,420	4,395
Rainier, Mt., Δ Washington (Δ Cascade Range)	14,410	4,392
Williamson, Mt., California	14,370	4,380
La Plata Pk., Colorado	14,361	4,377
Blanca Pk., Colorado (Δ Sangre de Cristo Mts.)	14,345	4,372
Uncompahgre Pk., Colorado (Δ San Juan Mts.)	14,309	4,361
Grays Pk., Colorado (Δ Front Range)	14,270	4,349
Evans, Mt., Colorado	14,264	4,348
Longs Pk., Colorado	14,255	4,345
Wrangell, Mt., Alaska	14,163	4,317
Shasta, Mt., California	14,162	4,317
Pikes Pk., Colorado	14,110	4,301
Colima, Nevado de, Mexico	13,991	4,240
Tajumulco, Volcán, Δ Guatemala (Δ Central America)	13,845	4,220
Gannett Pk., Δ Wyoming	13,804	4,207
Mauna Kea, Δ Hawaii	13,796	4,205
Grand Teton, Wyoming	13,770	4,197
Mauna Loa, Hawaii	13,679	4,169
Kings Pk., Δ Utah	13,528	4,123
Cloud Pk., Wyoming (Δ Bighorn Mts.)	13,167	4,013
Waddington, Mt., Canada (Δ Coast Mts.)	13,163	4,012
Wheeler Pk., Δ New Mexico	13,161	4,011
Boundary Pk., Δ Nevada	13,140	4,005
Robson, Mt., Canada (Δ Canadian Rockies)	12,972	3,954
Granite Pk., Δ Montana	12,799	3,901
Borah Pk., Δ Idaho	12,662	3,859
Humphreys Pk., Δ Arizona	12,633	3,851
Chirripó, Volcán, Δ Costa Rica	12,530	3,819
Columbia, Mt., Canada (Δ Alberta)	12,294	3,747
Adams, Mt., Washington	12,276	3,742
Gunnbjørn Fjeld, Δ Greenland	12,139	3,700
South America		
Aconcagua, Cerro, Δ Argentina (Δ Andes; Δ South America)	22,831	6,959
Ojos del Salado, Nevado, Argentina-Δ Chile	22,615	6,893
Bonete, Cerro, Argentina	22,546	6,872
Huascarán, Nevado, Δ Peru	22,133	6,746
Llullaillaco, Volcán, Argentina-Chile	22,110	6,739
Yerupaja, Nevado, Peru	21,765	6,634
Tupungato, Cerro, Argentina-Chile	21,555	6,570
Sajama, Nevado, Bolivia	21,463	6,542
Illampu, Nevado, Bolivia	21,066	6,421
Illimani, Nevado, Bolivia	20,741	6,322
Chimborazo, Δ Ecuador	20,702	6,310
Antofalla, Volcán, Argentina	20,013	6,100
Cotopaxi, Ecuador	19,347	5,897
Misti, Volcán, Peru	19,101	5,822
Huila, Nevado de, Colombia (Δ Cordillera Central)	18,865	5,750
Bolívar, Pico, Δ Venezuela	16,427	5,007

Notable Volcanic Eruptions

Year	Volcano Name, Location	Comments
ca. 4895 B.C.	Crater Lake, Oregon, U.S.	Collapse forms caldera that now contains Crater Lake.
ca. 4350 B.C.	Kikai, Ryukyu Islands, Japan	Japan's largest known eruption.
ca. 1628 B.C.	Santorini (Thira), Greece	Eruption devastates late Minoan civilization.
79 A.D.	Vesuvius (Vesuvio), Italy	Roman towns of Pompeii and Herculaneum are buried.
ca. 180	Taupo, New Zealand	Area measuring 6,200 square miles (16,000 sq km) is devastated.
ca. 260	Ilopango, El Salvador	Thousands killed, with major impact on Mayan civilization.
915	Towada, Honshu, Japan	Japan's largest historic eruption.
ca. 1000	Baitoushan, China/Korea	Largest known eruption on Asian mainland.
1259	Unknown	Evidence from polar ice cores suggests that a huge eruption, possibly the largest of the millennium, occurred in this year.
1586	Kelut, Java	Explosions in crater lake; mudflows kill 10,000.
1631	Vesuvius (Vesuvio), Italy	Eruption kills 4,000.
ca. 1660	Long Island, Papua New Guinea	"The time of darkness" in tribal legends on Papua New Guinea.
1672	Merapi, Java	Pyroclastic flows and mudflows kill 3,000.
1711	Awu, Sangihe Islands, Indonesia	Pyroclastic flows kill 3,000.
1760	Makian, Halmahera, Indonesia	Eruption kills 2,000; island evacuated for seven years.
1772	Papandayan, Java	Debris avalanche causes 2,957 fatalities.
1783	Lakagigar, Iceland	Largest historic lava flows; 9,350 deaths.
1790	Kilauea, Hawaii	Hawaii's last large explosive eruption.
1792	Unzen, Kyushu, Japan	Tsunami and debris avalanche kill 14,500.
1815	Tambora, Indonesia	History's most explosive eruption; 92,000 deaths.
1822	Galunggung, Java	Pyroclastic flows and mudflows kill 4,011.
1856	Awu, Sangihe Islands, Indonesia	Pyroclastic flows kill 2,806.
1883	Krakatau, Indonesia	Caldera collapse; 36,417 people killed, most by tsunami.
1888	Ritter Island, Papua New Guinea	3,000 killed, most by tsunami created by debris avalanche.
1902	Mont Pelee, West Indies	Town of St. Pierre destroyed; 28,000 people killed.
1902	Santa Maria, Guatemala	5,000 killed as 10 villages are buried by volcanic debris.
1912	Novarupta (Katmai), Alaska	Largest 20th-century eruption.
1914	Lassen, California, U.S.	California's last historic eruption.
1919	Kelut, Java	Mudflows devastate 104 villages and kill 5,110 people.
1930	Merapi, Java	1,369 people are killed as 42 villages are totally or partially destroyed.
1943	Parícutin, Mexico	Fissure in cornfield erupts, building cinder cone 1,500 feet (460 m) high within two years. One of the few volcano births ever witnessed.
1951	Lamington, Papua New Guinea	Pyroclastic flows kill 2,942.
1963	Surtsey, Iceland	Submarine eruption builds new island.
1977	Nyiragongo, Zaire	One of the shortest major eruptions and fastest lava flows ever recorded.
1980	St. Helens, Washington, U.S.	Lateral blast; 230-square-mile (600 sq km) area devastated.
1982	El Chichón, Mexico	Pyroclastic surges kill 1,877.
1985	Ruiz, Colombia	Mudflows kill 23,080.
1991	Pinatubo, Luzon, Philippines	Major eruption in densely populated area prompts evacuation of 250,000 people; fatalities number fewer than 800. Enormous amount of gas released into stratosphere lowers global temperatures for more than a year.
1993	Juan de Fuca Ridge, off the coast of Oregon, U.S.	Deep submarine rift eruptions account for three-fourths of all lava produced; this is one of the very few such eruptions that have been well-documented.

Sources: Smithsonian Institution Global Volcanism Program; Volcanoes of the World, Second Edition, by Tom Simkin and Lee Siebert, Geoscience Press and Smithsonian Institution, 1994.

Eruption of Mt. St. Helens in 1980

Significant Earthquakes through History

Year	Estimated Magnitude	Number of Deaths	Place
365		50,000	Knossos, Crete
844		50,000	Damascus, Syria; Antioch, Turkey
856		150,000	Dāmghān, Kashan, Qumis, Iran
893		150,000	Caucasus region
894		180,000	western India
1042		50,000	Palmyra, Baalbek, Syria
1138		230,000	Aleppo, Gansana, Syria
1139	6.8	300,000	Gäncä, Kiapas, Azerbaijan
1201		50,000	upper Egypt to Syria
1290	6.7	100,000	eastern China
1556		820,000	Shanxi Province, China
1662		300,000	China
1667	6.9	80,000	Caucasus region, northern Iran
1668		50,000	Shandong Province, China
1693		93,000	Sicily, Italy
1727		77,000	Tabrīz, Iran
1731		100,000	Beijing, China
1739		50,000	China
1755		62,000	Morocco, Portugal, Spain
1780	6.7	100,000	Tabrīz, Iran
1868	7.7	70,000	Ecuador, Colombia
1908	7.5	83,000	Calabria, Messina, Italy
1920	8.5	200,000	Gansu and Shanxi provinces, China

Year	Estimated Magnitude	Number of Deaths	Place
1923	8.2	142,807	Tokyo, Yokohama, Japan
1927	8.3	200,000	Gansu and Qinghai provinces, China
1932	7.6	70,000	Gansu Province, China
1970	7.8	66,794	northern Peru
1976	7.8	242,000	Tangshan, China
1990	7.7	50,000	northwestern Iran

Some Significant U.S. Earthquakes

Year	Estimated Magnitude	Number of Deaths	Place
1811–12	8.6, 8.4, 8.7	<10	New Madrid, Missouri (series)
1886	7.0	60	Charleston, South Carolina
1906	8.3	3,000	San Francisco, California
1933	6.3	115	Long Beach, California
1946	7.4	5 ‡	Alaska
1964	8.4	125	Anchorage, Alaska
1971	6.8	65	San Fernando, California
1989	7.1	62	San Francisco Bay Area, California
1994	6.8	58	Northridge, California

‡ A tsunami generated by this earthquake struck Hilo, Hawaii, killing 159 people.
Sources: Lowell S. Whiteside, National Geophysical Data Center; Catalog of Significant Earthquakes 2150 B.C.—1991 A.D. by Paula K. Dunbar, Patricia A. Lockridge, and Lowell S. Whiteside, National Geophysical Data Center, National Oceanic and Atmospheric Administration.

Oceans and Lakes

Oceans, Seas, Gulfs, and Bays

	Area sq. miles	Area sq. km.	Volume of water cubic miles	Volume of water cubic km.	Mean depth feet	Mean depth meters	Greatest known depth feet	Greatest known depth meters	
Pacific Ocean	63,800,000	165,200,000	169,650,000	707,100,000	12,987	3,957	35,810	10,922	Mariana Trench
Atlantic Ocean	31,800,000	82,400,000	79,199,000	330,100,000	11,821	3,602	28,232	8,610	Puerto Rico Trench
Indian Ocean	28,900,000	74,900,000	68,282,000	284,600,000	12,261	3,736	23,812	7,258	Weber Basin
Arctic Ocean	5,400,000	14,000,000	4,007,000	16,700,000	3,712	1,131	17,897	5,453	Lat. 77° 45'N, long. 175°W
Coral Sea	1,850,000	4,791,000	2,752,000	11,470,000	7,857	2,394	30,079	9,165	
Arabian Sea	1,492,000	3,864,000	2,416,000	10,070,000	8,973	2,734	19,029	5,803	
South China Sea	1,331,000	3,447,000	943,000	3,929,000	3,741	1,140	18,241	5,563	
Caribbean Sea	1,063,000	2,753,000	1,646,000	6,860,000	8,175	2,491	25,197	7,685	Off Cayman Islands
Mediterranean Sea	967,000	2,505,000	901,000	3,754,000	4,916	1,498	16,470	5,023	Off Cape Matapan, Greece
Bering Sea	876,000	2,269,000	911,000	3,796,000	5,382	1,640	25,194	7,684	Off Buldir Island
Bengal, Bay of	839,000	2,173,000	1,357,000	5,616,000	8,484	2,585	17,251	5,261	
Okhotsk, Sea of	619,000	1,603,000	316,000	1,317,000	2,694	821	1,029	3,374	Lat. 146° 10'E, long. 46° 50'N
Norwegian Sea	597,000	1,546,000	578,000	2,408,000	5,717	1,742	13,189	4,022	
Mexico, Gulf of	596,000	1,544,000	560,000	2,332,000	8,205	2,500	14,370	4,382	Sigsbee Deep
Hudson Bay	475,000	1,230,000	22,000	92,000	328	100	850	259	Near entrance
Greenland Sea	465,000	1,204,000	417,000	1,740,000	4,739	1,444	15,899	4,849	
Japan, Sea of	413,000	1,070,000	391,000	1,630,000	5,037	1,535	12,041	3,669	
Arafura Sea	400,000	1,037,000	49,000	204,000	646	197	12,077	3,680	
East Siberian Sea	357,000	926,000	14,000	61,000	216	66	508	155	
Kara Sea	349,000	903,000	24,000	101,000	371	113	2,034	620	
East China Sea	290,000	752,000	63,000	263,000	1,145	349	7,778	2,370	
Banda Sea	268,000	695,000	511,000	2,129,000	10,056	3,064	24,418	7,440	
Baffin Bay	263,000	681,000	142,000	593,000	2,825	861	7,010	2,136	
Laptev Sea	262,000	678,000	87,000	363,000	1,772	540	9,780	2,980	
Timor Sea	237,000	615,000	60,000	250,000	1,332	406	10,863	3,310	
Andaman Sea	232,000	602,000	158,000	660,000	3,597	1,096	13,777	4,198	
Chukchi Sea	228,000	590,000	11,000	45,000	252	77	525	160	
North Sea	214,000	554,000	12,000	52,000	315	96	2,655	809	
Java Sea	185,000	480,000	5,000	22,000	147	45	292	89	
Beaufort Sea	184,000	476,000	115,000	478,000	3,295	1,004	12,245	3,731	
Red Sea	174,000	450,000	60,000	251,000	1,831	558	8,648	2,635	
Baltic Sea	173,000	448,000	5,000	20,000	157	48	1,506	459	
Celebes Sea	168,000	435,000	380,000	1,586,000	11,962	3,645	19,173	5,842	
Black Sea	166,000	431,000	133,000	555,000	3,839	1,170	7,256	2,211	
Yellow Sea	161,000	417,000	4,000	17,000	131	40	344	105	
Sulu Sea	134,000	348,000	133,000	553,000	5,221	1,591	18,300	5,576	
Molucca Sea	112,000	291,000	133,000	554,000	6,242	1,902	16,311	4,970	
Ceram Sea	72,000	187,000	54,000	227,000	3,968	1,209	17,456	5,319	
Flores Sea	47,000	121,000	53,000	222,000	6,003	1,829	16,813	5,123	
Bali Sea	46,000	119,000	12,000	49,000	1,349	411	4,253	1,296	
Savu Sea	41,000	105,000	43,000	178,000	5,582	1,701	11,060	3,370	
White Sea	35,000	91,000	1,000	4,400	161	49	1,083	330	
Azov, Sea of	15,000	40,000	100	400	29	9	46	14	
Marmara, Sea of	4,000	11,000	1,000	4,000	1,171	357	4,138	1,261	

Source: Atlas of World Water Balance, USSR National Committee for the International Water Decade and UNESCO, 1977.

■ Potentially submerged areas

Fluctuating Sea Level

Changes in the Earth's climate have a dramatic effect on the sea level. Only 20,000 years ago, at the height of the most recent ice age, a vast amount of the Earth's water was locked up in ice sheets and glaciers, and the sea level was 330 feet (100 meters) lower than it is today. As the climate warmed slowly, the ice began to melt and the oceans began to rise.

Today there is still a tremendous amount of ice on the Earth. More than nine-tenths of it resides in the enormous ice cap which covers Antarctica. Measuring about 5.4 million square miles (14 million sq km) in surface area, the ice cap is on average one mile (1.6 km) thick but in some places is nearly three miles (4.8 km) thick. If it were to melt, the oceans would rise another 200 feet (60 m), and more than half of the world's population would have to relocate.

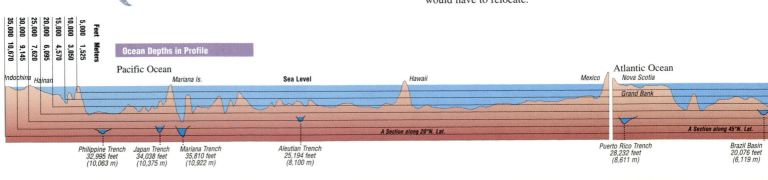

Ocean Depths in Profile

Deepest Lakes

Lake	Greatest depth feet	meters
1 Baikal, Lake, Russia	5,315	1,621
2 Tanganyika, Lake, Africa	4,800	1,464
3 Caspian Sea, Asia-Europe	3,363	1,025
4 Nyasa, Lake (Lake Malawi), Malawi-Mozambique-Tanzania	2,317	706
5 Issyk-Kul', Lake, Kyrgyzstan	2,303	702
6 Great Slave Lake, NWT, Canada	2,015	614
7 Matana, Lake, Indonesia	1,936	590
8 Crater Lake, Oregon, U.S.	1,932	589
9 Toba, Lake (Danau Toba), Indonesia	1,736	529
10 Sarez, Lake, Tajikistan	1,657	505
11 Tahoe, Lake, California-Nevada, U.S.	1,645	502
12 Kivu, Lake, Rwanda-Zaire	1,628	496
13 Chelan, Lake, Washington, U.S.	1,605	489
14 Quesnel Lake, BC, Canada	1,560	476
15 Adams Lake, BC, Canada	1,500	457

Lakes with the Greatest Volume of Water

Lake	Volume of water cubic mi	cubic km
1 Caspian Sea, Asia-Europe	18,900	78,200
2 Baikal, Lake, Russia	5,500	23,000
3 Tanganyika, Lake, Africa	4,500	18,900
4 Superior, Lake, Canada-U.S.	2,900	12,200
5 Nyasa, Lake (Lake Malawi), Malawi-Mozambique-Tanzania	1,900	7,725
6 Michigan, Lake, U.S.	1,200	4,910
7 Huron, Lake, Canada-U.S.	860	3,580
8 Victoria, Lake, Kenya-Tanzania-Uganda	650	2,700
9 Issyk-Kul', Lake, Kyrgyzstan	415	1,730
10 Ontario, Lake, Canada-U.S.	410	1,710
11 Great Slave Lake, Canada	260	1,070
12 Aral Sea, Kazakhstan-Uzbekistan	250	1,020
13 Great Bear Lake, Canada	240	1,010
14 Ladozhskoye, Ozero, Russia	220	908
15 Titicaca, Lago, Bolivia-Peru	170	710

Sources for volume and depth information: Atlas of World Water Balance, *USSR National Committee for the International Water Decade and UNESCO, 1977;* Principal Rivers and Lakes of the World, *National Oceanic and Atmospheric Administration, 1982.*

Principal Lakes

Lake	Area sq mi	sq km
1 Caspian Sea, Asia-Europe	143,240	370,990
2 Superior, Lake, Canada-U.S.	31,700	82,100
3 Victoria, Lake, Kenya-Tanzania-Uganda	26,820	69,463
4 Aral Sea, Kazakhstan-Uzbekistan	24,700	64,100
5 Huron, Lake, Canada-U.S.	23,000	60,000
6 Michigan, Lake, U.S.	22,300	57,800
7 Tanganyika, Lake, Africa	12,350	31,986
8 Baikal, Lake, Russia	12,200	31,500
9 Great Bear Lake, Canada	12,095	31,326
10 Nyasa, Lake (Lake Malawi), Malawi-Mozambique-Tanzania	11,150	28,878
11 Great Slave Lake, Canada	11,030	28,568
12 Erie, Lake, Canada-U.S.	9,910	25,667
13 Winnipeg, Lake, Canada	9,416	24,387
14 Ontario, Lake, Canada-U.S.	7,540	19,529
15 Balqash koli (Lake Balkhash), Kazakhstan	7,100	18,300
16 Ladozhskoye, Ozero, Russia	6,833	17,700
17 Chad, Lake (Lac Tchad), Cameroon-Chad-Nigeria	6,300	16,300
18 Onezhskoye, Ozero, Russia	3,753	9,720
19 Eyre, Lake, Australia	3,700	9,500
20 Titicaca, Lago, Bolivia-Peru	3,200	8,300
21 Nicaragua, Lago de, Nicaragua	3,150	8,158
22 Mai-Ndombe, Lac, Zaire	3,100	8,000
23 Athabasca, Lake, Canada	3,064	7,935
24 Reindeer Lake, Canada	2,568	6,650
25 Tônlé Sap, Cambodia	2,500	6,500
26 Rudolf, Lake, Ethiopia-Kenya	2,473	6,405
27 Issyk-Kul', Ozero, Kyrgyzstan	2,425	6,280
28 Torrens, Lake, Australia	2,300	5,900
29 Albert, Lake, Uganda-Zaire	2,160	5,594
30 Vänern, Sweden	2,156	5,584
31 Nettilling Lake, Canada	2,140	5,542
32 Winnipegosis, Lake, Canada	2,075	5,374
33 Bangweulu, Lake, Zambia	1,930	4,999
34 Nipigon, Lake, Canada	1,872	4,848
35 Orumiyeh, Daryacheh-ye, Iran	1,815	4,701
36 Manitoba, Lake, Canada	1,785	4,624
37 Woods, Lake of the, Canada-U.S.	1,727	4,472
38 Kyoga, Lake, Uganda	1,710	4,429
39 Great Salt Lake, U.S.	1,680	4,351

Lake Baikal

Russia's Great Lake

On a map of the world, Lake Baikal is easy to overlook — a thin blue crescent adrift in the vastness of Siberia. But its inconspicuousness is deceptive, for Baikal is one of the greatest bodies of fresh water on Earth.

Although lakes generally have a life span of less than one million years, Baikal has existed for perhaps as long as 25 million years, which makes it the world's oldest body of fresh water. It formed in a rift that tectonic forces had begun to tear open in the Earth's crust. As the rift grew, so did Baikal. Today the lake is 395 miles (636 km) long and an average of 30 miles (48 km) wide. Only seven lakes in the world have a greater surface area.

Baikal is the world's deepest lake. Its maximum depth is 5,315 feet (1,621 m) — slightly over a mile, and roughly equal to the greatest depth of the Grand Canyon. The lake bottom lies 4,250 feet (1,295 m) below sea level and two-and-a-third miles (3.75 km) below the peaks of the surrounding mountains. The crustal rift which Baikal occupies is the planet's deepest land depression, extending to a depth of more than five-and-a-half miles (9 km). The lake sits atop at least four miles (6.4 km) of sediment, the accumulation of 25 million years.

More than 300 rivers empty into Baikal, but only one, the Angara, flows out of it. Despite having only 38% of the surface area of North America's Lake Superior, Baikal contains more water than all five of the Great Lakes combined. Its volume of 5,500 cubic miles (23,000 cubic km) is greater than that of any other freshwater lake in the world and represents approximately one-fifth of all of the Earth's unfrozen fresh water.

Caspian Sea

Lake Superior

Lake Victoria

Aral Sea

Lake Huron

Lake Michigan

Lake Tanganyika

Lake Baikal

Great Bear Lake

Lake Nyasa (Malawi)

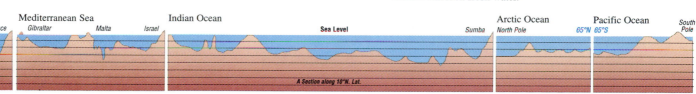

Mediterranean Sea — France — Gibraltar — Malta — Israel

Indian Ocean

Sea Level

Sumba

Arctic Ocean — North Pole — 65°N

Pacific Ocean — 65°S — South Pole

A Section along 10°N. Lat.

Rivers

World's Longest Rivers

Rank	River	Length Miles	Length Kilometers	Rank	River	Length Miles	Length Kilometers
1	Nile, Africa	4,145	6,671	36	Murray, Australia	1,566	2,520
2	Amazon (Amazonas)-Ucayali, South America	4,000	6,400	37	Ganges, Asia	1,560	2,511
3	Yangtze (Chang), Asia	3,900	6,300	38	Pilcomayo, South America	1,550	2,494
4	Mississippi-Missouri, North America	3,740	6,019	39	Euphrates, Asia	1,510	2,430
5	Huang (Yellow), Asia	3,395	5,464	40	Ural, Asia	1,509	2,428
6	Ob'-Irtysh, Asia	3,362	5,410	41	Arkansas, North America	1,459	2,348
7	Río de la Plata-Paraná, South America	3,030	4,876	42	Colorado, North America (U.S.-Mexico)	1,450	2,334
8	Congo (Zaïre), Africa	2,900	4,700	43	Aldan, Asia	1,412	2,273
9	Paraná, South America	2,800	4,500	44	Syr Darya, Asia	1,370	2,205
10	Amur-Argun, Asia	2,761	4,444	45	Dnieper, Europe	1,350	2,200
11	Lena, Asia	2,700	4,400	46	Araguaia, South America	1,350	2,200
12	Mackenzie, North America	2,635	4,241	47	Cassai (Kasai), Africa	1,338	2,153
13	Mekong, Asia	2,600	4,200	48	Tarim, Asia	1,328	2,137
14	Niger, Africa	2,600	4,200	49	Kolyma, Asia	1,323	2,129
15	Yenisey, Asia	2,543	4,092	50	Orange, Africa	1,300	2,100
16	Missouri-Red Rock, North America	2,533	4,076	51	Negro, South America	1,300	2,100
17	Mississippi, North America	2,348	3,779	52	Ayeyarwady (Irrawaddy), Asia	1,300	2,100
18	Murray-Darling, Australia	2,330	3,750	53	Red, North America	1,270	2,044
19	Missouri, North America	2,315	3,726	54	Juruá, South America	1,250	2,012
20	Volga, Europe	2,194	3,531	55	Columbia, North America	1,240	2,000
21	Madeira, South America	2,013	3,240	56	Xingu, South America	1,230	1,979
22	São Francisco, South America	1,988	3,199	57	Ucayali, South America	1,220	1,963
23	Grande, Rio (Río Bravo), North America	1,885	3,034	58	Saskatchewan-Bow, North America	1,205	1,939
24	Purús, South America	1,860	2,993	59	Peace, North America	1,195	1,923
25	Indus, Asia	1,800	2,900	60	Tigris, Asia	1,180	1,899
26	Danube, Europe	1,776	2,858	61	Don, Europe	1,162	1,870
27	Brahmaputra, Asia	1,770	2,849	62	Songhua, Asia	1,140	1,835
28	Yukon, North America	1,770	2,849	63	Pechora, Europe	1,124	1,809
29	Salween (Nu), Asia	1,750	2,816	64	Kama, Europe	1,122	1,805
30	Zambezi, Africa	1,700	2,700	65	Limpopo, Africa	1,120	1,800
31	Vilyuy, Asia	1,647	2,650	66	Angara, Asia	1,105	1,779
32	Tocantins, South America	1,640	2,639	67	Snake, North America	1,038	1,670
33	Orinoco, South America	1,615	2,600	68	Uruguay, South America	1,025	1,650
34	Paraguay, South America	1,610	2,591	69	Churchill, North America	1,000	1,600
35	Amu Darya, Asia	1,578	2,540	70	Marañón, South America	995	1,592

The World's Greatest River

Although the Nile is slightly longer, the Amazon surpasses all other rivers in volume, size of drainage basin, and in nearly every other important category. If any river is to be called the greatest in the world, surely it is the Amazon.

It has been estimated that one-fifth of all of the flowing water on Earth is carried by the Amazon. From its 150-mile (240-km)-wide mouth, the river discharges 6,180,000 cubic feet (174,900 cubic m) of water per second — four-and-a-half times as much as the Congo, ten times as much as the Mississippi, and fifty-six times as much as the Nile. The Amazon's tremendous outflow turns the waters of the Atlantic from salty to brackish for more than 100 miles (160 km) offshore.

Covering more than one-third of the entire continent of South America, the Amazon's vast drainage basin measures 2,669,000 square miles (6,915,000 sq km) and is nearly twice as large as that of the second-ranked Congo. The Amazon begins its 4,000-mile (6,400-km) journey to the Atlantic from high up in the Andes, only 100 miles (160 km) from the Pacific. Along its course it receives the waters of more than 1,000 tributaries, which rise principally from the Andes, the Guiana Highlands, and the Brazilian Highlands. Seven of the tributaries are more than 1,000 miles (1,600 km) long, and one, the Madeira, is more than 2,000 miles (3,200 km) long.

The depth of the Amazon throughout most of its Brazilian segment exceeds 150 feet (45 m). Depths of more than 300 feet (90 m) have been recorded at points near the mouth. The largest ocean-going vessels can sail as far inland as Manaus, 1,000 miles (1,600 km) from the mouth. Freighters and small passenger vessels can navigate to Iquitos, 2,300 miles (3,700 km) from the mouth, even during times of low water.

Drainage basin of the Amazon River

Rivers with the Greatest Volume of Water

Rank	River Name	Flow of water per second at mouth — cubic feet	cubic meters	Rank	River Name	Flow of water per second at mouth — cubic feet	cubic meters
1	Amazon (Amazonas), South America	6,180,000	174,900	18	Para-Tocantins, South America (joins Amazon at mouth)	360,000	10,200
2	Congo, Africa	1,377,000	39,000	19	Salween, Asia	353,000	10,000
3	Negro, South America (tributary of Amazon)	1,236,000	35,000	20	Cassai (Kasai), Africa (trib. of Congo)	351,000	9,900
4	Orinoco, South America	890,000	25,200	21	Mackenzie, North America	343,000	9,700
5	Río de la Plata-Paraná, South America	809,000	22,900	22	Volga, Europe	271,000	7,700
6	Yangtze (Chang), Asia;	770,000	21,800	23	Ohio, North America (trib. of Mississippi)	257,000	7,300
	Madeira, South America (trib. of Amazon)	770,000	21,800	24	Yukon, North America	240,000	6,800
7	Missouri, North America (trib. of Mississippi)	763,000	21,600	25	Indus, Asia	235,000	6,600
8	Mississippi, North America*	640,300	18,100	26	Danube, Europe	227,000	6,400
9	Yenisey, Asia	636,000	18,000	27	Niger, Africa	215,000	6,100
10	Brahmaputra, Asia	575,000	16,300	28	Atchafalaya, North America	181,000	5,100
11	Lena, Asia	569,000	16,100	29	Paraguay, South America	155,000	4,400
12	Zambezi, Africa	565,000	16,000	30	Ob'-Katun, Asia	147,000	4,200
13	Mekong, Asia	500,000	14,100	31	São Francisco, South America	120,000	3,400
14	Saint Lawrence, North America	460,000	13,000	32	Tunguska, Asia	118,000	3,350
15	Ayeyarwady (Irrawaddy), Asia	447,000	12,600	33	Huang (Yellow), Asia	116,000	3,300
16	Ob'-Irtysh, Asia; Ganges, Asia	441,000	12,500	34	Nile, Africa	110,000	3,100
17	Amur, Asia	390,000	11,000				

*Approximately one-third of the Mississippi's water is diverted above Baton Rouge, Louisiana, and reaches the Gulf of Mexico via the Atchafalaya River.

Principal Rivers of the Continents

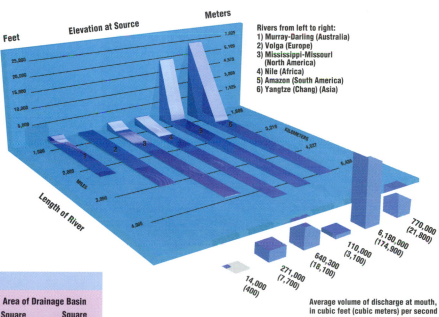

Rivers from left to right:
1) Murray-Darling (Australia)
2) Volga (Europe)
3) Mississippi-Missouri (North America)
4) Nile (Africa)
5) Amazon (South America)
6) Yangtze (Chang) (Asia)

Average volume of discharge at mouth, in cubic feet (cubic meters) per second

Rivers with the Largest Drainage Basins

Rank	River	Square Miles	Square Kilometers
1	Amazon (Amazonas), South America	2,669,000	6,915,000
2	Congo (Zaire), Africa	1,474,500	3,820,000
3	Mississippi-Missouri, North America	1,243,000	3,220,000
4	Río de la Plata-Paraná, South America	1,197,000	3,100,000
5	Ob'-Irtysh, Asia	1,154,000	2,990,000
6	Nile, Africa	1,108,000	2,870,000
7	Yenisey-Angara, Asia	1,011,000	2,618,500
8	Lena, Asia	961,000	2,490,000
9	Niger, Africa	807,000	2,090,000
10	Amur-Argun, Asia	792,000	2,051,300
11	Yangtze (Chang), Asia	705,000	1,826,000
12	Volga, Europe	525,000	1,360,000
13	Zambezi, Africa	513,500	1,330,000
14	St. Lawrence, North America	503,000	1,302,800
15	Huang (Yellow), Asia	486,000	1,258,700

Sources for volume and drainage basin information: Atlas of World Water Balance, USSR National Committee for the International Hydrological Decade and UNESCO, 1977; Principal Rivers and Lakes of the World, National Oceanic and Atmospheric Administration, 1982.

Climate and Weather

Temperature Extremes by Continent

Africa
Highest recorded temperature
Al 'Azīzīyah, Libya, September 13, 1922:
136° F (58° C),
Lowest recorded temperature
Ifrane, Morocco, February 11, 1935:
-11° F (-24° C)

Antarctica
Highest recorded temperature
Vanda Station, January 5, 1974:
59° F (15° C)
Lowest recorded temperature
Vostok, July 21, 1983:
-129° F (-89° C)

Asia
Highest recorded temperature
Tirat Zevi, Israel, June 21, 1942:
129° F (54° C)
Lowest recorded temperature
Oymyakon and Verkhoyansk,
Russia, February 5 and 7, 1892,
and February 6, 1933: -90° F (-68° C)

Australia / Oceania
Highest recorded temperature
Cloncurry, Queensland, January 16, 1889:
128° F (53° C)
Lowest recorded temperature
Charlottes Pass, New South Wales,
June 14, 1945, and July 22, 1947: -8° F (-22° C)

Europe
Highest recorded temperature
Sevilla, Spain, August 4, 1881:
122° F (50° C)
Lowest recorded temperature
Ust' Ščugor, Russia, (date not known):
-67° F (-55° C)

North America
Highest recorded temperature
Death Valley, California, United States,
July 10, 1913: 134° F (57° C)
Lowest recorded temperature
Northice, Greenland, January 9, 1954:
-87° F (-66° C)

South America
Highest recorded temperature
Rivadavia, Argentina, December 11, 1905:
120° F (49° C)
Lowest recorded temperature
Sarmiento, Argentina, June 1, 1907:
-27° F (-33° C)

World
Highest recorded temperature
Al 'Azīzīyah, Libya, September 13, 1922:
136° F (58° C)
Lowest recorded temperature
Vostok, Antarctica, July 21, 1983:
-129° F (-89° C)

World Temperature Extremes

Highest mean annual temperature Dalol, Ethiopia, 94° F (34° C)
Lowest mean annual temperature Plateau Station, Antarctica: -70° F (-57° C)

Greatest difference between highest and lowest recorded temperatures
Verkhoyansk, Russia. The highest temperature ever recorded there is 93.5° F (34.2° C); the lowest is -89.7° F (−67.6° C)
— a difference of 183° F (102° C).

Highest temperature ever recorded at the South Pole 7.5° F (-14° C) on December 27, 1978

Most consecutive days with temperatures of 100° F (38° C) or above Marble Bar, Australia, 162 days: October 30, 1923 to April 7, 1924

Greatest rise in temperature within a 12-hour period
Granville, North Dakota, on February 21, 1918. The temperature rose 83° F (46° C), from -33° F (-36° C)
in early morning to +50° F (10° C) in late afternoon

Greatest drop in temperature within a 12-hour period
Fairfield, Montana, on December 24, 1924. The temperature dropped 84° F (46° C), from 63° F (17° C)
at noon to -21° F (-29° C) by midnight

Temperature Ranges for 14 Major Cities around the World

City	Mean Temperature Coldest Winter Month	Mean Temperature Hottest Summer Month	City	Mean Temperature Coldest Winter Month	Mean Temperature Hottest Summer Month
Bombay, India	Jan: 74.3° F (23.5° C)	May: 85.5° F (29.7° C)	Moscow, Russia	Feb: 14.5° F (-9.7° C)	Jul: 65.8° F (18.8° C)
Buenos Aires, Argentina	Aug: 51.3° F (10.7° C)	Jan: 75.0° F (23.9° C)	New York City, U.S.	Jan: 32.9° F (0.5° C)	Jul: 77.0° F (25.0° C)
Calcutta, India	Jan: 67.5° F (19.7° C)	May: 88.5° F (31.4° C)	Osaka, Japan	Jan: 40.6° F (4.8° C)	Aug: 82.2° F (27.9° C)
London, England	Feb: 39.4° F (4.1° C)	Jul: 63.9° F (17.7° C)	Rio de Janeiro, Brazil	Jul: 70.2 ° F (21.2° C)	Jan: 79.9° F (26.6° C)
Los Angeles, U.S.	Jan: 56.3° F (13.5° C)	Jul: 74.1° F (23.4° C)	São Paulo, Brazil	Jul: 58.8° F (14.9° C)	Jan: 71.1° F (21.7° C)
Manila, Philippines	Jan: 77.7° F (25.4° C)	May: 84.9° F (29.4° C)	Seoul, South Korea	Jan: 23.2° F (-4.9° C)	Aug: 77.7° F (25.4° C)
Mexico City, Mexico	Jan: 54.1° F (12.3° C)	May: 64.9° F (18.3° C)	Tokyo, Japan	Jan: 39.6° F (4.2° C)	Aug: 79.3° F (26.3° C)

Precipitation

Greatest local average annual rainfall
Mt. Waialeale, Kauai, Hawaii,
460 inches (1,168 cm)

Lowest local average annual rainfall
Arica, Chile, .03 inches (.08 cm)

Greatest rainfall in 12 months
Cherrapunji, India, August 1860 to August 1861:
1,042 inches (2,647 cm)

Greatest rainfall in one month
Cherrapunji, India, July 1861: 366 inches (930 cm)

Greatest rainfall in 24 hours
Cilaos, Reunion, March 15 and 16, 1952:
74 inches (188 cm)

Greatest rainfall in 12 hours
Belouve, Reunion, February 28 and 29, 1964:
53 inches (135 cm)

Most thunderstorms annually
Kampala, Uganda, averages 242 days per
year with thunderstorms

Between 1916 and 1920, Bogor, Indonesia,
averaged 322 days per year with thunderstorms

Longest dry period
Arica, Chile, October, 1903
to January, 1918 — over 14 years

Largest hailstone ever recorded
Coffeyville, Kansas, U.S., September 3, 1970:
circumference 17.5 inches (44.5 cm)
diameter 5.6 inches (14 cm),
weight 1.67 pounds (758 grams)

Heaviest hailstone ever recorded
Kazakhstan, 1959: 4.18 pounds (1.9 kilograms)

North America's greatest snowfall in one season
Rainier Paradise Ranger Station, Washington,
U.S., 1971–1972: 1,122 inches (2,850 cm)

North America's greatest snowfall in one storm
Mt. Shasta Ski Bowl, California, U.S.,
February 13 to 19, 1959: 189 inches (480 cm)

North America's greatest snowfall in 24 hours
Silver Lake, Colorado, U.S., April 14 and 15, 1921:
76 inches (1 92.5 cm)

N. America's greatest depth of snowfall on the ground
Tamarack, California, U.S., March 11, 1911:
451 inches (1,145.5 cm)

Foggiest place on the U.S. West Coast
Cape Disappointment, Washington,
averages 2,552 hours of fog per year

Foggiest place on the U.S. East Coast
Mistake Island, Maine, averages
1,580 hours of fog per year

Wind

Highest 24-hour mean surface wind speed
Mt. Washington, New Hampshire, U.S.,
April 11 and 12, 1934: 128 mph (206 kph)

Highest 5-minute mean surface wind speed
Mt. Washington, New Hampshire, U.S.,
April 12, 1934: 188 mph (303 kph)

Highest surface wind peak gust:
Mt. Washington, New Hampshire, U.S.,
April 12, 1934: 231 mph (372 kph)

Windiest U.S. Cities

Chicago is sometimes called "The Windy City."
It earned this nickname because of long-winded politicians,
not because it has the strongest gales.

The windiest cities in the U.S. are as follows:

Cities	Average wind speed	
	mph	kph
Great Falls, Montana	13.1	21.0
Oklahoma City, Oklahoma	13.0	20.9
Boston, Massachusetts	12.9	20.7
Cheyenne, Wyoming	12.8	20.6
Wichita, Kansas	12.7	20.4

Chicago ranks 16th, with a 10.4 mph (16.7 kph) average.

Deadliest Hurricanes in the U.S. since 1900

Rank	Place	Year	Number of Deaths
1	Texas (Galveston)	1900	>6,000
2	Louisiana	1893	2,000
3	Florida (Lake Okeechobee)	1928	1,836
4	South Carolina, Georgia	1893	>1,000
5	Florida (Keys)	1919	>600
6	New England	1938	600
7	Florida (Keys)	1935	408
8	Southwest Louisiana, north Texas— "Hurricane Audrey"	1957	390
	Northeast U.S.	1944	390
9	Louisiana (Grand Isle)	1909	350
10	Louisana (New Orleans)	1915	275

Tornadoes in the U.S., 1950—1993

Rank	State	Total Number of Tornadoes	Yearly Average	Total Number of Deaths
1	Texas	5,303	120	471
2	Oklahoma	2,259	51	217
3	Kansas	2,068	47	199
4	Florida	1,932	44	81
5	Nebraska	1,618	37	51
	U.S. Total	33,120	753	4,045

Deadliest Floods in the U.S. since 1900

Rank	Place	Year	Number of Deaths
1	Ohio River and tributaries	1913	467
2	Mississippi Valley	1927	313
3	Black Hills, South Dakota	1972	237
4	Texas rivers	1921	215
5	Northeastern U.S., following Hurricane Dianne	1955	187
6	Texas rivers	1913	177
7	James River basin, Virginia	1969	153
8	Big Thompson Canyon, Colorado	1976	139
9	Ohio and Lower Mississippi river basins	1937	137
10	Buffalo Creek, West Virginia	1972	125

Population

During the first two million years of our species' existence, human population grew at a very slow rate, and probably never exceeded 10 million. With the development of agriculture circa 8000 B.C., the growth rate began to rise sharply: by the year A.D. 1, the world population stood at approximately 250 million.

By 1650 the population had doubled to 550 million, and within only 200 years it doubled again, reaching almost 1.2 billion by 1850. Each subsequent doubling has taken only about half as long as the previous one: 100 years to reach 2.5 billion, and 40 years to reach 5.2 billion.

Experts have estimated that today's world population of 5.6 billion represents 5.5% of all of the people who have ever lived on Earth.*

* *Population Today, Population Reference Bureau, February 1995*

World Population

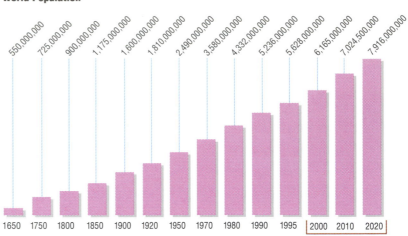

The World's Estimated Population (as of January 1, 1995): 5,628,000,000
Population Density: 97 people per square mile (37 people per square kilometer)

Projected Population

Historical Populations of the Continents and the World

Year	Africa	Asia	Australia	Europe	North America	Oceania, incl. Australia	South America	World
1650	*100,000,000*	335,000,000	*<1,000,000*	*100,000,000*	*5,000,000*	*2,000,000*	*8,000,000*	*550,000,000*
1750	*95,000,000*	476,000,000	*<1,000,000*	*140,000,000*	*5,000,000*	*2,000,000*	*7,000,000*	*725,000,000*
1800	*90,000,000*	593,000,000	*<1,000,000*	*190,000,000*	*13,000,000*	*2,000,000*	*12,000,000*	*900,000,000*
1850	*95,000,000*	754,000,000	*<1,000,000*	265,000,000	*39,000,000*	*2,000,000*	*20,000,000*	*1,175,000,000*
1900	*118,000,000*	932,000,000	4,000,000	400,000,000	106,000,000	6,000,000	38,000,000	*1,600,000,000*
1920	*140,000,000*	1,000,000,000	6,000,000	453,000,000	147,000,000	9,000,000	61,000,000	*1,810,000,000*
1950	199,000,000	1,418,000,000	8,000,000	530,000,000	219,000,000	13,000,000	111,000,000	*2,490,000,000*
1970	346,900,000	2,086,200,000	12,460,000	623,700,000	316,600,000	19,200,000	187,400,000	3,580,000,000
1980	463,800,000	2,581,000,000	14,510,000	660,000,000	365,000,000	22,700,000	239,000,000	4,332,000,000
1990	648,300,000	3,156,100,000	16,950,000	688,000,000	423,600,000	26,300,000	293,700,000	5,236,000,000

Figures for years prior to 1970 are rounded to the nearest million. Figures in italics represent rough estimates.

The 50 Most Populous Countries

Rank	Country	Population	Rank	Country	Population	Rank	Country	Population
1	China	1,196,980,000	18	United Kingdom	58,430,000	35	Algeria	27,965,000
2	India	909,150,000	19	Egypt	58,100,000	36	Morocco	26,890,000
3	United States	262,530,000	20	France	58,010,000	37	Sudan	25,840,000
4	Indonesia	193,680,000	21	Italy	57,330,000	38	Korea, North	23,265,000
5	Brazil	159,690,000	22	Ethiopia	55,070,000	39	Peru	23,095,000
6	Russia	150,500,000	23	Ukraine	52,140,000	40	Uzbekistan	22,860,000
7	Pakistan	129,630,000	24	Myanmar	44,675,000	41	Romania	22,745,000
8	Japan	125,360,000	25	Korea, South	44,655,000	42	Venezuela	21,395,000
9	Bangladesh	119,370,000	26	South Africa	44,500,000	43	Nepal	21,295,000
10	Nigeria	97,300,000	27	Zaire	43,365,000	44	Taiwan	21,150,000
11	Mexico	93,860,000	28	Spain	39,260,000	45	Iraq	20,250,000
12	Germany	81,710,000	29	Poland	38,730,000	46	Afghanistan	19,715,000
13	Vietnam	73,760,000	30	Colombia	34,870,000	47	Malaysia	19,505,000
14	Philippines	67,910,000	31	Argentina	34,083,000	48	Uganda	18,270,000
15	Iran	63,810,000	32	Kenya	28,380,000	49	Sri Lanka	18,240,000
16	Turkey	62,030,000	33	Tanzania	28,350,000	50	Australia	18,205,000
17	Thailand	59,870,000	34	Canada	28,285,000			

Most Densely Populated Countries

Rank	Country (Population)	Population per Square Mile	Population per Square Kilometer
1	Monaco (31,000)	44,286	16,316
2	Singapore (2,921,000)	11,874	4,593
3	Vatican City (1,000)	5,000	2,500
4	Malta (368,000)	3,016	1,165
5	Maldives (251,000)	2,183	842
6	Bangladesh (119,370,000)	2,147	829
7	Guernsey (64,000)	2,133	821
8	Bahrain (563,000)	2,109	815
9	Jersey (86,000)	1,911	741
10	Barbados (261,000)	1,572	607
11	Taiwan (21,150,000)	1,522	587
12	Mauritius (1,121,000)	1,423	550
13	Nauru (10,000)	1,235	476
14	Korea, South (44,655,000)	1,168	451
15	Puerto Rico (3,625,000)	1,031	398

Least Densely Populated Countries

Rank	Country (Population)	Population per Square Mile	Population per Square Kilometer
1	Greenland (57,000)	0.07	0.03
2	Mongolia (2,462,000)	4.1	1.6
3	Namibia (1,623,000)	5.1	2.0
4	Mauritania (2,228,000)	5.6	2.2
5	Australia (18,205,000)	6.1	2.4
6	Botswana (1,438,000)	6.4	2.5
7	Iceland (265,000), Suriname (426,000)	6.7	2.6
8	Canada (28,285,000)	7.3	2.8
9	Libya (5,148,000)	7.6	2.9
10	Guyana (726,000)	8.7	3.4
11	Gabon (1,035,000)	10.1	3.9
12	Chad (6,396,000)	12.9	5.0
13	Central African Republic (3,177,000)	13.0	5.1
14	Bolivia (6,790,000)	16.0	6.2
15	Kazakhstan (17,025,000)	16.3	6.3

Most Highly Urbanized Countries

Country	Urban pop. as a % of total pop.
Vatican City	100%
Singapore	100%
Monaco	100%
Belgium	96%
Kuwait	96%
San Marino	92%
Israel (excl. Occupied Areas)	92%
Venezuela	91%
Iceland	91%
Qatar	90%
Uruguay	89%
Netherlands	89%
United Kingdom	89%
Malta	87%
Argentina	86%

Least Urbanized Countries

Country	Urban pop. as a % of total pop.
Bhutan	5%
Burundi	5%
Rwanda	6%
Nepal	11%
Oman	11%
Uganda	11%
Ethiopia	12%
Cambodia (Kampuchea)	12%
Malawi	12%
Burkina Faso	15%
Eritrea	15%
Grenada	15%
Solomon Islands	15%
Bangladesh	16%
Northern Mariana Islands	16%

Fastest-Growing and Slowest-Growing Countries

A country's rate of natural increase is determined by subtracting the number of deaths from the number of births for a given period. Immigration and emigration are not included in this formulation.

The highest rate of natural increase among major countries today is Syria's 3.74%. At this rate, Syria's 1995 population of 14,100,000 will double in 19 years and triple in 30 years.

In Hungary and Ukraine deaths currently outnumber births, and the two countries share the same negative rate of natural increase, -0.026%, the lowest in the world.

When all of the countries of the world are compared, pronounced regional patterns become apparent. Of the 35 fastest-growing countries, 30 are found in either Africa or the Middle East. Of the 45 slowest-growing countries, 42 are found in Europe.

World's Largest Metropolitan Areas

Rank	Name	Population
1	Tokyo-Yokohama, Japan	30,300,000
2	New York City, U.S.	18,087,000
3	São Paulo, Brazil	16,925,000
4	Osaka-Kobe-Kyoto, Japan	16,900,000
5	Seoul, South Korea	15,850,000
6	Los Angeles, U.S.	14,531,000
7	Mexico City, Mexico	14,100,000
8	Moscow, Russia	13,150,000
9	Bombay, India	12,596,000
10	London, England	11,100,000
11	Rio de Janeiro, Brazil	11,050,000
12	Calcutta, India	11,022,000
13	Buenos Aires, Argentina	11,000,000
14	Paris, France	10,275,000
15	Jakarta, Indonesia	10,200,000

The World's Most Populous Cities

The following table lists the most populous cities of the world by continent and in descending order of population. It includes all cities with central city populations of 500,000 or greater. Cities with populations of less than 500,000 but with metropolitan area populations of 1,000,000 or greater have also been included in the table.

The city populations listed are the latest available census figures or official estimates. For a few cities, only unofficial estimates are available. The year in which the census was taken or to which the estimate refers is provided in parentheses preceding the city population. When comparing populations it is important to keep in mind that some figures are more current than others.

Figures in parentheses represent metropolitan area populations — the combined populations of the cities and their suburbs.

The sequence of information in each listing is as follows: city name, country name (metropolitan area population) (date of census or estimate) city population.

The Most Populous City in the World, through History

With more than 30 million people, Japan's Tokyo-Yokohama agglomeration ranks as the most populous metropolitan area in the world today. New York City held this title from the mid-1920's through the mid-1960's. But what city was the most populous in the world five hundred years ago? Five *thousand* years ago?

The following time line represents one expert's attempt to name the cities that have reigned as the most populous in the world since 3200 B.C. The time line begins with Memphis, the capital of ancient Egypt, which was possibly the first city in the world to attain a population of 20,000.

Listed after each city name is the name of the political entity to which the city belonged during the time that it was the most populous city in the world. The name of the modern political entity in which the city, its ruins, or its site is located, where this entity differs from the historic political entity, is listed in parentheses.

For the purpose of this time line, the word "city" is used in the general sense to denote a city, metropolitan area, or urban agglomeration.

It is important to note that reliable census figures are not available for most of the 5,200 years covered by this time line. Therefore the time line is somewhat subjective and conjectural.

Africa

Cairo (Al Qāhirah), Egypt (9,300,000) ('86)	6,068,695
Kinshasa, Zaire ('86)	3,000,000
Alexandria (Al Iskandarīyah), Egypt (3,350,000) ('86)	2,926,859
Casablanca (Dar-el-Beida), Morocco (2,475,000) ('82)	2,139,204
Abidjan, Cote d'Ivoire ('88)	1,929,079
Addis Ababa, Ethiopia (1,990,000) ('90)	1,912,500
Giza (Al Jīzah), Egypt ('86)	1,883,189
Algiers (El Djazaïr), Algeria (2,547,983)('87)	1,507,241
Nairobi, Kenya ('90)	1,505,000
Dakar, Senegal ('88)	1,490,450
Luanda, Angola ('89)	1,459,900
Antananarivo, Madagascar ('88)	1,250,000
Lagos, Nigeria (3,800,000) ('87)	1,213,000
Ibadan, Nigeria ('87)	1,144,000
Dar es Salaam, Tanzania ('85)	1,096,000
Maputo, Mozambique ('89)	1,069,727
Lusaka, Zambia ('90)	982,362
Accra, Ghana (1,390,000) ('87)	949,113
Cape Town, South Africa (1,900,000) ('91)	854,616
Conakry, Guinea ('86)	800,000
Kampala, Uganda ('91)	773,463
Durban, South Africa (1,740,000) ('91)	715,669
Shubrā al Khaymah, Egypt ('86)	714,594
Johannesburg, South Africa (4,000,000) ('91)	712,507
Douala, Cameroon ('87)	712,251
Brazzaville, Congo ('89)	693,712
Harare, Zimbabwe (955,000) ('83)	681,000
Bamako, Mali ('87)	658,275
Oran, Algeria ('87)	628,558
Mogadishu (Muqdisho), Somalia ('84)	600,000
Bangui, Central African Republic ('89)	596,800
Tunis, Tunisia (1,225,000) ('84)	596,654
Soweto, South Africa ('91)	596,632
Tripoli (Ṭarābulus), Libya (960,000) ('88)	591,062
Ogbomosho, Nigeria ('87)	582,900
Lubumbashi, Zaire ('84)	564,830
Yaoundé, Cameroon ('87)	560,785
Kano, Nigeria ('87)	538,300
Mombasa, Kenya ('90)	537,000
Cotonou, Benin ('92)	533,212
Omdurman (Umm Durmān), Sudan ('83)	526,192
Pretoria, South Africa (1,100,000) ('91)	525,583
Rabat, Morocco (980,000) ('82)	518,616
Lomé, Togo ('87)	500,000
N'Djamena, Chad ('88)	500,000
Khartoum (Al Khartūm), Sudan (1,450,000) ('83)	473,597

Asia

Seoul (Sŏul), South Korea (15,850,000) ('90)	10,627,790
Bombay, India (12,596,243) ('91)	9,925,891
Jakarta, Indonesia (10,200,000) ('90)	8,227,746
Tōkyō, Japan (30,300,000) ('90)	8,163,573
Shanghai, China (9,300,000) ('88)	7,220,000
Delhi, India (8,419,084) ('91)	7,206,704
Beijing (Peking), China (7,320,000) ('88)	6,710,000
İstanbul, Turkey (7,550,000) ('90)	6,620,241
Tehrān, Iran (7,550,000) ('86)	6,042,584
Bangkok (Krung Thep), Thailand (7,060,000) ('91)	5,620,591
Tianjin (Tientsin), China ('88)	4,950,000
Karāchi, Pakistan (5,300,000) ('81)	4,901,627
Calcutta, India (11,021,918) ('91)	4,399,819
Shenyang (Mukden), China ('88)	3,910,000
Madras, India (5,421,985) ('91)	3,841,396
Baghdād, Iraq ('87)	3,841,268
Pusan, South Korea (3,800,000) ('90)	3,797,566
Dhaka (Dacca), Bangladesh (6,537,308) ('91)	3,637,892
Wuhan, China ('88)	3,570,000
Yokohama, Japan ('90)	3,220,331
Guangzhou (Canton), China ('88)	3,100,000
Hyderābād, India (4,344,437) ('91)	3,043,896
Ahmadābād, India (3,312,216) ('91)	2,876,710
Ho Chi Minh City (Saigon), Vietnam (3,300,000) ('89)	2,796,229
Harbin, China ('88)	2,710,000
Lahore, Pakistan (3,025,000) ('81)	2,707,215
T'aipei, Taiwan (6,130,000) ('92)	2,706,453
Singapore, Singapore (3,025,000) ('90)	2,690,100
Bangalore, India (4,130,288) ('91)	2,660,088
Ōsaka, Japan (16,900,000) ('90)	2,623,801
Ankara, Turkey (2,650,000) ('90)	2,559,471
Rangoon (Yangon), Myanmar (2,650,000) ('83)	2,513,023
Chongqing (Chungking), China ('88)	2,502,000
Surabaya, Indonesia ('90)	2,473,272
Nanjing (Nanking), China ('88)	2,390,000
P'yŏngyang, North Korea ('81)	2,355,000
Dalian (Dairen), China ('88)	2,280,000
Taegu, South Korea ('90)	2,228,834
Xi'an (Sian), China ('88)	2,210,000
Nagoya, Japan (4,800,000) ('90)	2,154,793
Tashkent, Uzbekistan (2,325,000) ('91)	2,113,300
Bandung, Indonesia (2,220,000) ('90)	2,058,122
Chengdu (Chengtu), China ('88)	1,884,000
Kānpur, India (2,029,889) ('91)	1,874,409
Changchun, China ('88)	1,822,000
Inch'ŏn, South Korea ('90)	1,818,293
İzmir, Turkey (1,900,000) ('90)	1,757,414
Medan, Indonesia ('90)	1,730,052
Taiyuan, China ('88)	1,700,000
Sapporo, Japan (1,900,000) ('90)	1,671,742
Quezon City, Philippines ('90)	1,666,766
Nāgpur, India (1,664,006) ('91)	1,624,752
Lucknow, India (1,669,204) ('91)	1,619,115
Manila, Philippines (9,650,000) ('90)	1,598,918
Aleppo, Syria (1,640,000) ('94)	1,591,400
Pune, India (2,493,987) ('91)	1,566,651
Chittagong, Bangladesh (2,342,662) ('91)	1,566,070
Damascus (Dimashq), Syria (2,230,000) ('94)	1,549,932
Jinan (Tsinan), China ('88)	1,546,000
New Kowloon (Xinjiulong), Hong Kong ('86)	1,526,910
Sūrat, India (1,518,950) ('91)	1,498,817
Kōbe, Japan ('90)	1,477,410
Mashhad, Iran ('86)	1,463,508
Kyōto, Japan ('90)	1,461,103
Jaipur, India (1,518,235) ('91)	1,458,483
Novosibirsk, Russia (1,600,000) ('91)	1,446,300
Kābul, Afghanistan ('88)	1,424,400
Kaohsiung, Taiwan (1,845,000) ('92)	1,401,239
Anshan, China ('88)	1,330,000
Kunming, China ('88)	1,310,000
Jiddah, Saudi Arabia ('80)	1,300,000
Qingdao (Tsingtao), China ('88)	1,300,000
Lanzhou (Lanchow), China ('88)	1,297,000
Hangzhou (Hangchow), China ('88)	1,290,000

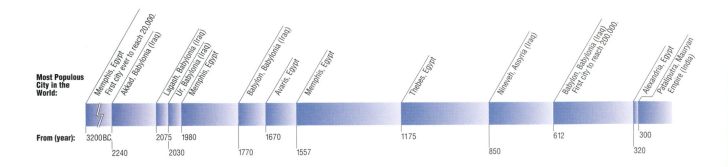

Most Populous City in the World:											
	Memphis, Egypt First city ever to reach 20,000.	Akkad, Babylonia (Iraq)	Lagash, Babylonia (Iraq)	Ur, Babylonia (Iraq) Memphis, Egypt	Babylon, Babylonia (Iraq)	Avaris, Egypt	Memphis, Egypt	Thebes, Egypt	Nineveh, Assyria (Iraq)	Babylon, Babylonia (Iraq) First city to reach 200,000.	Alexandria, Egypt Pataliputra, Mauryan Empire (India)

| From (year): | 3200 B.C. | 2240 | 2075 | 2030 1980 | 1770 | 1670 | 1557 | 1175 | 850 | 612 | 320 300 |

Fushun (Funan), China ('88) 1,290,000
Tbilisi, Georgia (1,460,000) ('91) 1,279,000
Victoria, Hong Kong (4,770,000) ('91) . . 1,250,993
Riyadh (Ar-Riyād), Saudi Arabia ('80) . . 1,250,000
Semarang, Indonesia ('90) 1,249,230
Fukuoka, Japan (1,750,000) ('90) 1,237,062
Changsha, China ('88) 1,230,000
Shijiazhuang, China ('88) 1,220,000
Jilin (Kirin), China ('88) 1,200,000
Yerevan, Armenia (1,315,000) ('89) . . . 1,199,000
Qiqihar (Tsitsihar), China ('88) 1,180,000
Kawasaki, Japan ('90) 1,173,603
Omsk, Russia (1,190,000) ('91) 1,166,800
Alma-Ata (Almaty),
  Kazakhstan (1,190,000) ('91) 1,156,200
Zhengzhou (Chengchow), China ('88) . . 1,150,000
Chelyabinsk, Russia (1,325,000) ('91) . . 1,148,300
Kwangju, South Korea ('90) 1,144,695
Palembang, Indonesia ('90) 1,144,047
Baotou (Paotow), China ('88) 1,130,000
Faisalabad (Lyallpur), Pakistan ('81) . . . 1,104,209
Indore, India (1,109,056) ('91) 1,091,674
Nanchang, China ('88) 1,090,000
Hiroshima, Japan (1,575,000) ('90) 1,085,705
Baku (Bakı),
  Azerbaijan (2,020,000) ('91) 1,080,500
Tangshan, China ('88) 1,080,000
Bhopāl, India ('91) 1,062,771
Taejŏn, South Korea ('90) 1,062,084
Ürümqi, China ('88) 1,060,000
Ludhiāna, India ('91) 1,042,740
Vadodara, India (1,126,824) ('91) 1,031,346
Guiyang (Kweiyang), China ('88) 1,030,000
Kitakyūshū, Japan (1,525,000) ('90) . . . 1,026,455
Kalyān, India ('91) 1,014,557
Eşfahān, Iran (1,175,000) ('86) 986,753
Tabrīz, Iran ('86) 971,482
Hāora, India ('91) 950,435
Ujungpandang (Makasar), Indonesia ('90) . 944,372
Madurai, India (1,085,914) ('91) 940,989

'Ammān, Jordan (1,625,000) ('89) 936,300
Vārānasi (Benares), India (1,030,863) ('91) 929,270
Krasnoyarsk, Russia ('91) 924,400
Kuala Lumpur, Malaysia (1,475,000) ('80) . 919,610
Sendai, Japan (1,175,000) ('90) 918,398
Patna, India (1,099,647) ('91) 917,243
Adana, Turkey ('90) 916,150
Fuzhou, China ('88) 910,000
Hanoi, Vietnam (1,275,000) ('89) 905,939
Āgra, India (948,063) ('91) 891,790
Wuxi (Wuhsi), China ('88) 880,000
Handan, China ('88) 870,000
Xuzhou (Süchow), China ('88) 860,000
Benxi (Penhsi), China ('88) 860,000
Shīrāz, Iran ('86) 848,289
Zibo (Zhangdian), China ('88) 840,000
Yichun, China ('88) 840,000
Bursa, Turkey ('90) 834,576

Chiba, Japan ('90) 829,455
Coimbatore, India (1,100,746) ('91) 816,321
Datong, China ('88) 810,000
Sakai, Japan ('90) 807,765
Thāna, India ('91) 803,369
Allahābād, India (844,546) ('91) 792,858
T'aichung, Taiwan ('92) 785,182
Kowloon (Jiulong), Hong Kong ('86) . . . 774,781
Caloocan, Philippines ('90) 761,011
Luoyang (Loyang), China ('88) 760,000
Meerut, India (849,799) ('91) 753,778
Vishākhapatnam, India (1,057,118) ('91) . 752,037
Jabalpur, India (888,916) ('91) 741,927
Suzhou (Soochow), China ('88) 740,000
Hefei, China ('88) 740,000
Nanning, China ('88) 720,000
Jinzhou (Chinchou), China ('88) 710,000
Amritsar, India ('91) 708,835
Hyderābād, Pakistan (800,000) ('81) . . . 702,539
Vijayawāda, India (845,756) ('91) 701,827
Fuxin, China ('88) 700,000
Jixi, China ('88) 700,000
Huainan, China ('88) 700,000
Multān, Pakistan (732,070) ('81) 696,316
Malang, Indonesia ('90) 695,089
T'ainan, Taiwan ('92) 692,116
Gwalior, India (717,780) ('91) 690,765
Ulsan, South Korea ('90) 682,978
Liuzhou, China ('88) 680,000
Hohhot, China ('88) 670,000
Bucheon, South Korea ('90) 667,777
Jodhpur, India ('91) 666,279
Nāshik, India (725,341) ('91) 656,925
Mudanjiang, China ('88) 650,000
Hubli-Dhārwār, India ('91) 648,298
Vladivostok, Russia ('91) 648,000
Suwŏn, South Korea ('90) 644,968
Hims, Syria ('94) 644,204
Irkutsk, Russia ('91) 640,500
Daqing, China ('88) 640,000
Bishkek, Kyrgyzstan ('91) 631,300
Phnum Pénh, Cambodia ('90) 620,000
Xining (Sining), China ('88) 620,000
Farīdabad, India ('91) 617,717
Al Basrah, Iraq ('85) 616,700
Khabarovsk, Russia ('91) 613,300
Colombo, Sri Lanka (2,050,000) ('89) . . 612,000
Cebu, Philippines (825,000) ('90) 610,417
Qaraghandy, Kazakhstan ('91) 608,600
Barnaul, Russia (673,000) ('91) 606,800
Solāpur, India (620,846) ('91) 604,215
Gaziantep, Turkey ('90) 603,434
Novokuznetsk, Russia ('91) 601,900
Khulna, Bangladesh (966,096) ('91) . . . 601,051
Gujrānwāla, Pakistan (658,753) ('81) . . 600,993
Rānchi, India (614,795) ('91) 599,306
Srīnagar, India (606,002) ('81) 594,775
Okayama, Japan ('90) 593,730
Hegang, China ('86) 588,300
Bareilly, India (617,350) ('91) 587,211
Guwāhāti, India ('91) 584,342
Dushanbe, Tajikistan ('91) 582,400
Ahvāz, Iran ('86) 579,826
Dandong, China ('86) 579,800
Kumamoto, Japan ('90) 579,306
Ulan Bator, Mongolia ('91) 575,000
Aurangābād, India (592,709) ('91) 573,272
Al-Mawşil, Iraq ('85) 570,926
Ningbo, China ('88) 570,000
Cochin, India (1,140,605) ('91) 564,589
Bākhtarān (Kermānshāh), Iran ('86) . . . 560,514
Shantou (Swatow), China ('88) 560,000
Rājkot, India (654,490) ('91) 559,407

Mecca (Makkah), Saudi Arabia ('80) 550,000
Qom, Iran ('86) 543,139
Söngnam, South Korea ('90) 540,764
T'aipeihsien, Taiwan ('91) 538,954
Kota, India ('91) 537,371
Kagoshima, Japan ('90) 536,752
Hamamatsu, Japan ('90) 534,620
Funabashi, Japan ('90) 533,270
Mandalay, Myanmar ('83) 532,949
Sagamihara, Japan ('90) 531,542
Jerusalem (Yerushalayim) (Al-Quds),
  Israel (560,000) ('91) 524,500
Trivandrum, India (826,225) ('91) 524,006
Changzhou (Changchow), China ('86) . . . 522,700
Davao, Philippines ('90) 521,525
Kemerovo, Russia ('91) 520,700
Higashiōsaka, Japan ('90) 518,319

Chŏnju, South Korea ('90) 517,104
Pimpri-Chinchwad, India ('91) 517,083
Tsuen Wan (Quanwan), Hong Kong ('86) . 514,241
Konya, Turkey ('90) 513,346
Jalandhar, India ('91) 509,510
Beirut (Bayrūt), Lebanon (1,675,000) ('82) 509,000
Peshāwar, Pakistan (566,248) ('81) 506,896
Tomsk, Russia ('91) 505,600
Gorakhpur, India ('91) 505,566
Chandīgarh, India (575,829) ('91) 504,094
Surakarta, Indonesia (590,000) ('90) . . . 503,827
Zhangjiakou (Kalgan), China ('88) 500,000
Rāwalpindi, Pakistan (1,040,000) ('81) . . 457,091
Tel Aviv-Yafo, Israel (1,735,000) ('91) . . . 339,400
Kuwait (Al-Kuwayt),
  Kuwait (1,375,000) ('85) 44,335

Brisbane, Australia (1,334,017) ('91) 751,115
Perth, Australia (1,143,249) ('91) 80,517
Melbourne, Australia (3,022,439) ('91) . . . 60,476
Adelaide, Australia (1,023,597) ('91) 14,843
Sydney, Australia (3,538,749) ('91) 13,501

Moscow (Moskva),
  Russia (13,150,000) ('91) 8,801,500
London, England, U.K. (11,100,000) ('81) 6,574,009
Saint Petersburg (Leningrad),
  Russia (5,525,000) ('91) 4,466,800
Berlin, Germany (4,150,000) ('91) 3,433,695
Madrid, Spain (4,650,000) ('88) 3,102,846
Rome (Roma), Italy (3,175,000) ('91) . . 2,693,383
Kiev (Kyyiv), Ukraine (3,250,000) ('91) . 2,635,000
Paris, France (10,275,000) ('90) 2,152,423
Bucharest (Bucureşti),
  Romania (2,300,000) ('92) 2,064,474
Budapest, Hungary (2,515,000) ('90) . . 2,016,774
Barcelona, Spain (4,040,000) ('88) 1,714,355
Hamburg, Germany (2,385,000) ('91) . . 1,652,363

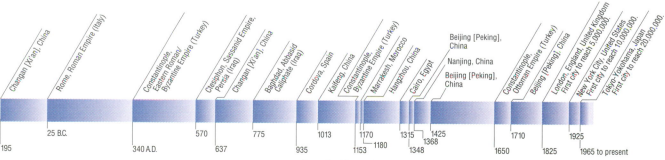

Source: Four Thousand Years of Urban Growth *by Tertius Chandler, Edwin Mellen Press, 1987.*

Warsaw (Warszawa),
Poland (2,312,000) ('93) . . . 1,644,500
Minsk, Belarus (1,694,000) ('91) . . . 1,633,600
Kharkiv (Kharkov),
Ukraine (2,050,000) ('91) . . . 1,622,800
Vienna (Wien), Austria (1,900,000) ('91) . 1,539,848
Nizhniy Novgorod (Gorky),
Russia (2,025,000) ('91) . . . 1,445,000
Yekaterinburg, Russia (1,620,000) ('91) . 1,375,400
Milan (Milano), Italy (3,750,000) ('91) . . 1,371,008
Samara (Kuybyshev),
Russia (1,505,000) ('91) . . . 1,257,300
Munich (München),
Germany (1,900,000) ('91) . . . 1,229,026
Prague (Praha),
Czech Republic (1,328,000) ('91) . . . 1,212,010
Dnipropetrovs'k,
Ukraine (1,600,000) ('91) . . . 1,189,300
Sofia (Sofiya), Bulgaria (1,205,000) ('89) 1,136,875
Belgrade (Beograd),
Yugoslavia (1,554,826) ('91) . . . 1,136,786
Donets'k, Ukraine (2,125,000) ('91) . . . 1,121,300
Perm', Russia (1,180,000) ('91) . . . 1,110,400
Kazan', Russia (1,165,000) ('91) . . . 1,107,300
Odesa, Ukraine (1,185,000) ('91) . . . 1,100,700
Ufa, Russia (1,118,000) ('91) . . . 1,097,000
Rostov-na-Donu,
Russia (1,165,000) ('91) . . . 1,027,600
Naples (Napoli), Italy (2,875,000) ('91) . 1,024,601
Birmingham,
England, U.K. (2,675,000) ('81) . . . 1,013,995
Volgograd (Stalingrad),
Russia (1,360,000) ('91) . . . 1,007,300
Turin (Torino), Italy (1,550,000) ('91) . . . 961,916
Cologne, Germany (1,810,000) ('91) . . . 953,551
Łódź, Poland (950,000) ('93) . . . 938,400
Saratov, Russia (1,155,000) ('91) . . . 911,100
Rīga, Latvia (1,005,000) ('91) . . . 910,200
Voronezh, Russia ('91) . . . 900,000
Zaporizhzhya, Ukraine ('91) . . . 896,600
Lisbon (Lisboa), Portugal (2,250,000) ('81) 807,167
L'viv (L'vov), Ukraine ('91) . . . 802,200
Marseille, France (1,225,000) ('90) . . . 800,550
Athens (Athínai), Greece (3,096,775) ('91) . 748,110
Kraków, Poland (823,000) ('93) . . . 744,000
València, Spain (1,270,000) ('88) . . . 743,933
Kryvyy Rih, Ukraine ('91) . . . 724,000
Amsterdam, Netherlands (1,875,000) ('92) . 713,407
Zagreb, Croatia ('87) . . . 697,925
Palermo, Italy ('91) . . . 697,162
Glasgow, Scotland, U.K. (1,800,000) ('90) . 689,210
Chişinău (Kishinev), Moldova ('91) . . . 676,700
Genoa (Genova), Italy (805,000) ('91) . . . 675,639
Stockholm, Sweden (1,491,726) ('91) . . . 674,452
Sevilla, Spain (945,000) ('88) . . . 663,132
Tol'yatti, Russia ('91) . . . 654,700
Ul'yanovsk, Russia ('91) . . . 648,300
Izhevsk, Russia ('91) . . . 646,800
Frankfurt (Frankfurt am Main),
Germany (1,935,000) ('91) . . . 644,865
Wrocław (Breslau), Poland ('93) . . . 640,700
Yaroslavl', Russia ('91) . . . 638,100
Krasnodar, Russia ('91) . . . 631,200
Essen, Germany (5,050,000) ('91) . . . 626,973
Dortmund, Germany ('91) . . . 599,055
Vilnius, Lithuania ('92) . . . 596,900
Rotterdam, Netherlands (1,120,000) ('92) . 589,707
Poznań, Poland (666,000) ('93) . . . 582,900
Zaragoza, Spain ('88) . . . 582,239
Stuttgart, Germany (2,005,000) ('91) . . . 579,988
Düsseldorf, Germany (1,225,000) ('91) . . . 575,794
Málaga, Spain ('88) . . . 574,456
Orenburg, Russia ('91) . . . 556,500
Bremen, Germany (790,000) ('91) . . . 551,219
Penza, Russia ('91) . . . 551,100
Tula, Russia (640,000) ('91) . . . 543,600
Liverpool, England, U.K. (1,525,000) ('81) . 538,809
Duisburg, Germany ('91) . . . 535,447
Ryazan', Russia ('91) . . . 527,200
Mariupol' (Zhdanov), Ukraine ('91) . . . 521,800
Hannover, Germany (1,000,000) ('91) . . . 513,010
Astrakhan', Russia ('91) . . . 511,900
Mykolayiv, Ukraine ('91) . . . 511,600
Leipzig, Germany (720,000) ('91) . . . 511,079
Naberezhnyye Chelny,
Russia ('91) . . . 510,100
Luhans'k, Ukraine (650,000) ('91) . . . 503,900
Gomel', Belarus ('91) . . . 503,300
Dublin, Ireland (1,140,000) ('86) . . . 502,749
Helsinki (Helsingfors),
Finland (1,045,000) ('93) . . . 501,514
Nürnberg, Germany (1,065,000) ('91) . . . 493,692
Antwerp, Belgium (1,140,000) ('91) . . . 467,518
Copenhagen (København),
Denmark (1,670,000) ('92) . . . 464,566
Leeds, England, U.K. (1,540,000) ('81) . . . 445,242
Manchester,
England, U.K. (2,775,000) ('81) . . . 437,612
Lyon, France (1,335,000) ('90) . . . 415,487
Katowice, Poland (2,770,000) ('93) . . . 359,900
Porto, Portugal (1,225,000) ('81) . . . 327,368
Mannheim, Germany (1,525,000) ('91) . . . 310,411
Newcastle upon Tyne,
England, U.K. (1,300,000) ('81) . . . 199,064
Lille, France (1,050,000) ('90) . . . 172,142
Brussels (Bruxelles),
Belgium (2,385,000) ('91) . . . 136,424

North America

Mexico City (Ciudad de México),
Mexico (14,100,000) ('90) . . . 8,235,744
New York, N.Y., U.S. (18,087,251) ('90) . 7,322,564
Los Angeles, Ca., U.S. (14,531,529) ('90) 3,485,398
Chicago, Il., U.S. (8,065,633) ('90) . . . 2,783,726
Santo Domingo,
Dominican Republic ('90) . . . 2,411,900
Havana (La Habana),
Cuba (2,210,000) ('91) . . . 2,119,059
Guadalajara, Mexico (2,325,000) ('90) . . 1,650,042
Houston, Tx., U.S. (3,711,043) ('90) . . . 1,630,553
Philadelphia, Pa., U.S. (5,899,345) ('90) . 1,585,577
Nezahualcóyotl, Mexico ('90) . . . 1,255,456
Ecatepec, Mexico ('90) . . . 1,218,135
San Diego, Ca., U.S. (2,949,000) ('90) . . 1,110,549
Monterrey, Mexico (2,015,000) ('90) . . . 1,068,996
Guatemala, Guatemala (1,400,000) ('89) . 1,057,210
Detroit, Mi., U.S. (4,665,236) ('90) . . . 1,027,974
Montréal, P.Q., Canada (3,127,242) ('91) . 1,017,666
Puebla, Mexico (1,200,000) ('90) . . . 1,007,170
Dallas, Tx., U.S. (3,885,415) ('90) . . . 1,006,877
Phoenix, Az., U.S. (2,122,101) ('90) . . . 983,403
San Antonio, Tx., U.S. (1,302,099) ('90) . . 935,933
Naucalpan de Juárez, Mexico ('90) . . . 845,960
Port-au-Prince, Haiti (880,000) ('87) . . . 797,000
Ciudad Juárez, Mexico ('90) . . . 789,522
San Jose, Ca., U.S. (1,497,577) ('90) . . . 782,248
León, Mexico ('90) . . . 758,279
Baltimore, Md., U.S. (2,382,172) ('90) . . . 736,014
Indianapolis, In., U.S. (1,249,822) ('90) . . 731,327
San Francisco, Ca., U.S. (6,253,311) ('90) . 723,959
Calgary, Ab., Canada (754,033) ('91) . . . 710,677

Tlalnepantla, Mexico ('90) . . . 702,270
Tijuana, Mexico ('90) . . . 698,752
Managua, Nicaragua ('85) . . . 682,000
Zapopan, Mexico ('90) . . . 668,323
Toronto, On., Canada (3,893,046) ('91) . . . 635,395
Jacksonville, Fl., U.S. (906,727) ('90) . . . 635,230
Columbus, Oh., U.S. (1,377,419) ('90) . . . 632,910
Milwaukee, Wi., U.S. (1,607,183) ('90) . . . 628,088
Winnipeg, Mb., Canada (652,354) ('91) . . . 616,790
Edmonton, Ab., Canada (839,924) ('91) . . . 616,741
Memphis, Tn., U.S. (981,747) ('90) . . . 610,337
Washington, D.C., U.S. (3,923,574) ('90) . . 606,900
Kingston, Jamaica (890,000) ('91) . . . 587,798
Tegucigalpa, Honduras ('88) . . . 576,661
Boston, Ma., U.S. (4,171,643) ('90) . . . 574,283
North York, On., Canada ('91) . . . 562,564
Guadalupe, Mexico ('90) . . . 535,332
Scarborough, On., Canada ('91) . . . 524,598
Mérida, Mexico ('90) . . . 523,422
Seattle, Wa., U.S. (2,559,164) ('90) . . . 516,259
Chihuahua, Mexico ('90) . . . 516,153
Acapulco de Juárez, Mexico ('90) . . . 515,374
El Paso, Tx., U.S. (1,211,300) ('90) . . . 515,342
Cleveland, Oh., U.S. (2,759,823) ('90) . . . 505,616
New Orleans, La., U.S. (1,238,816) ('90) . . 496,938
Vancouver, B.C., Canada (1,602,502) ('91) . 471,844
Denver, Co., U.S. (1,848,319) ('90) . . . 467,610
Fort Worth, Tx., U.S. (1,332,053) ('90) . . . 447,619
Portland, Or., U.S. (1,477,895) ('90) . . . 437,319
Kansas City, Mo., U.S. (1,566,280) ('90) . . 435,146
San Juan, Puerto Rico (1,877,000) ('90) . . 426,832
Saint Louis, Mo., U.S. (2,444,099) ('90) . . 396,685
Charlotte, N.C., U.S. (1,162,093) ('90) . . . 395,934
Atlanta, Ga., U.S. (2,833,511) ('90) . . . 394,017
Oakland, Ca., U.S. (2,082,914) ('90) . . . 372,242
Pittsburgh, Pa., U.S. (2,242,798) ('90) . . . 369,879
Sacramento, Ca., U.S. (1,481,102) ('90) . . 369,365
Minneapolis, Mn., U.S. (2,464,124) ('90) . 368,383
Cincinnati, Oh., U.S. (1,744,124) ('90) . . . 364,040
Miami, Fl., U.S. (3,192,582) ('90) . . . 358,548
Buffalo, N.Y., U.S. (1,189,288) ('90) . . . 328,123
Tampa, Fl., U.S. (2,067,959) ('90) . . . 280,015
San José, Costa Rica (1,355,000) ('88) . . 278,600
Newark, N.J., U.S. (1,824,321) ('90) . . . 275,221
Anaheim, Ca., U.S. (2,410,556) ('90) . . . 266,406
Norfolk, Va., U.S. (1,396,107) ('90) . . . 261,229
Rochester, N.Y., U.S. (1,002,410) ('90) . . . 231,636
Riverside, Ca., U.S. (2,588,793) ('90) . . . 226,505
Orlando, Fl., U.S. (1,072,748) ('90) . . . 164,693
Providence, R.I., U.S. (1,141,510) ('90) . . . 160,728
Salt Lake City, Ut., U.S. (1,072,227) ('90) . 159,936
Fort Lauderdale, Fl., U.S. (1,255,488) ('90) 149,377
Hartford, Ct., U.S. (1,085,837) ('90) . . . 139,739

South America

São Paulo, Brazil (16,925,000) ('91) . . . 9,393,753
Rio de Janeiro, Brazil (11,050,000) ('91) . 5,473,909
Bogotá (Santa Fe de Bogotá),
Colombia (4,260,000) ('85) . . . 3,982,941
Buenos Aires,
Argentina (11,000,000) ('91) . . . 2,960,976
Salvador, Brazil (2,340,000) ('91) . . . 2,070,296
Caracas, Venezuela (4,000,000) ('90) . . . 1,824,654
Belo Horizonte, Brazil (3,340,000) ('91) . 1,529,566
Brasília, Brazil ('91) . . . 1,513,470
Guayaquil, Ecuador ('90) . . . 1,508,444
Medellín, Colombia (2,095,000) ('85) . . . 1,468,089
Cali, Colombia (1,400,000) ('85) . . . 1,350,565
Recife, Brazil (2,880,000) ('91) . . . 1,296,995
Montevideo, Uruguay (1,550,000) ('85) . 1,251,647
Maracaibo, Venezuela ('90) . . . 1,249,670
Porto Alegre, Brazil (2,850,000) ('91) . . . 1,247,352
Córdoba, Argentina (1,260,000) ('91) . . . 1,148,305
San Justo, Argentina ('91) . . . 1,111,811
Quito, Ecuador (1,300,000) ('90) . . . 1,100,847
Manaus, Brazil ('91) . . . 1,005,634
Goiânia, Brazil (1,130,000) ('91) . . . 912,136
Valencia, Venezuela ('90) . . . 903,621
Barranquilla, Colombia (1,140,000) ('85) . 899,781
Rosario, Argentina (1,190,000) ('91) . . . 894,645
Curitiba, Brazil (1,815,000) ('91) . . . 841,882
Belém, Brazil (1,355,000) ('91) . . . 765,476
Campinas, Brazil (1,290,000) ('91) . . . 759,032
Fortaleza, Brazil (2,040,000) ('91) . . . 743,335
La Paz, Bolivia (1,120,000) ('92) . . . 713,378
Santa Cruz de la Sierra, Bolivia ('92) . . . 697,278
General Sarmiento (San Miguel),
Argentina ('91) . . . 646,891
Morón, Argentina ('91) . . . 641,541
Barquisimeto, Venezuela ('90) . . . 625,450
Lomas de Zamora, Argentina ('91) . . . 572,769
Osasco, Brazil ('91) . . . 566,949
Nova Iguaçu, Brazil ('91) . . . 562,062
Teresina, Brazil (665,000) ('91) . . . 556,073
Maceió, Brazil ('91) . . . 554,727
São Bernardo do Campo, Brazil ('91) . . . 550,030
Guarulhos, Brazil ('91) . . . 546,417
Cartagena, Colombia ('85) . . . 531,426
La Plata, Argentina ('91) . . . 520,449
Mar del Plata, Argentina ('91) . . . 519,707
Santo André, Brazil ('91) . . . 518,272
Campo Grande, Brazil ('91) . . . 516,403
Quilmes, Argentina ('91) . . . 509,445
Asunción, Paraguay (700,000) ('92) . . . 502,426
Santos, Brazil (1,165,000) ('91) . . . 415,554
Lima, Perú (4,608,010) ('81) . . . 371,122
Santiago, Chile (4,100,000) ('82) . . . 232,667

Countries and Flags

This 12-page section presents basic information about each of the world's countries, along with an illustration of each country's flag. A total of 199 countries are listed: the world's 191 fully independent countries, and 8 internally independent countries which are under the protection of other countries in matters of defense and foreign affairs. Colonies and other dependent political entities are not listed.

The categories of information provided for each country are as follows.

Flag: In many countries two or more versions of the national flag exist. For example, there is often a "civil" version which the average person flies, and a "state" version which is flown only at government buildings and government functions. A common difference between the two is the inclusion of a coat of arms on the state version. The flag versions shown here are the ones that each country has chosen to fly at the United Nations.

Country name: The short form of the English translation of the official country name.

Official name: The long form of the English translation of the official country name.

Population: The population figures listed are 1995 estimates based on U.S. census bureau figures and other available information.

Area: Figures provided represent total land area and all inland water. They are based on official data or U.N. data.

Population density: The number of people per square mile and square kilometer, calculated by dividing the country's population figure by its area figure.

Capital: The city that serves as the official seat of government. Population figures follow the capital name. These figures are based upon the latest official data.

AFGHANISTAN
Official Name: Islamic State of
  Afghanistan
Population: 19,715,000
Area: 251,826 sq mi (652,225 sq km)
Density: 78/sq mi (30/sq km)
Capital: Kābul, 1,424,400

ALGERIA
Official Name: Democratic and
  Popular Republic of Algeria
Population: 27,965,000
Area: 919,595 sq mi (2,381,741 sq km)
Density: 30/sq mi (12/sq km)
Capital: Algiers (El Djazaïr),1,507,241

ANGUILLA
Official Name: Anguilla
Population: 7,100
Area: 35 sq mi (91 sq km)
Density: 203/sq mi (78/sq km)
Capital: The Valley, 1,042

ALBANIA
Official Name: Republic of Albania
Population: 3,394,000
Area: 11,100 sq mi (28,748 sq km)
Density: 306/sq mi (118/sq km)
Capital: Tiranë, 238,100

ANDORRA
Official Name: Principality of Andorra
Population: 59,000
Area: 175 sq mi (453 sq km)
Density: 337/sq mi (130/sq km)
Capital: Andorra, 20,437

ANTIGUA AND BARBUDA
Official Name: Antigua and Barbuda
Population: 67,000
Area: 171 sq mi (442 sq km)
Density: 392/sq mi (152/sq km)
Capital: St. John's, 24,359

ANGOLA
Official Name: Republic of Angola
Population: 10,690,000
Area: 481,354 sq mi (1,246,700 sq km)
Density: 22/sq mi (8.6/sq km)
Capital: Luanda, 1,459,900

Countries
and Flags
continued

BAHAMAS
Official Name: Commonwealth of the
Bahamas
Population: 275,000
Area: 5,382 sq mi (13,939 sq km)
Pop. Density: 51/sq mi (20/sq km)
Capital: Nassau, 141,000

BELIZE
Official Name: Belize
Population: 212,000
Area: 8,866 sq mi (22,963 sq km)
Pop. Density: 24/sq mi (9.2/sq km)
Capital: Belmopan, 5,256

ARGENTINA
Official Name: Argentine Republic
Population: 34,083,000
Area: 1,073,519 sq mi (2,780,400 sq km)
Pop. Density: 32/sq mi (12/sq km)
Capital: Buenos Aires (de facto), 2,960,976,
and Viedma (future), 40,452

BAHRAIN
Official Name: State of Bahrain
Population: 563,000
Area: 267 sq mi (691 sq km)
Pop. Density: 2,109/sq mi (815/sq km)
Capital: Al Manāmah, 82,700

BENIN
Official Name: Republic of Benin
Population: 5,433,000
Area: 43,475 sq mi (112,600 sq km)
Pop. Density: 125/sq mi (48/sq km)
Capital: Porto-Novo (designated), 164,000,
and Cotonou (de facto), 533,212

ARMENIA
Official Name: Republic of Armenia
Population: 3,794,000
Area: 11,506 sq mi (29,800 sq km)
Pop. Density: 330/sq mi (127/sq km)
Capital: Yerevan, 1,199,000

BANGLADESH
Official Name: People's Republic of
Bangladesh
Population: 119,370,000
Area: 55,598 sq mi (143,998 sq km)
Pop. Density: 2,147/sq mi (829/sq km)
Capital: Dhaka (Dacca), 3,637,892

BHUTAN
Official Name: Kingdom of Bhutan
Population: 1,758,000
Area: 17,954 sq mi (46,500 sq km)
Pop. Density: 98/sq mi (38/sq km)
Capital: Thimphu, 12,000

AUSTRALIA
Official Name: Commonwealth of Australia
Population: 18,205,000
Area: 2,966,155 sq mi (7,682,300 sq km)
Pop. Density: 6.1/sq mi (2.4/sq km)
Capital: Canberra, 276,162

BARBADOS
Official Name: Barbados
Population: 261,000
Area: 166 sq mi (430 sq km)
Pop. Density: 1,572/sq mi (607/sq km)
Capital: Bridgetown, 5,928

BOLIVIA
Official Name: Republic of Bolivia
Population: 6,790,000
Area: 424,165 sq mi (1,098,581 sq km)
Pop. Density: 16/sq mi (6.2/sq km)
Capital: La Paz (seat of government),
713,378, and Sucre (legal capital), 131,769

AUSTRIA
Official Name: Republic of Austria
Population: 7,932,000
Area: 32,377 sq mi (83,856 sq km)
Pop. Density: 245/sq mi (95/sq km)
Capital: Vienna (Wien), 1,539,848

BELARUS
Official Name: Republic of Belarus
Population: 10,425,000
Area: 80,155 sq mi (207,600 sq km)
Pop. Density: 130/sq mi (50/sq km)
Capital: Minsk, 1,633,600

BOSNIA AND HERZEGOVINA
Official Name: Republic of Bosnia and
Herzegovina
Population: 4,481,000
Area: 19,741 sq mi (51,129 sq km)
Pop. Density: 227/sq mi (88/sq km)
Capital: Sarajevo, 341,200

AZERBAIJAN
Official Name: Azerbaijani Republic
Population: 7,491,000
Area: 33,436 sq mi (86,600 sq km)
Pop. Density: 224/sq mi (87/sq km)
Capital: Baku (Bakı), 1,080,500

BELGIUM
Official Name: Kingdom of Belgium
Population: 10,075,000
Area: 11,783 sq mi (30,518 sq km)
Pop. Density: 855/sq mi (330/sq km)
Capital: Brussels (Bruxelles), 136,424

BOTSWANA
Official Name: Republic of Botswana
Population: 1,438,000
Area: 224,711 sq mi (582,000 sq km)
Pop. Density: 6.4/sq mi (2.5/sq km)
Capital: Gaborone, 133,468

BRAZIL
Official Name: Federative Republic of Brazil
Population: 159,690,000
Area: 3,286,500 sq mi (8,511,996 sq km)
Pop. Density: 49/sq mi (19/sq km)
Capital: Brasília, 1,513,470

CAMEROON
Official Name: Republic of Cameroon
Population: 13,330,000
Area: 183,568 sq mi (475,440 sq km)
Pop. Density: 73/sq mi (28/sq km)
Capital: Yaoundé, 560,785

CHINA
Official Name: People's Republic of China
Population: 1,196,980,000
Area: 3,689,631 sq mi (9,556,100 sq km)
Pop. Density: 324/sq mi (125/sq km)
Capital: Beijing (Peking), 6,710,000

BRUNEI
Official Name: Negara Brunei Darussalam
Population: 289,000
Area: 2,226 sq mi (5,765 sq km)
Pop. Density: 130/sq mi (50/sq km)
Capital: Bandar Seri Begawan, 22,777

CANADA
Official Name: Canada
Population: 28,285,000
Area: 3,849,674 sq mi (9,970,610 sq km)
Pop. Density: 7.3/sq mi (2.8/sq km)
Capital: Ottawa, 313,987

COLOMBIA
Official Name: Republic of Colombia
Population: 34,870,000
Area: 440,831 sq mi (1,141,748 sq km)
Pop. Density: 79/sq mi (31/sq km)
Capital: Santa Fe de Bogotá (Bogotá), 3,982,941

BULGARIA
Official Name: Republic of Bulgaria
Population: 8,787,000
Area: 42,855 sq mi (110,994 sq km)
Pop. Density: 205/sq mi (79/sq km)
Capital: Sofia (Sofiya), 1,136,875

CAPE VERDE
Official Name: Republic of Cape Verde
Population: 429,000
Area: 1,557 sq mi (4,033 sq km)
Pop. Density: 276/sq mi (106/sq km)
Capital: Praia, 61,644

COMOROS
Official Name: Federal Islamic Republic of the Comoros
Population: 540,000
Area: 863 sq mi (2,235 sq km)
Pop. Density: 626/sq mi (242/sq km)
Capital: Moroni, 23,432

BURKINA FASO
Official Name: Burkina Faso
Population: 10,275,000
Area: 105,792 sq mi (274,000 sq km)
Pop. Density: 97/sq mi (38/sq km)
Capital: Ouagadougou, 441,514

CENTRAL AFRICAN REPUBLIC
Official Name: Central African Republic
Population: 3,177,000
Area: 240,535 sq mi (622,984 sq km)
Pop. Density: 13/sq mi (5.1/sq km)
Capital: Bangui, 596,800

CONGO
Official Name: Republic of the Congo
Population: 2,474,000
Area: 132,047 sq mi (342,000 sq km)
Pop. Density: 19/sq mi (7.2/sq km)
Capital: Brazzaville, 693,712

BURUNDI
Official Name: Republic of Burundi
Population: 6,192,000
Area: 10,745 sq mi (27,830 sq km)
Pop. Density: 576/sq mi (222/sq km)
Capital: Bujumbura, 226,628

CHAD
Official Name: Republic of Chad
Population: 6,396,000
Area: 495,755 sq mi (1,284,000 sq km)
Pop. Density: 13/sq mi (5/sq km)
Capital: N'Djamena, 500,000

COOK ISLANDS
Official Name: Cook Islands
Population: 19,000
Area: 91 sq mi (236 sq km)
Pop. Density: 209/sq mi (81/sq km)
Capital: Avarua, 10,886

CAMBODIA
Official Name: Kingdom of Cambodia
Population: 9,713,000
Area: 69,898 sq mi (181,035 sq km)
Pop. Density: 139/sq mi (54/sq km)
Capital: Phnum Pénh (Phnom Penh), 620,000

CHILE
Official Name: Republic of Chile
Population: 14,050,000
Area: 292,135 sq mi (756,626 sq km)
Pop. Density: 48/sq mi (19/sq km)
Capital: Santiago, 232,667

COSTA RICA
Official Name: Republic of Costa Rica
Population: 3,379,000
Area: 19,730 sq mi (51,100 sq km)
Pop. Density: 171/sq mi (66/sq km)
Capital: San José, 278,600

Countries
and Flags
continued

CZECH REPUBLIC
Official Name: Czech Republic
Population: 10,430,000
Area: 30,450 sq mi (78,864 sq km)
Pop. Density: 343/sq mi (132/sq km)
Capital: Prague (Praha), 1,212,010

EGYPT
Official Name: Arab Republic of Egypt
Population: 58,100,000
Area: 386,662 sq mi (1,001,449 sq km)
Pop. Density: 150/sq mi (58/sq km)
Capital: Cairo (Al Qāhirah), 6,068,695

COTE D'IVOIRE
Official Name: Republic of Cote d'Ivoire
Population: 14,540,000
Area: 124,518 sq mi (322,500 sq km)
Pop. Density: 117/sq mi (45/sq km)
Capital: Abidjan (de facto), 1,929,079, and
  Yamoussoukro (future), 106,786

DENMARK
Official Name: Kingdom of Denmark
Population: 5,207,000
Area: 16,639 sq mi (43,094 sq km)
Pop. Density: 313 sq mi (121/sq km)
Capital: Copenhagen (København), 464,566

EL SALVADOR
Official Name: Republic of El Salvador
Population: 5,280,000
Area: 8,124 sq mi (21,041 sq km)
Pop. Density: 650/sq mi (251/sq km)
Capital: San Salvador, 462,652

CROATIA
Official Name: Republic of Croatia
Population: 4,801,000
Area: 21,829 sq mi (56,538 sq km)
Pop. Density: 220/sq mi (85/sq km)
Capital: Zagreb, 697,925

DJIBOUTI
Official Name: Republic of Djibouti
Population: 557,000
Area: 8,958 sq mi (23,200 sq km)
Pop. Density: 62/sq mi (24/sq km)
Capital: Djibouti, 329,337

EQUATORIAL GUINEA
Official Name: Republic of Equatorial Guinea
Population: 394,000
Area: 10,831 sq mi (28,051 sq km)
Pop. Density: 36/sq mi (14/sq km)
Capital: Malabo, 31,630

CUBA
Official Name: Republic of Cuba
Population: 11,560,000
Area: 42,804 sq mi (110,861 sq km)
Pop. Density: 270/sq mi (104/sq km)
Capital: Havana (La Habana), 2,119,059

DOMINICA
Official Name: Commonwealth of Dominica
Population: 89,000
Area: 305 sq mi (790 sq km)
Pop. Density: 292/sq mi (113/sq km)
Capital: Roseau, 9,348

ERITREA
Official Name: State of Eritrea
Population: 3,458,000
Area: 36,170 sq mi (93,679 sq km)
Pop. Density: 96/sq mi (37/sq km)
Capital: Asmera, 358,100

CYPRUS
Official Name: Republic of Cyprus
Population: 551,000
Area: 2,276 sq mi (5,896 sq km)
Pop. Density: 242/sq mi (93/sq km)
Capital: Nicosia (Levkosía), 48,221

DOMINICAN REPUBLIC
Official Name: Dominican Republic
Population: 7,896,000
Area: 18,704 sq mi (48,442 sq km)
Pop. Density: 422/sq mi (163/sq km)
Capital: Santo Domingo, 2,411,900

ESTONIA
Official Name: Republic of Estonia
Population: 1,515,000
Area: 17,413 sq mi (45,100 sq km)
Pop. Density: 87/sq mi (34/sq km)
Capital: Tallinn, 481,500

CYPRUS, NORTH
Official Name: Turkish Republic of
  Northern Cyprus
Population: 182,000
Area: 1,295 sq mi (3,355 sq km)
Pop. Density: 141/sq mi (54/sq km)
Capital: Nicosia (Lefkoşa), 37,400

ECUADOR
Official Name: Republic of Ecuador
Population: 11,015,000
Area: 105,037 sq mi (272,045 sq km)
Pop. Density: 105/sq mi (40/sq km)
Capital: Quito, 1,100,847

ETHIOPIA
Official Name: Ethiopia
Population: 55,070,000
Area: 446,953 sq mi (1,157,603 sq km)
Pop. Density: 123/sq mi (48/sq km)
Capital: Addis Ababa (Adis Abeba), 1,912,500

FIJI
Official Name: Republic of Fiji
Population: 775,000
Area: 7,056 sq mi (18,274 sq km)
Pop. Density: 110/sq mi (42/sq km)
Capital: Suva, 69,665

GERMANY
Official Name: Federal Republic of Germany
Population: 81,710,000
Area: 137,822 sq mi (356,955 sq km)
Pop. Density: 593/sq mi (229/sq km)
Capital: Berlin (designated), 3,433,695, and Bonn (de facto), 292,234

GUINEA
Official Name: Republic of Guinea
Population: 6,469,000
Area: 94,926 sq mi (245,857 sq km)
Pop. Density: 68/sq mi (26/sq km)
Capital: Conakry, 800,000

FINLAND
Official Name: Republic of Finland
Population: 5,098,000
Area: 130,559 sq mi (338,145 sq km)
Pop. Density: 39/sq mi (15/sq km)
Capital: Helsinki (Helsingfors), 501,514

GHANA
Official Name: Republic of Ghana
Population: 17,210,000
Area: 92,098 sq mi (238,533 sq km)
Pop. Density: 187/sq mi (72/sq km)
Capital: Accra, 949,113

GUINEA-BISSAU
Official Name: Republic of Guinea-Bissau
Population: 1,111,000
Area: 13,948 sq mi (36,125 sq km)
Pop. Density: 80/sq mi (31/sq km)
Capital: Bissau, 125,000

FRANCE
Official Name: French Republic
Population: 58,010,000
Area: 211,208 sq mi (547,026 sq km)
Pop. Density: 275/sq mi (106/sq km)
Capital: Paris, 2,152,423

GREECE
Official Name: Hellenic Republic
Population: 10,475,000
Area: 50,949 sq mi (131,957 sq km)
Pop. Density: 206/sq mi (79/sq km)
Capital: Athens (Athínai), 748,110

GUYANA
Official Name: Co-operative Republic of Guyana
Population: 726,000
Area: 83,000 sq mi (214,969 sq km)
Pop. Density: 8.7/sq mi (3.4/sq km)
Capital: Georgetown, 78,500

GABON
Official Name: Gabonese Republic
Population: 1,035,000
Area: 103,347 sq mi (267,667 sq km)
Pop. Density: 10/sq mi (3.9/sq km)
Capital: Libreville, 235,700

GREENLAND
Official Name: Greenland
Population: 57,000
Area: 840,004 sq mi (2,175,600 sq km)
Pop. Density: 0.1/sq mi (0.03/sq km)
Capital: Godthåb (Nuuk), 12,217

HAITI
Official Name: Republic of Haiti
Population: 7,069,000
Area: 10,714 sq mi (27,750 sq km)
Pop. Density: 660/sq mi (255/sq km)
Capital: Port-au-Prince, 797,000

GAMBIA
Official Name: Republic of the Gambia
Population: 1,082,000
Area: 4,127 sq mi (10,689 sq km)
Pop. Density: 262/sq mi (101/sq km)
Capital: Banjul, 44,188

GRENADA
Official Name: Grenada
Population: 92,000
Area: 133 sq mi (344 sq km)
Pop. Density: 692/sq mi (267/sq km)
Capital: St. George's, 4,439

HONDURAS
Official Name: Republic of Honduras
Population: 5,822,000
Area: 43,277 sq mi (112,088 sq km)
Pop. Density: 135/sq mi (52/sq km)
Capital: Tegucigalpa, 576,661

GEORGIA
Official Name: Republic of Georgia
Population: 5,704,000
Area: 26,911 sq mi (69,700 sq km)
Pop. Density: 212/sq mi (82/sq km)
Capital: Tbilisi, 1,279,000

GUATEMALA
Official Name: Republic of Guatemala
Population: 10,420,000
Area: 42,042 sq mi (108,889 sq km)
Pop. Density: 248/sq mi (96/sq km)
Capital: Guatemala, 1,057,210

HUNGARY
Official Name: Republic of Hungary
Population: 10,270,000
Area: 35,919 sq mi (93,030 sq km)
Pop. Density: 286/sq mi (110/sq km)
Capital: Budapest, 2,016,774

Countries
and Flags
continued

IRELAND
Official Name: Ireland
Population: 3,546,000
Area: 27,137 sq mi (70,285 sq km)
Pop. Density: 131/sq mi (50/sq km)
Capital: Dublin (Baile Átha Cliath), 502,749

KAZAKHSTAN
Official Name: Republic of Kazakhstan
Population: 17,025,000
Area: 1,049,156 sq mi (2,717,300 sq km)
Pop. Density: 16/sq mi (6.3/sq km)
Capital: Alma-Ata (Almaty), 1,156,200, and
  Akmola (future), 286,000

ICELAND
Official Name: Republic of Iceland
Population: 265,000
Area: 39,769 sq mi (103,000 sq km)
Pop. Density: 6.7/sq mi (2.6/sq km)
Capital: Reykjavik, 100,850

ISRAEL
Official Name: State of Israel
Population: 5,059,000
Area: 8,019 sq mi (20,770 sq km)
Pop. Density: 631/sq mi (244/sq km)
Capital: Jerusalem (Yerushalayim), 524,500

KENYA
Official Name: Republic of Kenya
Population: 28,380,000
Area: 224,961 sq mi (582,646 sq km)
Pop. Density: 126/sq mi (49/sq km)
Capital: Nairobi, 1,505,000

INDIA
Official Name: Republic of India
Population: 909,150,000
Area: 1,237,062 sq mi (3,203,975 sq km)
Pop. Density: 735/sq mi (284/sq km)
Capital: New Delhi, 301,297

ITALY
Official Name: Italian Republic
Population: 57,330,000
Area: 116,324 sq mi (301,277 sq km)
Pop. Density: 493/sq mi (190/sq km)
Capital: Rome (Roma), 2,693,383

KIRIBATI
Official Name: Republic of Kiribati
Population: 79,000
Area: 313 sq mi (811 sq km)
Pop. Density: 252/sq mi (97/sq km)
Capital: Bairiki, 2,226

INDONESIA
Official Name: Republic of Indonesia
Population: 193,680,000
Area: 752,410 sq mi (1,948,732 sq km)
Pop. Density: 257/sq mi (99/sq km)
Capital: Jakarta, 8,227,746

JAMAICA
Official Name: Jamaica
Population: 2,568,000
Area: 4,244 sq mi (10,991 sq km)
Pop. Density: 605/sq mi (234/sq km)
Capital: Kingston, 587,798

KOREA, NORTH
Official Name: Democratic People's Republic
  of Korea
Population: 23,265,000
Area: 46,540 sq mi (120,538 sq km)
Pop. Density: 500/sq mi (193/sq km)
Capital: P'yŏngyang, 2,355,000

IRAN
Official Name: Islamic Republic of Iran
Population: 63,810,000
Area: 632,457 sq mi (1,638,057 sq km)
Pop. Density: 101/sq mi (39/sq km)
Capital: Tehrān, 6,042,584

JAPAN
Official Name: Japan
Population: 125,360,000
Area: 145,870 sq mi (377,801 sq km)
Pop. Density: 859/sq mi (332/sq km)
Capital: Tōkyō, 8,163,573

KOREA, SOUTH
Official Name: Republic of Korea
Population: 44,655,000
Area: 38,230 sq mi (99,016 sq km)
Pop. Density: 1,168/sq mi (451/sq km)
Capital: Seoul (Sŏul), 10,627,790

IRAQ
Official Name: Republic of Iraq
Population: 20,250,000
Area: 169,235 sq mi (438,317 sq km)
Pop. Density: 120/sq mi (46/sq km)
Capital: Baghdād, 3,841,268

JORDAN
Official Name: Hashemite Kingdom of
  Jordan
Population: 4,028,000
Area: 35,135 sq mi (91,000 sq km)
Pop. Density: 115/sq mi (44/sq km)
Capital: 'Ammān, 936,300

KUWAIT
Official Name: State of Kuwait
Population: 1,866,000
Area: 6,880 sq mi (17,818 sq km)
Pop. Density: 271/sq mi (105/sq km)
Capital: Kuwait (Al Kuwayt), 44,335

KYRGYZSTAN
Official Name: Kyrgyz Republic
Population: 4,541,000
Area: 76,641 sq mi (198,500 sq km)
Pop. Density: 59/sq mi (23/sq km)
Capital: Bishkek, 631,300

LIBYA
Official Name: Socialist People's Libyan
  Arab Jamahiriya
Population: 5,148,000
Area: 679,362 sq mi (1,759,540 sq km)
Pop. Density: 7.6/sq mi (2.9/sq km)
Capital: Tripoli (Ṭarābulus), 591,062

MALAWI
Official Name: Republic of Malawi
Population: 8,984,000
Area: 45,747 sq mi (118,484 sq km)
Pop. Density: 196/sq mi (76/sq km)
Capital: Lilongwe, 223,318

LAOS
Official Name: Lao People's Democratic
  Republic
Population: 4,768,000
Area: 91,429 sq mi (236,800 sq km)
Pop. Density: 52/sq mi (20/sq km)
Capital: Viangchan (Vientiane), 377,409

LIECHTENSTEIN
Official Name: Principality of Liechtenstein
Population: 30,000
Area: 62 sq mi (160 sq km)
Pop. Density: 484/sq mi (188/sq km)
Capital: Vaduz, 4,887

MALAYSIA
Official Name: Malaysia
Population: 19,505,000
Area: 127,320 sq mi (329,758 sq km)
Pop. Density: 153/sq mi (59/sq km)
Capital: Kuala Lumpur, 919,610

LATVIA
Official Name: Republic of Latvia
Population: 2,532,000
Area: 24,595 sq mi (63,700 sq km)
Pop. Density: 103/sq mi (40/sq km)
Capital: Rīga, 910,200

LITHUANIA
Official Name: Republic of Lithuania
Population: 3,757,000
Area: 25,212 sq mi (65,300 sq km)
Pop. Density: 149/sq mi (58/sq km)
Capital: Vilnius, 596,900

MALDIVES
Official Name: Republic of Maldives
Population: 251,000
Area: 115 sq mi (298 sq km)
Pop. Density: 2,183/sq mi (842/sq km)
Capital: Male', 55,130

LEBANON
Official Name: Republic of Lebanon
Population: 3,660,000
Area: 4,015 sq mi (10,400 sq km)
Pop. Density: 912/sq mi (352/sq km)
Capital: Beirut (Bayrūt), 509,000

LUXEMBOURG
Official Name: Grand Duchy of Luxembourg
Population: 396,000
Area: 998 sq mi (2,586 sq km)
Pop. Density: 397/sq mi (153/sq km)
Capital: Luxembourg, 75,377

MALI
Official Name: Republic of Mali
Population: 9,585,000
Area: 482,077 sq mi (1,248,574 sq km)
Pop. Density: 20 ̧mi (7.7/sq km)
Capital: Bamako 658,275

LESOTHO
Official Name: Kingdom of Lesotho
Population: 1,967,000
Area: 11,720 sq mi (30,355 sq km)
Pop. Density: 168/sq mi (65/sq km)
Capital: Maseru, 109,382

MACEDONIA
Official Name: Republic of Macedonia
Population: 2,102,000
Area: 9,928 sq mi (25,713 sq km)
Pop. Density: 212/sq mi (82/sq km)
Capital: Skopje, 444,900

MALTA
Official Name: Republic of Malta
Population: 368,000
Area: 122 sq mi (316 sq km)
Pop. Density: 3,016/sq mi (1,165/sq km)
Capital: Valletta, 9,199

LIBERIA
Official Name: Republic of Liberia
Population: 2,771,000
Area: 38,250 sq mi (99,067 sq km)
Pop. Density: 72/sq mi (28/sq km)
Capital: Monrovia, 465,000

MADAGASCAR
Official Name: Republic of Madagascar
Population: 13,645,000
Area: 226,658 sq mi (587,041 sq km)
Pop. Density: 60/sq mi (23/sq km)
Capital: Antananarivo, 1,250,000

MARSHALL ISLANDS
Official Name: Republic of the Marshall
  Islands
Population: 55,000
Area: 70 sq mi (181 sq km)
Pop. Density: 786/sq mi (304/sq km)
Capital: Majuro (island)

Countries and Flags
continued

MONACO
Official Name: Principality of Monaco
Population: 31,000
Area: 0.7 sq mi (1.9 sq km)
Pop. Density: 44,286/sq mi (16,316/sq km)
Capital: Monaco, 31,000

NAURU
Official Name: Republic of Nauru
Population: 10,000
Area: 8.1 sq mi (21 sq km)
Pop. Density: 1,235/sq mi (476/sq km)
Capital: Yaren District

MAURITANIA
Official Name: Islamic Republic of Mauritania
Population: 2,228,000
Area: 395,956 sq mi (1,025,520 sq km)
Pop. Density: 5.6/sq mi (2.2/sq km)
Capital: Nouakchott, 285,000

MONGOLIA
Official Name: Mongolia
Population: 2,462,000
Area: 604,829 sq mi (1,566,500 sq km)
Pop. Density: 4.1/sq mi (1.6/sq km)
Capital: Ulan Bator (Ulaanbaatar), 575,000

NEPAL
Official Name: Kingdom of Nepal
Population: 21,295,000
Area: 56,827 sq mi (147,181 sq km)
Pop. Density: 375/sq mi (145/sq km)
Capital: Kathmandu, 421,258

MAURITIUS
Official Name: Republic of Mauritius
Population: 1,121,000
Area: 788 sq mi (2,040 sq km)
Pop. Density: 1,423/sq mi (550/sq km)
Capital: Port Louis, 141,870

MOROCCO
Official Name: Kingdom of Morocco
Population: 26,890,000
Area: 172,414 sq mi (446,550 sq km)
Pop. Density: 156/sq mi (60/sq km)
Capital: Rabat, 518,616

NETHERLANDS
Official Name: Kingdom of the Netherlands
Population: 15,425,000
Area: 16,164 sq mi (41,864 sq km)
Pop. Density: 954/sq mi (368/sq km)
Capital: Amsterdam (designated), 713,407, and The Hague ('s-Gravenhage) (seat of government), 445,287

MEXICO
Official Name: United Mexican States
Population: 93,860,000
Area: 759,534 sq mi (1,967,183 sq km)
Pop. Density: 124/sq mi (48/sq km)
Capital: Mexico City (Ciudad de México), 8,235,744

MOZAMBIQUE
Official Name: Republic of Mozambique
Population: 17,860,000
Area: 308,642 sq mi (799,380 sq km)
Pop. Density: 58/sq mi (22/sq km)
Capital: Maputo, 1,069,727

NEW ZEALAND
Official Name: New Zealand
Population: 3,558,000
Area: 104,454 sq mi (270,534 sq km)
Pop. Density: 34/sq mi (13/sq km)
Capital: Wellington, 150,301

MICRONESIA, FEDERATED STATES OF
Official Name: Federated States of Micronesia
Population: 122,000
Area: 271 sq mi (702 sq km)
Pop. Density: 450/sq mi (174/sq km)
Capital: Kolonia (de facto), 6,169, and Paliker (future)

MYANMAR
Official Name: Union of Myanmar
Population: 44,675,000
Area: 261,228 sq mi (676,577 sq km)
Pop. Density: 171/sq mi (66/sq km)
Capital: Rangoon (Yangon), 2,513,023

NICARAGUA
Official Name: Republic of Nicaragua
Population: 4,438,000
Area: 50,054 sq mi (129,640 sq km)
Pop. Density: 89/sq mi (34/sq km)
Capital: Managua, 682,000

MOLDOVA
Official Name: Republic of Moldova
Population: 4,377,000
Area: 13,012 sq mi (33,700 sq km)
Pop. Density: 336/sq mi (130/sq km)
Capital: Chișinău (Kishinev), 676,700

NAMIBIA
Official Name: Republic of Namibia
Population: 1,623,000
Area: 318,253 sq mi (824,272 sq km)
Pop. Density: 5.1/sq mi (2.0/sq km)
Capital: Windhoek, 114,500

NIGER
Official Name: Republic of Niger
Population: 9,125,000
Area: 489,191 sq mi (1,267,000 sq km)
Pop. Density: 19/sq mi (7.2/sq km)
Capital: Niamey, 392,165

NIGERIA
Official Name: Federal Republic of Nigeria
Population: 97,300,000
Area: 356,669 sq mi (923,768 sq km)
Pop. Density: 273/sq mi (105/sq km)
Capital: Lagos (de facto),1,213,000, and
  Abuja (designated), 250,000

NIUE
Official Name: Niue
Population: 1,900
Area: 100 sq mi (259 sq km)
Pop. Density: 19/sq mi (7.3/sq km)
Capital: Alofi, 706

NORTHERN MARIANA ISLANDS
Official Name: Commonwealth of the
  Northern Mariana Islands
Population: 51,000
Area: 184 sq mi (477 sq km)
Pop. Density: 277/sq mi (107/sq km)
Capital: Saipan (island)

NORWAY
Official Name: Kingdom of Norway
Population: 4,339,000
Area: 149,412 sq mi (386,975 sq km)
Pop. Density: 29/sq mi (11/sq km)
Capital: Oslo, 470,204

OMAN
Official Name: Sultanate of Oman
Population: 2,089,000
Area: 82,030 sq mi (212,457 sq km)
Pop. Density: 25/sq mi (9.8/sq km)
Capital: Muscat (Masqat), 30,000

PAKISTAN
Official Name: Islamic Republic of Pakistan
Population: 129,630,000
Area: 339,732 sq mi (879,902 sq km)
Pop. Density: 382/sq mi (147/sq km)
Capital: Islāmābād, 204,364

PALAU
Official Name: Republic of Palau
Population: 17,000
Area: 196 sq mi (508 sq km)
Pop. Density: 87/sq mi (33/sq km)
Capital: Koror (de facto), 9,018, and
  Melekeok (future)

PANAMA
Official Name: Republic of Panama
Population: 2,654,000
Area: 29,157 sq mi (75,517 sq km)
Pop. Density: 91/sq mi (35/sq km)
Capital: Panamá, 411,549

PAPUA NEW GUINEA
Official Name: Independent State of Papua
  New Guinea
Population: 4,057,000
Area: 178,704 sq mi (462,840 sq km)
Pop. Density: 23/sq mi (8.8/sq km)
Capital: Port Moresby, 193,242

PARAGUAY
Official Name: Republic of Paraguay
Population: 4,400,000
Area: 157,048 sq mi (406,752 sq km)
Pop. Density: 28/sq mi (11/sq km)
Capital: Asunción, 502,426

PERU
Official Name: Republic of Peru
Population: 23,095,000
Area: 496,225 sq mi (1,285,216 sq km)
Pop. Density: 47/sq mi (18/sq km)
Capital: Lima, 371,122

PHILIPPINES
Official Name: Republic of the Philippines
Population: 67,910,000
Area: 115,831 sq mi (300,000 sq km)
Pop. Density: 586/sq mi (226/sq km)
Capital: Manila, 1,598,918

POLAND
Official Name: Republic of Poland
Population: 38,730,000
Area: 121,196 sq mi (313,895 sq km)
Pop. Density: 320/sq mi (123/sq km)
Capital: Warsaw (Warszawa), 1,644,500

PORTUGAL
Official Name: Portuguese Republic
Population: 9,907,000
Area: 35,516 sq mi (91,985 sq km)
Pop. Density: 279/sq mi (108/sq km)
Capital: Lisbon (Lisboa), 807,167

PUERTO RICO
Official Name: Commonwealth of Puerto Rico
Population: 3,625,000
Area: 3,515 sq mi (9,104 sq km)
Pop. Density: 1,031/sq mi (398/sq km)
Capital: San Juan, 426,832

QATAR
Official Name: State of Qatar
Population: 519,000
Area: 4,412 sq mi (11,427 sq km)
Pop. Density: 118/sq mi (45/sq km)
Capital: Ad Dawḥah (Doha), 217,294

ROMANIA
Official Name: Romania
Population: 22,745,000
Area: 91,699 sq mi (237,500 sq km)
Pop. Density: 248/sq mi (96/sq km)
Capital: Bucharest (Bucureşti), 2,064,474

RUSSIA
Official Name: Russian Federation
Population: 150,500,000
Area: 6,592,849 sq mi (17,075,400 sq km)
Pop. Density: 23/sq mi (8.8/sq km)
Capital: Moscow (Moskva), 8,801,500

Countries
and Flags
continued

SAO TOME AND PRINCIPE
Official Name: Democratic Republic of Sao
  Tome and Principe
Population: 127,000
Area: 372 sq mi (964 sq km)
Pop. Density: 341/sq mi (132/sq km)
Capital: São Tomé, 5,245

SLOVAKIA
Official Name: Slovak Republic
Population: 5,353,000
Area: 18,933 sq mi (49,035 sq km)
Pop. Density: 283/sq mi (109/sq km)
Capital: Bratislava, 441,453

RWANDA
Official Name: Republic of Rwanda
Population: 7,343,000
Area: 10,169 sq mi (26,338 sq km)
Pop. Density: 722/sq mi (279/sq km)
Capital: Kigali, 232,733

SAUDI ARABIA
Official Name: Kingdom of Saudi Arabia
Population: 18,190,000
Area: 830,000 sq mi (2,149,690 sq km)
Pop. Density: 22/sq mi (8.5/sq km)
Capital: Riyadh (Ar Riyād), 1,250,000

SLOVENIA
Official Name: Republic of Slovenia
Population: 1,993,000
Area: 7,820 sq mi (20,253 sq km)
Pop. Density: 255/sq mi (98/sq km)
Capital: Ljubljana, 233,200

ST. KITTS AND NEVIS
Official Name: Federation of St. Kitts and
  Nevis
Population: 42,000
Area: 104 sq mi (269 sq km)
Pop. Density: 404/sq mi (156/sq km)
Capital: Basseterre, 14,725

SENEGAL
Official Name: Republic of Senegal
Population: 8,862,000
Area: 75,951 sq mi (196,712 sq km)
Pop. Density: 117/sq mi (45/sq km)
Capital: Dakar, 1,490,450

SOLOMON ISLANDS
Official Name: Solomon Islands
Population: 393,000
Area: 10,954 sq mi (28,370 sq km)
Pop. Density: 36/sq mi (14/sq km)
Capital: Honiara, 30,413

ST. LUCIA
Official Name: St. Lucia
Population: 138,000
Area: 238 sq mi (616 sq km)
Pop. Density: 580/sq mi (224/sq km)
Capital: Castries, 11,147

SEYCHELLES
Official Name: Republic of Seychelles
Population: 75,000
Area: 175 sq mi (453 sq km)
Pop. Density: 429/sq mi (166/sq km)
Capital: Victoria, 23,000

SOMALIA
Official Name: Somalia
Population: 7,187,000
Area: 246,201 sq mi (637,657 sq km)
Pop. Density: 29/sq mi (11/sq km)
Capital: Mogadishu (Muqdisho), 600,000

ST. VINCENT AND THE GRENADINES
Official Name: St. Vincent and the Grenadines
Population: 110,000
Area: 150 sq mi (388 sq km)
Pop. Density: 733/sq mi (284/sq km)
Capital: Kingstown, 15,466

SIERRA LEONE
Official Name: Republic of Sierra Leone
Population: 4,690,000
Area: 27,925 sq mi (72,325 sq km)
Pop. Density: 168/sq mi (65/sq km)
Capital: Freetown, 469,776

SOUTH AFRICA
Official Name: Republic of South Africa
Population: 44,500,000
Area: 471,010 sq mi (1,219,909 sq km)
Pop. Density: 94/sq mi (36/sq km)
Capital: Pretoria (administrative), 525,583,
  Cape Town (legislative), 854,616, and
  Bloemfontein (judicial), 126,867

SAN MARINO
Official Name: Republic of San Marino
Population: 24,000
Area: 24 sq mi (61 sq km)
Pop. Density: 1,000/sq mi (393/sq km)
Capital: San Marino, 2,794

SINGAPORE
Official Name: Republic of Singapore
Population: 2,921,000
Area: 246 sq mi (636 sq km)
Pop. Density: 11,874/sq mi (4,593/sq km)
Capital: Singapore, 2,921,000

SPAIN
Official Name: Kingdom of Spain
Population: 39,260,000
Area: 194,885 sq mi (504,750 sq km)
Pop. Density: 201/sq mi (78/sq km)
Capital: Madrid, 3,102,846

SRI LANKA
Official Name: Democratic Socialist Republic
  of Sri Lanka
Population: 18,240,000
Area: 24,962 sq mi (64,652 sq km)
Pop. Density: 731/sq mi (282/sq km)
Capital: Colombo (designated), 612,000, and
  Sri Jayawardenepura (seat of government),
  108,000

SUDAN
Official Name: Republic of the Sudan
Population: 25,840,000
Area: 967,500 sq mi (2,505,813 sq km)
Pop. Density: 27/sq mi (10/sq km)
Capital: Khartoum (Al Kharţum), 473,597

SURINAME
Official Name: Republic of Suriname
Population: 426,000
Area: 63,251 sq mi (163,820 sq km)
Pop. Density: 6.7/sq mi (2.6/sq km)
Capital: Paramaribo, 241,000

SWAZILAND
Official Name: Kingdom of Swaziland
Population: 889,000
Area: 6,704 sq mi (17,364 sq km)
Pop. Density: 133/sq mi (51/sq km)
Capital: Mbabane (administrative), 38,290,
  and Lobamba (legislative)

SWEDEN
Official Name: Kingdom of Sweden
Population: 8,981,000
Area: 173,732 sq mi (449,964 sq km)
Pop. Density: 52/sq mi (20/sq km)
Capital: Stockholm, 674,452

SWITZERLAND
Official Name: Swiss Confederation
Population: 7,244,000
Area: 15,943 sq mi (41,293 sq km)
Pop. Density: 454/sq mi (175/sq km)
Capital: Bern (Berne), 136,338

SYRIA
Official Name: Syrian Arab Republic
Population: 14,100,000
Area: 71,498 sq mi (185,180 sq km)
Pop. Density: 197/sq mi (76/sq km)
Capital: Damascus (Dimashq), 1,549,932

TAIWAN
Official Name: Republic of China
Population: 21,150,000
Area: 13,900 sq mi (36,002 sq km)
Pop. Density: 1,522/sq mi (587/sq km)
Capital: T'aipei, 2,706,453

TAJIKISTAN
Official Name: Republic of Tajikistan
Population: 6,073,000
Area: 55,251 sq mi (143,100 sq km)
Pop. Density: 110/sq mi (42/sq km)
Capital: Dushanbe, 582,400

TANZANIA
Official Name: United Republic of Tanzania
Population: 28,350,000
Area: 341,217 sq mi (883,749 sq km)
Pop. Density: 83/sq mi (32/sq km)
Capital: Dar es Salaam (de facto), 1,096,000,
  and Dodoma (legislative), 85,000

THAILAND
Official Name: Kingdom of Thailand
Population: 59,870,000
Area: 198,115 sq mi (513,115 sq km)
Pop. Density: 302/sq mi (117/sq km)
Capital: Bangkok (Krung Thep), 5,620,591

TOGO
Official Name: Republic of Togo
Population: 4,332,000
Area: 21,925 sq mi (56,785 sq km)
Pop. Density: 198/sq mi (76/sq km)
Capital: Lomé, 500,000

TONGA
Official Name: Kingdom of Tonga
Population: 110,000
Area: 288 sq mi (747 sq km)
Pop. Density: 382/sq mi (147/sq km)
Capital: Nuku'alofa, 21,265

TRINIDAD AND TOBAGO
Official Name: Republic of Trinidad and
  Tobago
Population: 1,281,000
Area: 1,980 sq mi (5,128 sq km)
Pop. Density: 647/sq mi (250/sq km)
Capital: Port of Spain, 50,878

TUNISIA
Official Name: Republic of Tunisia
Population: 8,806,000
Area: 63,170 sq mi (163,610 sq km)
Pop. Density: 139/sq mi (54/sq km)
Capital: Tunis, 596,654

TURKEY
Official Name: Republic of Turkey
Population: 62,030,000
Area: 300,948 sq mi (779,452 sq km)
Pop. Density: 206/sq mi (80/sq km)
Capital: Ankara, 2,559,471

TURKMENISTAN
Official Name: Turkmenistan
Population: 4,035,000
Area: 188,456 sq mi (488,100 sq km)
Pop. Density: 21/sq mi (8.3/sq km)
Capital: Ashkhabad, 412,200

TUVALU
Official Name: Tuvalu
Population: 10,000
Area: 10 sq mi (26 sq km)
Pop. Density: 1,000/sq mi (385/sq km)
Capital: Funafuti, 2,191

Countries
and Flags
continued

URUGUAY
Official Name: Oriental Republic of Uruguay
Population: 3,317,000
Area: 68,500 sq mi (177,414 sq km)
Pop. Density: 48/sq mi (19/sq km)
Capital: Montevideo, 1,251,647

WESTERN SAMOA
Official Name: Independent State of Western
Samoa
Population: 172,000
Area: 1,093 sq mi (2,831 sq km)
Pop. Density: 157/sq mi (61/sq km)
Capital: Apia, 34,126

UGANDA
Official Name: Republic of Uganda
Population: 18,270,000
Area: 93,104 sq mi (241,139 sq km)
Pop. Density: 196/sq mi (76/sq km)
Capital: Kampala, 773,463

UZBEKISTAN
Official Name: Republic of Uzbekistan
Population: 22,860,000
Area: 172,742 sq mi (447,400 sq km)
Pop. Density: 132/sq mi (51/sq km)
Capital: Tashkent, 2,113,300

YEMEN
Official Name: Republic of Yemen
Population: 12,910,000
Area: 203,850 sq mi (527,968 sq km)
Pop. Density: 63/sq mi (24/sq km)
Capital: San'ā', 427,150

UKRAINE
Official Name: Ukraine
Population: 52,140,000
Area: 233,090 sq mi (603,700 sq km)
Pop. Density: 224/sq mi (86/sq km)
Capital: Kiev (Kyyiv), 2,635,000

VANUATU
Official Name: Republic of Vanuatu
Population: 161,000
Area: 4,707 sq mi (12,190 sq km)
Pop. Density: 34/sq mi (13/sq km)
Capital: Port Vila, 18,905

YUGOSLAVIA
Official Name: Socialist Federal Republic of
Yugoslavia
Population: 10,765,000
Area: 39,449 sq mi (102,173 sq km)
Pop. Density: 273/sq mi (105/sq km)
Capital: Belgrade (Beograd), 1,136,786

UNITED ARAB EMIRATES
Official Name: United Arab Emirates
Population: 2,855,000
Area: 32,278 sq mi (83,600 sq km)
Pop. Density: 88/sq mi (34/sq km)
Capital: Abū Ẓaby (Abu Dhabi), 242,975

VATICAN CITY
Official Name: State of the Vatican City
Population: 1,000
Area: 0.2 sq mi (0.4 sq km)
Pop. Density: 5,000/sq mi (2,500/sq km)
Capital: Vatican City, 1,000

ZAIRE
Official Name: Republic of Zaire
Population: 43,365,000
Area: 905,355 sq mi (2,344,858 sq km)
Pop. Density: 48/sq mi (18/sq km)
Capital: Kinshasa, 3,000,000

UNITED KINGDOM
Official Name: United Kingdom of Great
Britain and Northern Ireland
Population: 58,430,000
Area: 94,249 sq mi (244,101 sq km)
Pop. Density: 620/sq mi (239/sq km)
Capital: London, 6,574,009

VENEZUELA
Official Name: Republic of Venezuela
Population: 21,395,000
Area: 352,145 sq mi (912,050 sq km)
Pop. Density: 61/sq mi (23/sq km)
Capital: Caracas, 1,822,465

ZAMBIA
Official Name: Republic of the Zambia
Population: 8,809,000
Area: 290,587 sq mi (752,618 sq km)
Pop. Density: 30/sq mi (12/sq km)
Capital: Lusaka, 982,362

UNITED STATES
Official Name: United States of America
Population: 262,530,000
Area: 3,787,425 sq mi (9,809,431 sq km)
Pop. Density: 69/sq mi (27/sq km)
Capital: Washington, D.C., 606,900

VIETNAM
Official Name: Socialist Republic of Vietnam
Population: 73,760,000
Area: 127,428 sq mi (330,036 sq km)
Pop. Density: 579/sq mi (223/sq km)
Capital: Hanoi, 905,939

ZIMBABWE
Official Name: Republic of Zimbabwe
Population: 11,075,000
Area: 150,872 sq mi (390,757 sq km)
Pop. Density: 73/sq mi (28/sq km)
Capital: Harare (Salisbury), 681,000

Legend

Continental and regional coverage of the world's land areas is provided by the following section of physical-political reference maps. The section falls into a continental arrangement: North America, South America, Europe, Africa, Asia, and Oceania. Introducing each regional reference map section are several basic thematic maps.

To aid the reader in understanding the relative sizes of continents and of some of the countries and regions, uniform scales for comparable areas were used as far as possible. Most of the world is covered by a series of regional maps at scales of 1:16,000,000 and 1:12,000,000. Maps at 1:10,000,000 provide even greater detail for parts of Europe. The United States and parts of South America are mapped at 1:4,000,000.

Many of the symbols used are self-explanatory. A complete legend below provides a key to the symbols on the reference maps in the atlas.

The color tints on the maps depict the varying elevations and depths of land areas and bodies of water. The Relief legend that accompanies each map shows the specific elevation or depth that each color tint represents.

The surface configuration is represented by hill-shading, which gives the three-dimensional impression of landforms. This terrain representation is superimposed on the layer tints to convey a realistic and readily visualized impression of the surface. The combination of altitudinal tints and hill-shading best shows elevation, relief, steepness of slope, and ruggedness of terrain.

If the world used one alphabet and language, no particular difficulty would arise in understanding place-names. However, some of the people of the world, the Chinese and the Japanese, for example, use non-alphabetic languages. Their symbols are transliterated into the Roman alphabet. In this atlas, a "local-name" policy generally was used for naming cities, towns, and all local topographic and water features. However, for a few major cities the Anglicized name was preferred and the local name given in parentheses: for instance, Moscow (Moskva), Vienna (Wien), Bangkok (Krung Thep). In countries where more than one official language is used, a name appears in the dominant local language. The generic parts of local names for topographic and water features are self-explanatory in many cases because of the associated map symbols or type styles. A complete list of foreign generic names is given in the Glossary.

Physical-Political Reference Map Legend

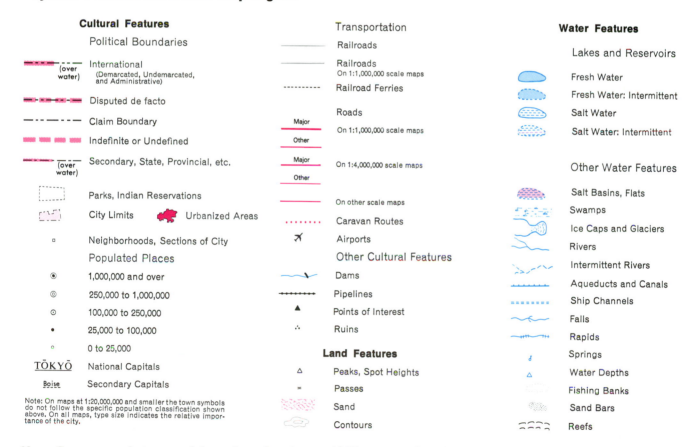

Note: Country populations used throughout the atlas are 1995 estimates based on U.S. Census Bureau figures and other available information. City populations reflect the latest available official data.

ARCTIC OCEAN

ZEML'A FRANCA-IOSIFA
NOVOSIBIRSKIJE OSTROVA
More Laptevych
NOVAJA ZEML'A   Karskoje More
Barents Sea
Arctic Circle
SVALBARD (Nor.)

SWEDEN   Noril'sk
FINLAND   Jenisej
Stockholm   Archangel'sk
Helsinki   Lena   Jakutsk   Anadyr
SANKT-PETERBURG   Bering Sea
MOSKVA   R U S S I A   Sea of Okhotsk   ALEUTIAN IS. (U.S.)
GERMANY   Niznij Novgorod   Petropavlovsk-Kamcatskij
POLAND   Jekaterinburg   OSTROV SACHALIN
UKRAINE   Novosibirsk   Harbin
BELA   Karaganda   Ozero Bajkal   Sea of Japan
ROM.   KAZAKHSTAN   MONGOLIA   KOREA   JAPAN
Volga   Aral Sea   ALTAJ   BEIJING PEKING   SEOUL   OSAKA   TOKYO
Gora El'brus 5633   UZBEK.   GOBI
ITALY   Caspian Sea   Taskent   KYRG.   Xi'an   Yellow Sea
ROMA   Black Sea   TURKMENISTAN   TAJIK.   C H I N A   Wuhan   SHANGHAI
GREECE   GEOR.   AZER.   Chongqing
TURKEY   Istanbul   AFGHANISTAN   HIMALAYA   Guangzhou
MALTA   SYRIA   IRAN   NEPAL   Everest 8848   HONG KONG (U.K.)   TAIWAN
Mediterranean Sea   ISRAEL   IRAQ   PAKISTAN   DELHI   BHU.   PACIFIC OCEAN
LIBYA   JORDAN   KUWAIT   Karachi   Tropic of Cancer   BNGL.   MYANMAR (BURMA)   Philippine Sea   WAKE ISLAND (U.S.)
AL-QAHIRAH CAIRO   QATAR   CALCUTTA   LAOS   South
EGYPT   SAUDI   UNITED ARAB EMIRATES   I N D I A   Bay of   THAILAND   China   MANILA   GUAM (U.S.)
NIGER   CHAD   ARABIA   OMAN   BOMBAY   Bengal   Krung Thep   VIETNAM   Sea   PHILIPPINES   MICRONESIA
ERITREA   Madras   Bangkok   CAMB.
Red Sea   YEMEN   Arabian Sea   China
SUDAN   DJIBOUTI   Adan   Sea
ETHIOPIA   SOMALIA   SRI LANKA   BRUNEI
CEN. AFR. REP.   Colombo   MALDIVES   MALAYSIA
UGANDA   KENYA   Muqdisho   Singapore   BORNEO   SULAWESI
GABON   ZAIRE   RWANDA   Nairobi   SEYCHELLES   SUMATERA   IRIAN JAYA   PAPUA NEW GUINEA   SOLOMON ISLANDS
Kinshasa   BURUNDI   Victoria   Equator   JAKARTA   I N D O N E S I A   NEW GUINEA   KIRIBATI
TANZANIA   Kilimanjaro 5895   CHAGOS ARCHIPELAGO (B.I.O.T.)   JAWA   TIMOR   Port Moresby   TUVALU
Luanda   ANGOLA   ZAMBIA   CHRISTMAS ISLAND (Aust.)   MELANESIA   SOLOMON ISLANDS
I N D I A N   Equator
ZIMBABWE   O C E A N   Cairns   VANUATU
NAMIBIA   BOTSWANA   MADAGASCAR   MAURITIUS   Coral Sea   FIJI
Mozambique Channel   REUNION (Fr.)   NEW CALEDONIA (Fr.)
Johannesburg   SWAZILAND   Tropic of Capricorn   A U S T R A L I A   Brisbane
LESOTHO   Durban   Perth   Sydney
SOUTH AFRICA   Melbourne   Mount Kosciusko 2230   Tasman Sea   NEW ZEALAND
Cape Town   CAPE OF GOOD HOPE   TASMANIA   Wellington

ÎLES KERGUELEN (F.S.A.T.)

Antarctic Circle

ENDERBY LAND   WILKES LAND

A N T A R C T I C A

Kilometers   0   1000   2000   3000   Km.
Miles   0   1000   2000   3000   Mi.
Robinson Projection

WORLD TERRAIN

Arctic Ocean

QUEEN ELIZABETH ISLANDS

GREENLAND

RUSSIA

UNITED STATES

BAFFIN ISLAND

Arctic Cir

ICELAND

C A N A D A

N O R T H

PORTUGAL

A M E R I C A

UNITED STATES

Chicago

New York

Atlantic

WESTERN SAHARA

Pacific

GREAT BASIN

APPALACHIAN MOUNTAINS

Ocean

MAUR

Los Angeles

Mississippi

TANK

Tropic of Cancer

Ocean

MEXICO

GUINEA

Mexico City

WEST INDIES

Equator

Equator

VENEZUELA

COLOMBIA

Pacific

ARCHIPELAGO DE COLON
GALAPAGOS ISLANDS

Amazon

S O U T H

Atlantic

B R A Z I L

PERU

A M E R I C A

Ocean

BOLIVIA

Ocean

Tropic of Capricorn

Rio de Janeiro

PARAGUAY

Ocean

ARGENTINA

URUGUAY

PAMPA

Buenos Aires

BRAZ

IS

A

150°

120°

90°

60°

30°

Terrain

Land Elevations in Profile

OCEANIA	NORTH AMERICA	SOUTH AMERICA	AFRICA

LOS ANDES

30000 9145   NEW ZEALAND
25000 7620   HAWAII   ALASKA RANGE   SIERRA   Aconcagua (Vol.)   ATLAS
20000 6095   Mt. McKinley   CASCADE RANGE   NEVADA   ROCKY MTS. Citlaltépetl   Chimborazo   22 831   Nev. Illimani   Jebel Toubkal
15000 4570   Mt. Cook   Mauna Kea (Vol.)   20 320   Mt. Rainier   Mt. Whitney   Pikes Peak 18 701   20 561   21 151   Pico da Bandeira   13 665   Cameroon Mtn.   15 15
10000 3050   12 349   13 796   14 410   14 491   14 110   Irazú (Vol.)   Mt.   CANARIAS   13 451
 5000 1525   TAHITI   GREAT   11 200   Mitchell   HISPANIOLA   PLATEAU OF BOLIVIA 9 482   Pico de Teide
                                                               BASIN   6 084   Pico Duarte   12 188
Feet Meters   7 352   10 417

Ocean Depths in Profile

P A C I F I C   O C E A N   A T L A N T I C

INDOCHINA HAINAN   Sea Level   HAWAII   MEXICO   NOVA SCOTIA
5000 1525   MARIANA IS.   GRAND BANK   ATLANT
10000 3050   PHILIPPINES BASIN
15000 4570   20 384   BRAZ
20000 6095   ALEUTIAN TRENCH
25000 7620   PHILIPPINES TRENCH   JAPAN TRENCH   20 374   PUERTO RICO TRENCH
30000 9145   34 440   34 038   MARIANA TRENCH   A Section along 20°N. Lat.   28 374   A Section along
35000 10670   35 201

Feet Meters

Elevations and dep

Map Labels

Oceans and Seas:
Arctic Ocean
Pacific Ocean
Indian Ocean
Mediterranean Sea
Black Sea
Caspian Sea
Red Sea

Lines:
Arctic Circle
Tropic of Cancer
Equator
Tropic of Capricorn
Antarctic Circle

Europe:
NORWAY
SWEDEN
FINLAND
Berlin
GERMANY
POLAND
BELARUS
Moscow
Volga
Ob'
EUROPE
ALPS
ITALY
Rome
UKRAINE
ROMANIA
Paris

Asia/Russia:
RUSSIA
ASIA
KAZAKHSTAN
MONGOLIA
GOBI
TURKMENISTAN
TURKEY
SYRIA
Tehran
IRAN
IRAQ
ISRAEL
PAKISTAN
HIMALAYAS
Ganges
INDIA
Calcutta
Bombay
CHINA
Beijing
Shanghai
JAPAN
Tokyo
THAILAND
VIETNAM
CAMB.
MALAYSIA
PHILIPPINES

Africa:
LIBYA
EGYPT
SAUDI ARABIA
Cairo
Nile
SAHARA
NIGER
CHAD
SUDAN
NIGERIA
CENTRAL AFRICAN REPUBLIC
ETHIOPIA
SOMALIA
GABON
CONGO
ZAIRE
Congo
RIFT VALLEY
Lake Victoria
TANZANIA
AFRICA
ANGOLA
ZAMBIA
ZIMBABWE
MOZAMBIQUE
NAMIBIA
KALAHARI DESERT
BOTSWANA
SOUTH AFRICA
Cape Town
MADAGASCAR

Oceania:
INDONESIA
Jakarta
PAPUA NEW GUINEA
AUSTRALIA
GREAT SANDY DESERT
GREAT VICTORIA DESERT
GREAT DIVIDING RANGE
Sydney
NEW ZEALAND

Antarctica:
ANTARCTICA

Scale
0 1000 2000 Mi.
0 1000 2000 Km.
Scale

A-510000-792-1E-1E-1-2*

©1990 Rand McNally & Co.

Cross-section profile (top)

EUROPE — ASIA — OCEANIA

Peak	Meters	Feet
	9145	30000
	7620	25000
	6095	20000
	4570	15000
	3050	10000
	1525	5000

ALPS
Mt. Blanc 15,771
PYRENEES
Pico de Aneto 11,168
KJÖLEN
Glittertinden 8,110
Etna (Vol.) 10,902
Dj. esh-Sheikh (Hermon) 9,232
Narodnaya 6,217
MADAGASCAR
Maromokotro 9,436
Hekla (Vol.) 4,892
CAUCASUS
Gora El'brus 18,510
ELBURZ
Demavend 18,386
K2 28,250
PLATEAU OF TIBET
IRAN
Patandanga
BURMA
PAMIRS
Everest 29,028
Känchenjunga 28,208
Gongga Shan 24,790
GOBI DESERT
SUMATRA
JAVA
Kerinci 12,467
Semeru
Klyuchevskaya 15,584
BORNEO
Kinabalu 13,455
Puti-San (Vol.) 12,388
Mt. Apo 9,692
G. Rantja... 12,060
NEW GUINEA
AUSTRALIA 6,095
Puncak Jaya 16,503
Mt. Kosciusko 7,310

Meters Feet

Cross-section profile (bottom): A Section along 10°S. Lat.

FRANCE — MEDITERRANEAN SEA — GIBRALTAR — MALTA — ISRAEL — INDIAN OCEAN — Sea Level — SOEMBA — ARCTIC OCEAN — NORTH POLE — PACIFIC OCEAN — SOUTH POLE — LITTLE AMERICA

16,420

Meters	Feet
1525	5000
3050	10000
4570	15000
6095	20000
7620	25000
9145	30000
10670	35000

in feet

Meters Feet

World Climate

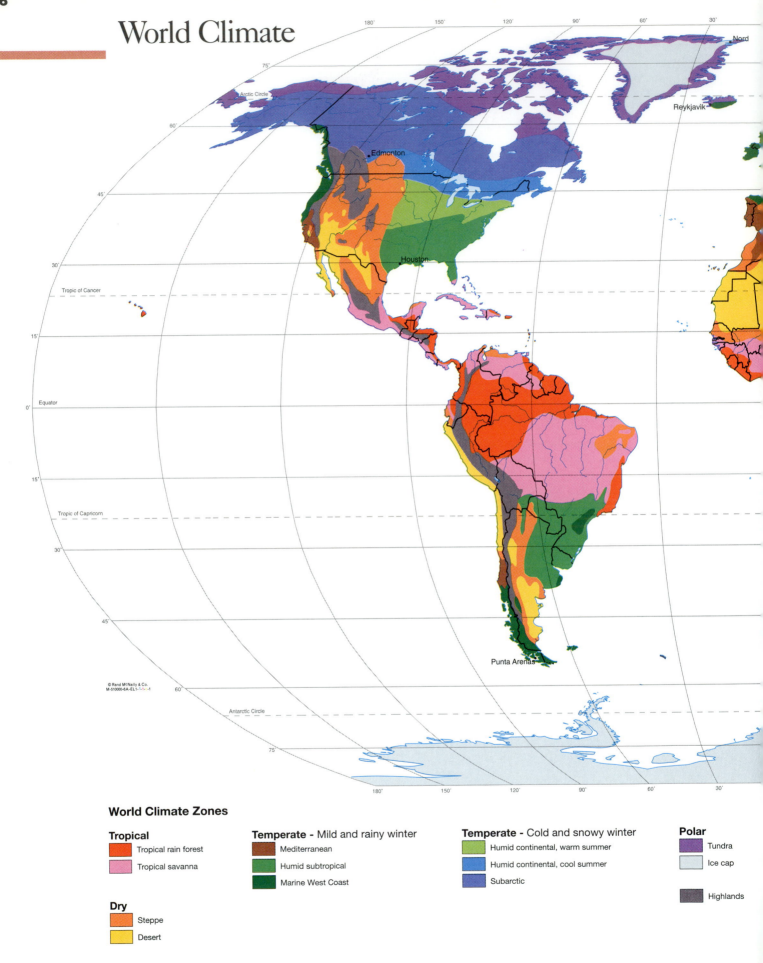

World Climate Zones

Tropical
- Tropical rain forest
- Tropical savanna

Dry
- Steppe
- Desert

Temperate - Mild and rainy winter
- Mediterranean
- Humid subtropical
- Marine West Coast

Temperate - Cold and snowy winter
- Humid continental, warm summer
- Humid continental, cool summer
- Subarctic

Polar
- Tundra
- Ice cap
- Highlands

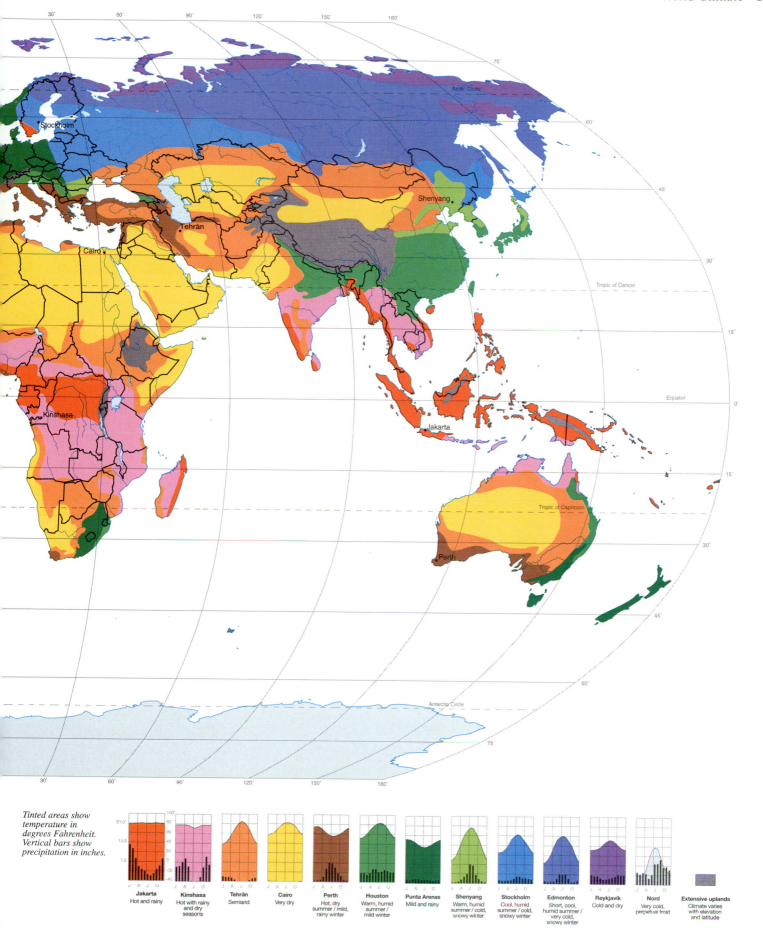

Tinted areas show temperature in degrees Fahrenheit. Vertical bars show precipitation in inches.

Jakarta
Hot and rainy

Kinshasa
Hot with rainy and dry seasons

Tehrān
Semiarid

Cairo
Very dry

Perth
Hot, dry summer / mild, rainy winter

Houston
Warm, humid summer / mild winter

Punta Arenas
Mild and rainy

Shenyang
Warm, humid summer / cold, snowy winter

Stockholm
Cool, humid summer / cold, snowy winter

Edmonton
Short, cool, humid summer / very cold, snowy winter

Reykjavík
Cold and dry

Nord
Very cold, perpetual frost

Extensive uplands
Climate varies with elevation and latitude

World Vegetation

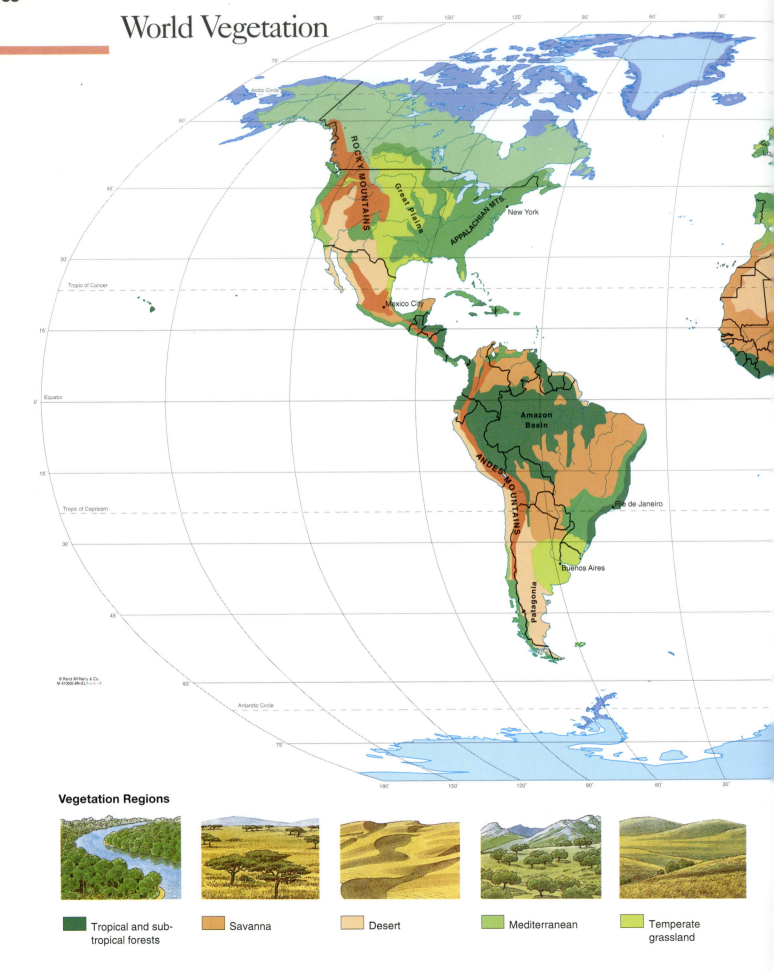

Vegetation Regions

Tropical and sub-tropical forests

Savanna

Desert

Mediterranean

Temperate grassland

© Rand McNally & Co.
M-510000-8N-EL1-|-|-·|-·-·1

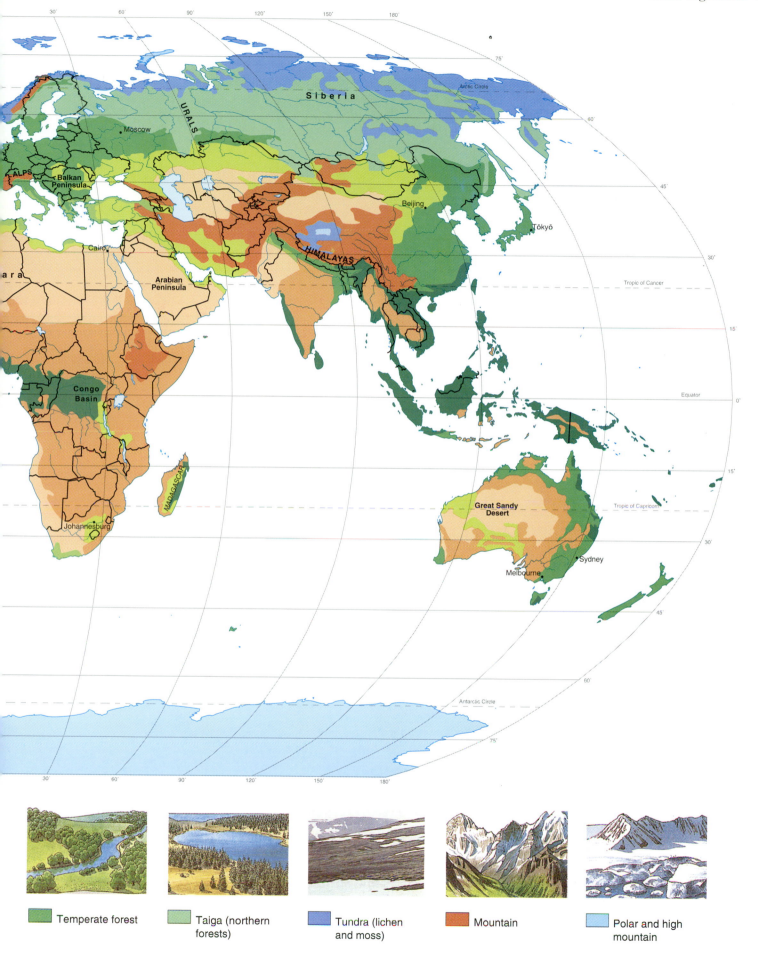

30° 60° 90° 120° 150° 180°

75°

Arctic Circle

60°

S i b e r i a

Moscow

U R A L S

45°

ALPS

Balkan
Peninsula

Beijing

Tōkyō

Cairo

30°

HIMALAYAS

Tropic of Cancer

Arabian
Peninsula

a r a

15°

Congo
Basin

Equator 0°

MADAGASCAR

15°

Great Sandy
Desert

Tropic of Capricorn

Johannesburg

Sydney

Melbourne

30°

45°

60°

Antarctic Circle

75°

30° 60° 90° 120° 150° 180°

Temperate forest   **Taiga (northern forests)**   **Tundra (lichen and moss)**   **Mountain**   **Polar and high mountain**

World Population

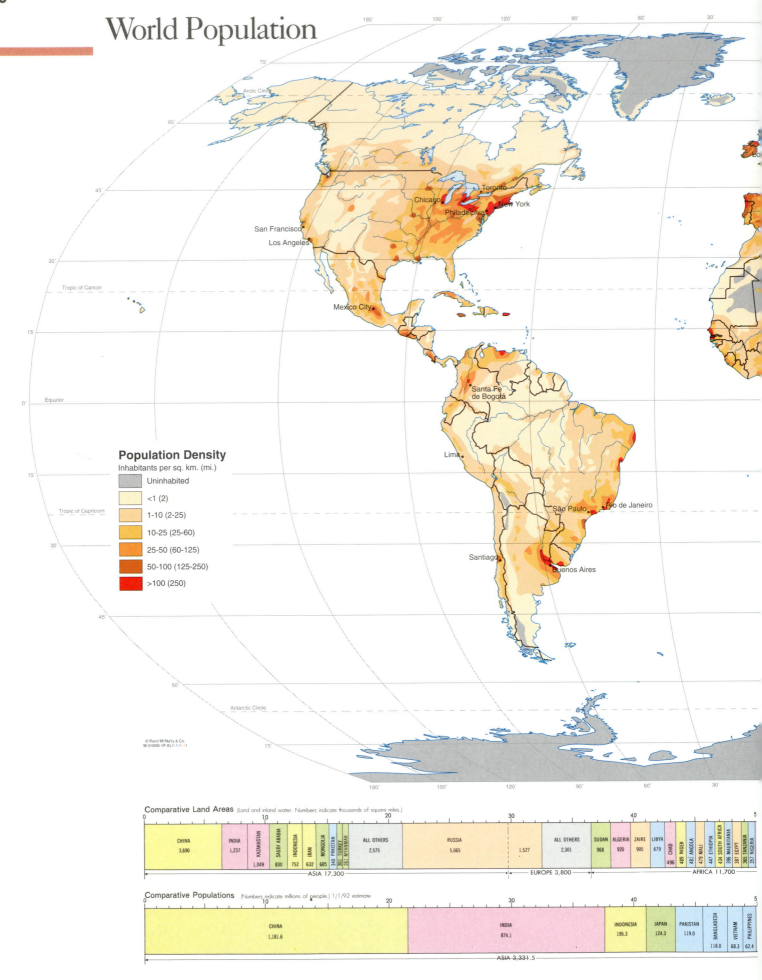

Population Density
Inhabitants per sq. km. (mi.)

- Uninhabited
- <1 (2)
- 1-10 (2-25)
- 10-25 (25-60)
- 25-50 (60-125)
- 50-100 (125-250)
- >100 (250)

© Rand McNally & Co.
M-510000-1P-EL1-1-1-...-1

Comparative Land Areas (Land and inland water. Numbers indicate thousands of square miles.)

CHINA 3,690	INDIA 1,237	KAZAKHSTAN 1,049	SAUDI ARABIA 830	INDONESIA 752	IRAN 632	MONGOLIA 605	PAKISTAN 340	TURKEY 301	MYANMAR 261	ALL OTHERS 2,575	RUSSIA 5,065	1,527	ALL OTHERS 2,301	SUDAN 968	ALGERIA 920	ZAIRE 905	LIBYA 679	CHAD 496	NIGER 489	ANGOLA 481	MALI 479	ETHIOPIA 447	SOUTH AFRICA 434	MAURITANIA 396	EGYPT 387

ASIA 17,300 · EUROPE 3,800 · AFRICA 11,700

(TANZANIA 365, NIGERIA 357)

Comparative Populations (Numbers indicate millions of people.) 1/1/92 estimate

CHINA 1,181.6	INDIA 874.1	INDONESIA 195.3	JAPAN 124.3	PAKISTAN 119.0	BANGLADESH 118.0	VIETNAM 68.3	PHILIPPINES 62.4

ASIA 3,331.5

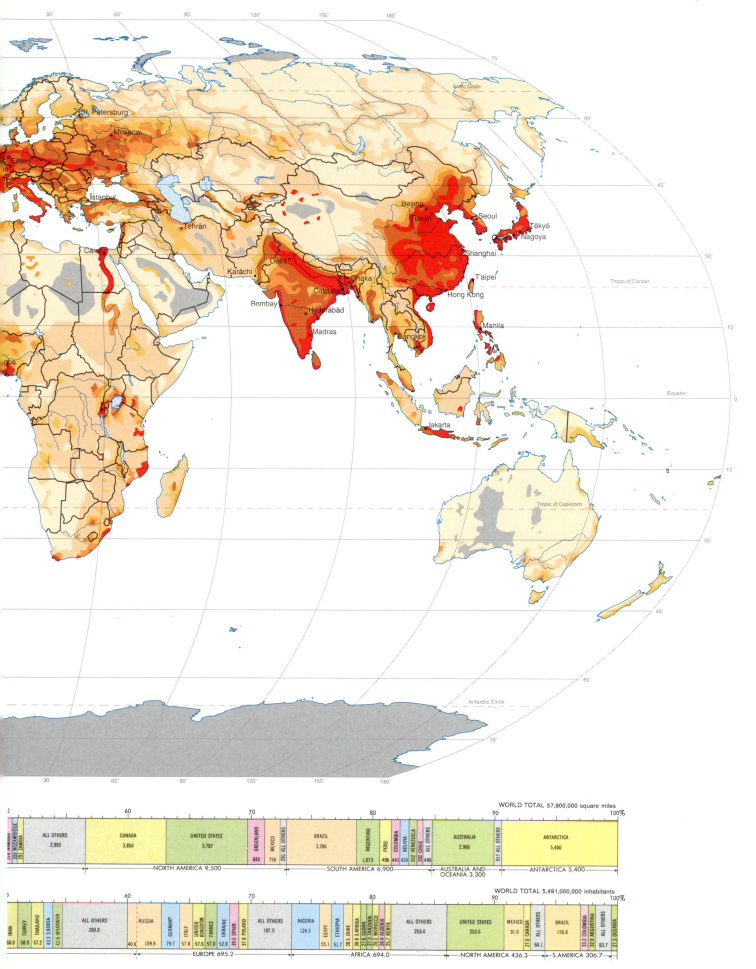

WORLD TOTAL 57,900,000 square miles

NAMIBIA 318	MOZAMBIQUE 303	ZAMBIA 291	ALL OTHERS 2,993	CANADA 3,850	UNITED STATES 3,787	GREENLAND 840	MEXICO 756	ALL OTHERS 291	BRAZIL 3,286	ARGENTINA 1,073	PERU 496	COLOMBIA 441	VENEZUELA 424	CHILE 292	ALL OTHERS 490	AUSTRALIA 2,966	ALL OTHERS 317	ANTARCTICA 5,400

NORTH AMERICA 9,500 — SOUTH AMERICA 6,900 — AUSTRALIA AND OCEANIA 3,300 — ANTARCTICA 5,400

WORLD TOTAL 5,491,000,000 inhabitants

IRAN 50.0	TURKEY 58.9	THAILAND 57.2	S. KOREA 43.3	MYANMAR 42.6	ALL OTHERS 289.8	RUSSIA 109.9	GERMANY 79.7	ITALY 57.8	UNITED KINGDOM 57.6	FRANCE 57.0	UKRAINE 52.8	POLAND 39.5	ALL OTHERS 197.3	NIGERIA 124.3	EGYPT 55.1	ETHIOPIA 51.7	S.AFRICA 38.5	ZAIRE 36.8	SUDAN 27.6	TANZANIA 26.5	MOROCCO 26.4	ALGERIA 25.7	KENYA	ALL OTHERS 253.4	UNITED STATES 253.5	MEXICO 91.0	CANADA 27.0	ALL OTHERS 64.1	BRAZIL 156.8	COLOMBIA 33.2	ARGENTINA 32.9	ALL OTHERS 83.7	OCEANIA 27.3

EUROPE 695.2 — AFRICA 694.0 — NORTH AMERICA 436.3 — S.AMERICA 306.7

World Environments

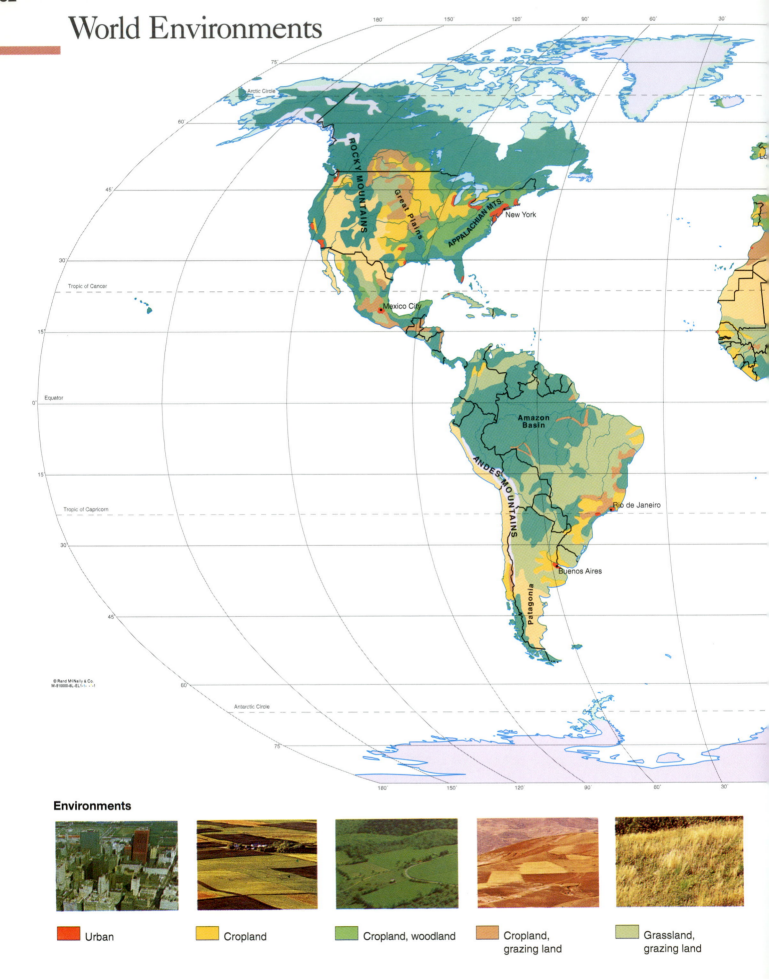

Environments

Urban

Cropland

Cropland, woodland

Cropland, grazing land

Grassland, grazing land

Siberia

URALS

Moscow

ALPS

Balkan
Peninsula

Cairo

r a

Arabian
Peninsula

Beijing

Tōkyō

HIMALAYAS

Congo
Basin

MADAGASCAR

Johannesburg

Great Sandy
Desert

Sydney

Melbourne

Arctic Circle

Tropic of Cancer

Equator

Tropic of Capricorn

Antarctic Circle

| | Forest, woodland | | Swamp, marsh | | Tundra | | Shrub, sparse grass, wasteland | | Barren land |

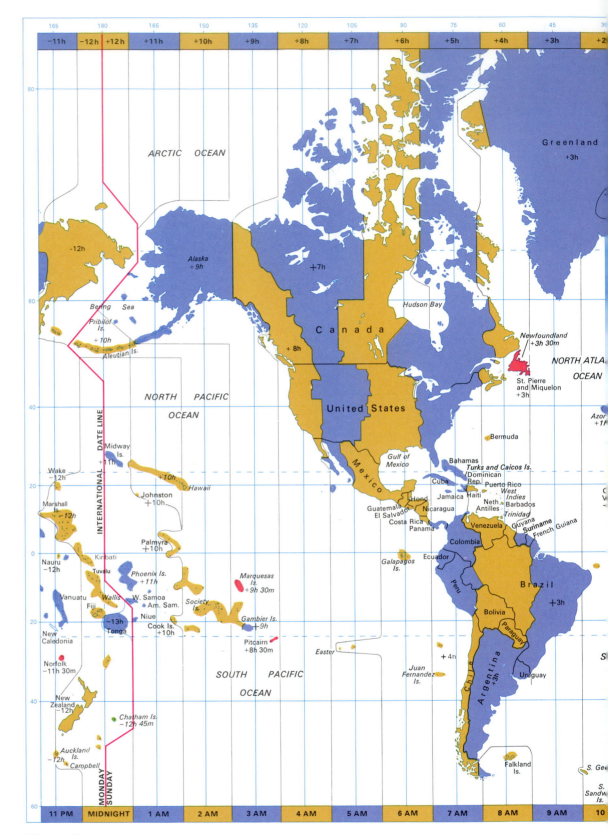

Time Zones

🟨	Standard time zone of even-numbered hours from Greenwich time
🟦	Standard time zone of odd-numbered hours from Greenwich time
🟥	Time varies from the standard time zone by half an hour
🟩	Time varies from the standard time zone by other than half an hour

h m hours, minutes

The standard time zone system, fixed by international agreement and by law in each country, is based on a theoretical division of the globe into 24 zones of 15° longitude each. The mid-meridian of each zone fixes the hour for the entire zone. The zero time zone extends 7½° east and 7½° west of the Greenwich meridian, 0° longitude. Since the earth rotates toward the east, time zones to the west of Greenwich are earlier, to the east, later.

Plus and minus hours at the top of the map are added to or subtracted from local time to find Greenwich time. Local standard time can be determined for any area in the world by adding one hour for each time zone counted in an easterly direction from one's own, or by subtracting one hour for each zone counted in a westerly direction. To separate one day from the next, the 180th meridian has been designated as the international date line. On both sides of the line the time of day is the same, but west of the line it is one day later than it is to the east. Countries that adhere to the international zone system adopt the zone applicable to their location. Some countries, however, establish time zones based on political boundaries, or adopt the time zone of a neighboring unit. For all or part of the year some countries also advance their time by one hour, thereby utilizing more daylight hours each day.

North America

North America is the world's third-largest continent, covering an area of 9.5 million square miles (24.7 million sq km). It lies primarily between the Arctic Circle and the Tropic of Cancer, and comes within 500 miles (800 km) of both the North Pole and the Equator. The continent's western flank is dominated by the spectacular Rocky Mountains. Covering vast stretches of the central United States and Canada are the fertile Great Plains, a large part of which is drained by the Mississippi River and its tributaries.

In the north, Hudson Bay is frozen for much of the year. Mexico, located in the continent's southern third, is mostly mountainous and dry, but farther south, the climate is wet. Many of the small Central American countries have volcanoes along the Pacific Coast.

North America at a glance

Land area: 9,500,000 square miles (24,700,000 sq km)

Estimated population (January 1, 1995): 453,300,000

Population density: 48/square mile (18/sq km)

Mean elevation: 2,000 feet (610 m)

Highest point: Mt. McKinley, Alaska, U.S. 20,230 feet (6,194 m)

Lowest point: Death Valley, California, U.S., 282 feet (86 m) below sea level

Longest river: Mississippi-Missouri, 3,740 mi (6,019 km)

Number of countries (incl. dependencies): 38

Largest independent country: Canada, 3,849,674 square miles (9,970,610 sq km)

Smallest independent country: St. Kitts and Nevis, 101 square miles (261 sq km)

Most populous independent country: United States, 262,530,000

Least populous independent country: St. Kitts and Nevis, 44,000

Largest city: Mexico City, pop. 8,235,744 (1990)

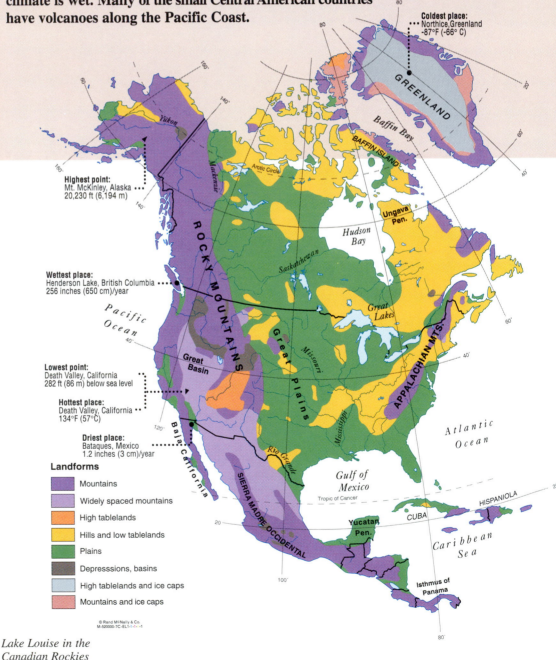

Coldest place: Northice, Greenland -87°F (-66° C)

Highest point: Mt. McKinley, Alaska 20,230 ft (6,194 m)

Wettest place: Henderson Lake, British Columbia 256 inches (650 cm)/year

Lowest point: Death Valley, California 282 ft (86 m) below sea level

Hottest place: Death Valley, California 134°F (57°C)

Driest place: Bataques, Mexico 1.2 inches (3 cm)/year

Landforms

- Mountains
- Widely spaced mountains
- High tablelands
- Hills and low tablelands
- Plains
- Depresssions, basins
- High tablelands and ice caps
- Mountains and ice caps

© Rand McNally & Co.
M-520000-7C-EL1-1-1- -1

Lake Louise in the Canadian Rockies

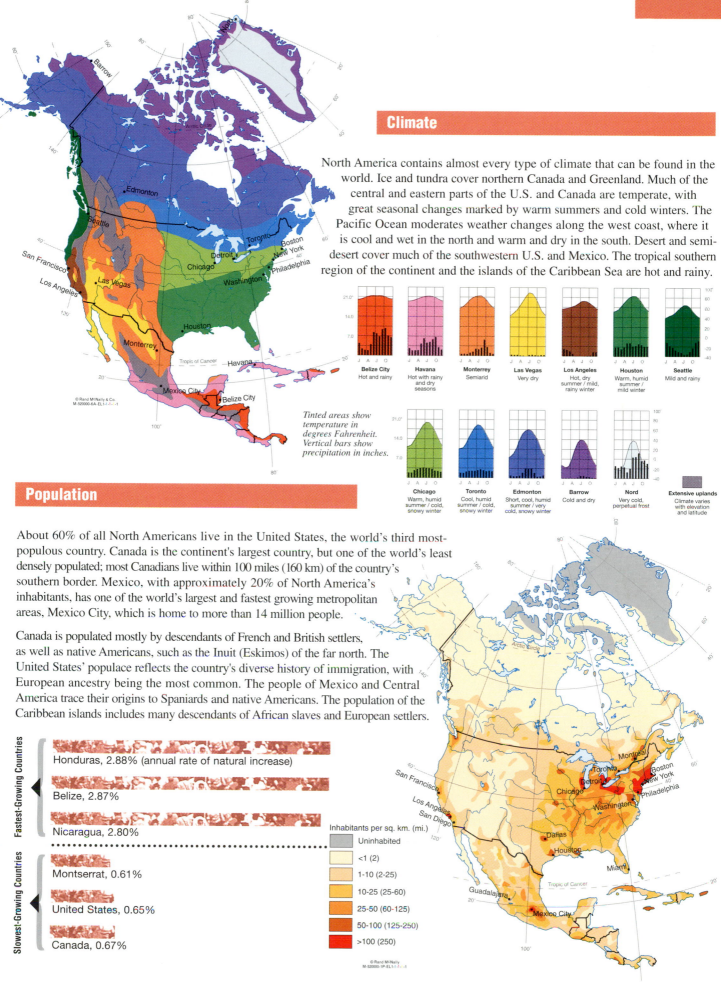

Climate

North America contains almost every type of climate that can be found in the world. Ice and tundra cover northern Canada and Greenland. Much of the central and eastern parts of the U.S. and Canada are temperate, with great seasonal changes marked by warm summers and cold winters. The Pacific Ocean moderates weather changes along the west coast, where it is cool and wet in the north and warm and dry in the south. Desert and semi-desert cover much of the southwestern U.S. and Mexico. The tropical southern region of the continent and the islands of the Caribbean Sea are hot and rainy.

Belize City — Hot and rainy

Havana — Hot with rainy and dry seasons

Monterrey — Semiarid

Las Vegas — Very dry

Los Angeles — Hot, dry summer / mild, rainy winter

Houston — Warm, humid summer / mild winter

Seattle — Mild and rainy

Tinted areas show temperature in degrees Fahrenheit. Vertical bars show precipitation in inches.

Chicago — Warm, humid summer / cold, snowy winter

Toronto — Cool, humid summer / cold, snowy winter

Edmonton — Short, cool, humid summer / very cold, snowy winter

Barrow — Cold and dry

Nord — Very cold, perpetual frost

Extensive uplands — Climate varies with elevation and latitude

Population

About 60% of all North Americans live in the United States, the world's third most-populous country. Canada is the continent's largest country, but one of the world's least densely populated; most Canadians live within 100 miles (160 km) of the country's southern border. Mexico, with approximately 20% of North America's inhabitants, has one of the world's largest and fastest growing metropolitan areas, Mexico City, which is home to more than 14 million people.

Canada is populated mostly by descendants of French and British settlers, as well as native Americans, such as the Inuit (Eskimos) of the far north. The United States' populace reflects the country's diverse history of immigration, with European ancestry being the most common. The people of Mexico and Central America trace their origins to Spaniards and native Americans. The population of the Caribbean islands includes many descendants of African slaves and European settlers.

Fastest-Growing Countries

Honduras, 2.88% (annual rate of natural increase)

Belize, 2.87%

Nicaragua, 2.80%

Slowest-Growing Countries

Montserrat, 0.61%

United States, 0.65%

Canada, 0.67%

Inhabitants per sq. km. (mi.)

- Uninhabited
- <1 (2)
- 1-10 (2-25)
- 10-25 (25-60)
- 25-50 (60-125)
- 50-100 (125-250)
- >100 (250)

Environments and Land Use

Although only 12% of the continent is suitable for agriculture, North America is the world's leading food producer. Unlike other parts of the world, famine is virtually unknown. Large quantities of food, such as grains from the central U.S. and Canada, are exported worldwide. Sixteen percent of the continent is used for grazing, and the livestock raised on these lands are also an important source of food at home and abroad.

Forests cover one-third of the land, and the timber and paper industries are important to the U.S. and Canada. The continent has an extremely long coastline, and many countries send great fishing fleets to sea. This is especially true of Canada, whose eastern-most provinces are fittingly known as the "Maritime Provinces." However, sharp declines in catches due to over-fishing have put the industry in economic turmoil.

Blue waters, sunny skies, and idyllic beaches draw millions of tourists to the Caribbean each year. While tourism provides income for island countries that have few other assets, the economic gap between the visitors and the people who serve them remains dramatic.

One of the greatest challenges facing North America in the coming decades is a familiar one: coping with a growing population and dwindling resources. Pollution and the environment are divisive issues. Although the United States has begun to clean up its air and water, economic pressures will continue to be an argument for a relaxation of policies. Meanwhile, in Mexico, environmental issues have been pushed aside by concerns about the economy and the exploding population.

Legend:

- Urban
- Cropland
- Cropland and woodland
- Cropland and grazing land
- Grassland, grazing land
- Forest, woodland
- Swamp, marsh
- Tundra
- Shrub, sparse grass, wasteland
- Barren land

© Rand McNally & Co.
M-520000-8L-EL1-1-1- -1

0   200   400   600   800   1000 Miles
0   300   600   900   1200   1500 Kilometers

Field of corn in the midwestern United States

Map labels: GREENLAND, BAFFIN ISLAND, Arctic Circle, Hudson Bay, Ungava Pen., Edmonton, ROCKY MOUNTAINS, Pacific Ocean, Great Lakes, Montreal, Great Plains, Great Basin, Chicago, Denver, APPALACHIAN MTS., New York, Los Angeles, Atlantic Ocean, Gulf of Mexico, Tropic of Cancer, Yucatan Pen., Mexico City, Caribbean Sea

Urbanization in North America

Seen from the air, large portions of North America still bear the checkerboard imprint left by the people who settled the continent: a vast array of small farms that could be worked by one man and a horse. As industrialization swept through the United States in the second half of the 19th century, many farmers left their farms. Great numbers moved to fast-growing cities such as Chicago and St. Louis. Many small towns saw their populations dwindle.

In the cities, change was continuous. The former farm families were joined by waves of European immigrants. Over the next 100 years, urban populations continued to grow, and cities that had once been separate became part of vast urban megalopolises. An example can be seen in the eastern United States, where a band of urban centers stretches almost continuously from Boston south through New York City to Washington D.C. (see map at right).

After World War II, as the U. S. middle class expanded, large numbers of families moved out of the city centers into suburban communities of mass-produced, affordable homes. Many of those who remained were economically disadvantaged. A shrinking tax base meant that cities could not support their infrastructures, and conditions in the inner cities worsened. In the suburbs the opposite was true: vast sums were spent building new roads, houses, and shopping centers.

The same process that transformed the U.S. is now occurring in Mexico. In 1945, 25% of the population was considered urban, but today the figure surpasses 70% (see graph above). Not content to lead lives as subsistence farmers, scores of Mexicans arrive in the cities each day in search of jobs that will enable them to provide a better life for their families.

Sadly, these dreams are often elusive. Most of the people end up in low-paying jobs, with their meager wages going to pay for the food that they once grew themselves. City officials are hard-pressed to provide clean water to their ever-growing populations, let alone electricity, transportation and education.

As elsewhere in the world, coping with the pressures of growing populations is one of the greatest challenges facing North Americans today.

Rising Urban Population
Urban population as a percentage of total population, 1900-2000 (estimated)

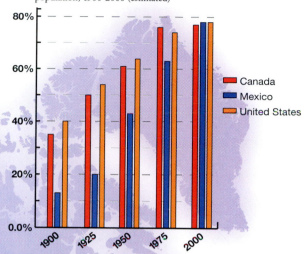

Legend:
- Canada
- Mexico
- United States

(The definition of "urban" varies from country to country. In Canada, all towns with more than 1,000 people are considered urban, while in the U.S. and Mexico only towns with more than 2,500 people are defined as urban.)

Urban Centers

- 50,000-99,999 people
- 100,000-500,000 people
- Over 500,000 people

© Rand McNally
M-520000-9E-EL1-1-1- -1

Mexico City, whose metropolitan area population exceeds 14 million, sprawls toward the distant mountains.

40,000 SQ MI
AREA

0   300   600
Miles

A-520000-26—5EL—5EL—15EL
COPYRIGHT BY
RAND McNALLY & COMPANY
MADE IN U.S.A.

0   200   400   600   800   1000 Miles
0   400   800   1200   1600 Kilometers

120°   110°   Longitude   West 100° of Greenwich   90°

Scale 1:40 000 000: one inch to 630 miles. Lambert's Azimuthal Equal Area Projection
Elevations and depressions are given in feet

Relief

Meters		Feet
3050		10 000
1525		5000
610		2000
305		1000
0	Sea Level	0
		Below Sea Level
152.5		500
1525		5000
3050		10 000
6100		20 000

A-520000-76-2-5-5.15
COPYRIGHT BY
RAND McNALLY & COMPANY
MADE IN U.S.A.

Longitude West of Greenwich

Scale 1:40 000 000: one inch to 630 miles. Lambert's Azimuthal Equal Area Projection
Elevations and depressions are given in feet

200 400 600 800 1000 Miles
400 800 1200 1600 Kilometers

Scale 1: 12 000 000; one inch to 190 miles. Conic Projection
Elevations and depressions are given in feet

Scale 1:12 000 000; one inch to 190 miles. Polyconic Project
Elevations and depressions are given in feet

95° 90° 85° 80° 75° 70° 65°

ONTARIO

QUEBEC

NEW BRUNSWICK

PRINCE EDWARD ISLAND

Chicoutimi

Roberval

Chatham

MONTAGNE TREMBLANTE PROVINCIAL PARK

Cochrane

LAURENTIDES PROVINCIAL PARK

Trois-Rivières

Campbellton

NOVA SCOTIA

Kenora

Lake of the Woods

QUETICO PROV. PARK

Rainy

North Bay

Ottawa

Sorel

St-Jean

Sherbrooke

Québec

Saint John

Fredericton

Charlottetown

Moncton

Windsor

Truro

Halifax

C. SABLE

Thunder Bay

International Falls

ISLE ROYALE NAT'L PARK

Sudbury

ALGONQUIN PROVINCIAL PARK

Pembroke

Brockville

Ogdensburg

Burlington

Montpelier

MAINE

Bangor

Augusta

ACADIA NAT'L PARK

Yarmouth

Hibbing

Virginia

Duluth

Superior

Ashland

LAKE SUPERIOR

Hancock

Marquette

Sault Ste. Marie

Sault Ste. Marie

North Bay

Nipissing

Party Sound

Georgian Bay

LAKE HURON

Peterborough

Kingston

Watertown

ADIRONDACK MTS.

VT. N.H.

Portland

Portsmouth

Manchester

Concord

Lowell

Lynn

BOSTON

Worcester

Providence

C. COD

MINNESOTA

St. Cloud

St. Paul

MINNEAPOLIS

Eau Claire

Wausau

Marinette

Escanaba

Alpena

MICHIGAN

Owen Sound

Guelph

TORONTO

Hamilton

LAKE ONTARIO

Rochester

Oswego

Syracuse

Utica

Schenectady

Troy

Albany

Pittsfield

Springfield

Hartford

MASS.

New Bedford

Fall River

Nantucket

WISCONSIN

Appleton

Oshkosh

Fond du Lac

Green Bay

Sheboygan

Saginaw

Bay City

Flint

Grand Rapids

Muskegon

Lansing

LAKE MICHIGAN

Port Huron

Brantford

Niagara Falls

BUFFALO

NEW YORK

Binghamton

Jamestown

Ithaca

Poughkeepsie

Kingston

Catskill

Bridgeport

N.Y.

NEW YORK

CONN.

New Haven

LONG I.

R.I.

Mankato

Winona

Rochester

La Crosse

Madison

MILWAUKEE

Racine

Kenosha

Beloit

Waukegan

Evanston

Battle Creek

Kalamazoo

Ann Arbor

Jackson

Windsor

DETROIT

Lakewood

CLEVELAND

Erie

Ashtabula

Youngstown

PENN.

Altoona

Scranton

Wilkes-Barre

Allentown

Reading

Jersey City

Newark

Trenton

PHILADELPHIA

Camden

Fort Dodge

Mason City

Waterloo

Dubuque

IOWA

Cedar Rapids

Freeport

Rockford

Elgin

Aurora

CHICAGO

Hammond

Gary

South Bend

Fort Wayne

Toledo

Sandusky

Lima

Akron

Canton

PITTSBURGH

Johnstown

Harrisburg

Lancaster

York

Wilmington

BALTIMORE

Atlantic City

Des Moines

Iowa City

Davenport

Rock Island

Galesburg

Peoria

Bloomington

Lafayette

Logansport

Marion

Muncie

Springfield

Dayton

Columbus

Hagerstown

Frederick

MD.

Annapolis

Dover

Delaware Bay

DEL.

Ottumwa

Burlington

Keokuk

ILLINOIS

Champaign

Decatur

Springfield

Terre Haute

INDIANA

Indianapolis

Hamilton

CINCINNATI

Parkersburg

Cumberland

WASHINGTON D.C.

Alexandria

Council Bluffs

Omaha

Kirksville

St. Joseph

Quincy

Hannibal

Moberly

Columbia

Mattoon

Vincennes

Evansville

Covington

Frankfort

Lexington

Newport

Portsmouth

Huntington

WEST VIRGINIA

Charleston

Clarksburg

Roanoke

Lynchburg

SHENANDOAH NAT'L PARK

Charlottesville

Richmond

Kansas City

KANSAS CITY

Sedalia

Jefferson City

ST. LOUIS

East St. Louis

Alton

Louisville

Owensboro

KENTUCKY

MAMMOTH CAVE NAT'L PARK

Bowling Green

Hopkinsville

Paducah

Cairo

Bristol

Johnson City

Danville

Petersburg

Portsmouth

Norfolk

Newport News

VIRGINIA

APPALACHIAN

Fort Scott

MISSOURI

Cape Girardeau

Joplin

Springfield

OZARK PLATEAU

Lake of the Ozarks

Nashville

Knoxville

Asheville

GREAT SMOKY MTS. NAT'L PARK

Winston-Salem

Greensboro

Durham

Raleigh

NORTH CAROLINA

New Bern

C. HATTERAS

Buggs Island Lake

Muskogee

BOSTON MTS.

Jonesboro

TENNESSEE

Chattanooga

Memphis

Jackson

Florence

Gadsden

Rome

Spartanburg

Rock Hill

Charlotte

New Bern

Wilmington

Fort Smith

ARKANSAS

Hot Springs

Little Rock

HOT SPRINGS NAT'L PARK

OUACHITA MTS.

Pine Bluff

Helena

Greenville

Birmingham

Anniston

Tuscaloosa

Athens

Greenville

Anderson

SOUTH CAROLINA

Columbia

Charleston

Texarkana

El Dorado

Monroe

Vicksburg

MISSISSIPPI

Meridian

ALABAMA

Selma

Montgomery

Columbus

ATLANTA

La Grange

Macon

Augusta

GEORGIA

Savannah

Tyler

Shreveport

Alexandria

Natchez

Jackson

Laurel

Hattiesburg

Mobile

Dothan

Americus

Albany

Waycross

Brunswick

Marshall

LOUISIANA

Baton Rouge

Biloxi

Pensacola

Tallahassee

Gainesville

Jacksonville

St. Augustine

Daytona Beach

Beaumont

Lake Charles

Lafayette

Port Arthur

HOUSTON

Galveston

Galveston Bay

New Orleans

C. SAN BLAS

Apalachee Bay

FLORIDA

Sanford

Orlando

CAPE CANAVERAL

Tampa

St. Petersburg

Lakeland

Tampa Bay

Okeechobee

W. Palm Beach

GT. ABACO

BAHAMAS

EVERGLADES NAT'L PARK

C. SABLE

MIAMI

Key West

FLORIDA KEYS

Straits of Florida

ANDROS

GULF OF MEXICO

ATLANTIC OCEAN

40°

35°

30°

25°

Cities and Towns

0 to 50,000

50,000 to 500,000

500,000 to 1,000,000

1,000,000 and over

50 75 100   200   300   400   500 Miles

100   200   400   600   800 Kilometers

40,000 SQ MI AREA

0   100   200

Miles

Scale 1:12 000 000; one inch to 190 miles. Polyconic Project
Elevations and depressions are given in feet

AVERAGE ANNUAL PRECIPITATION

After U. S. Dept. of Agriculture and Canada Dept. of Transport

A-520500-6A6-2-2-2-4
Copyright by Rand McNally & Co.
Made in U.S.A.

Centimeters	Inches
Under 25	Under 10
25–50	10–20
50–75	20–30
75–100	30–40
100–125	40–50
125–150	50–60
150–200	60–80
200–250	80–100
Over 250	Over 100

PRECIPITATION
NOV. 1 TO APRIL 30

Copyright by Rand McNally & Co.
Made in U.S.A.

Inches
Under 5
5–10
10–20
20–40
Over 40

PRECIPITATION
MAY 1 TO OCT. 31

Copyright by Rand McNally & Co.
Made in U.S.A.

Inches
Under 5
5–10
10–20
20–40
Over 40

GLACIAL LAKE AGASSIZ

After Warren Upham, U. S. G. S., and others

0 50 100 150 200 Miles
0 100 200 300 Km.

Present lakes and rivers are shown in black.

ANCIENT LAKES LAHONTAN AND BONNEVILLE

Lahontan after I. Russell
Bonneville after G. K. Gilbert, U. S. G. S.

GLACIAL LAURENTIAN LAKES
EARLY STAGE
After Taylor and Leverett

Marginal moraines in red

GLACIAL LAURENTIAN LAKES
LATER STAGE
After Taylor and Leverett

Marginal moraines in red

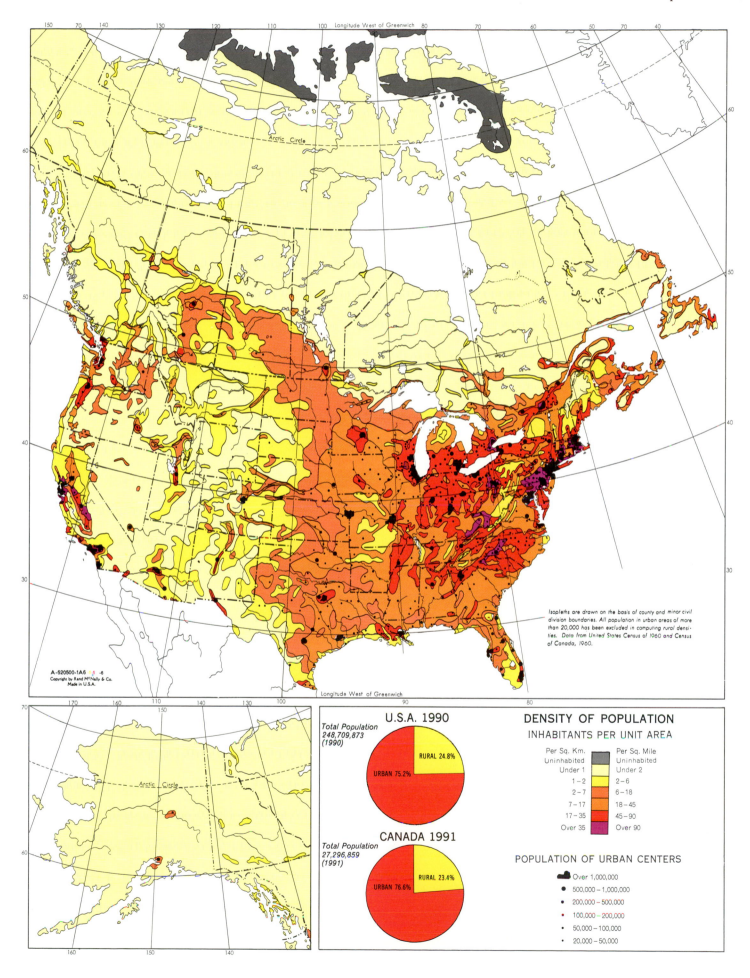

Isopleths are drawn on the basis of county and minor civil division boundaries. All population in urban areas of more than 20,000 has been excluded in computing rural densities. Data from United States Census of 1960 and Census of Canada, 1960.

A-520500-1A6 -6
Copyright by Rand McNally & Co.
Made in U.S.A.

U.S.A. 1990

Total Population
248,709,873
(1990)

URBAN 75.2%   RURAL 24.8%

CANADA 1991

Total Population
27,296,859
(1991)

URBAN 76.6%   RURAL 23.4%

DENSITY OF POPULATION
INHABITANTS PER UNIT AREA

Per Sq. Km.	Per Sq. Mile
Uninhabited	Uninhabited
Under 1	Under 2
1–2	2–6
2–7	6–18
7–17	18–45
17–35	45–90
Over 35	Over 90

POPULATION OF URBAN CENTERS

Over 1,000,000
500,000 – 1,000,000
200,000 – 500,000
100,000 – 200,000
50,000 – 100,000
20,000 – 50,000

Scale 1:32 000 000; One inch to 500 miles.   LAMBERT CONFORMAL CONIC PROJECTION

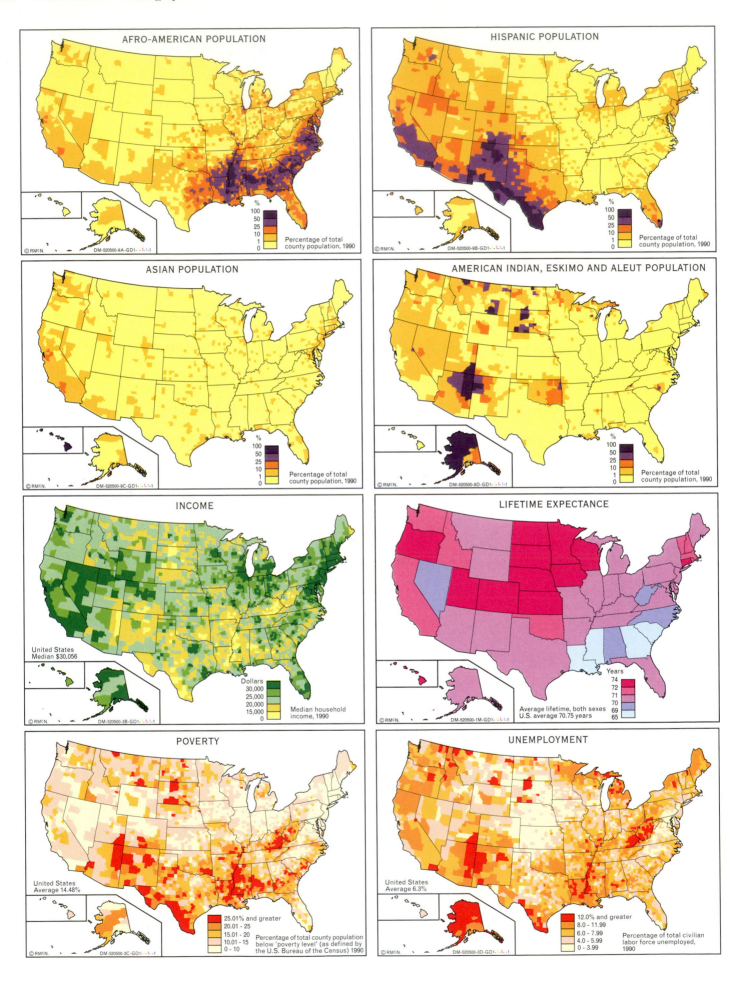

AFRO-AMERICAN POPULATION

%
100
50
25
10
1
0
Percentage of total
county population, 1990

© RMcN.   DM-520500-9A-GD1- -1- 1-1

HISPANIC POPULATION

%
100
50
25
10
1
0
Percentage of total
county population, 1990

© RMcN.   DM-520500-9B-GD1- -1- 1-1

ASIAN POPULATION

%
100
50
25
10
1
0
Percentage of total
county population, 1990

© RMcN.   DM-520500-9C-GD1- -1- 1-1

AMERICAN INDIAN, ESKIMO AND ALEUT POPULATION

%
100
50
25
10
1
0
Percentage of total
county population, 1990

© RMcN.   DM-520500-9D-GD1- -1- 1-1

INCOME

United States
Median $30,056

Dollars
30,000
25,000
20,000
15,000
0
Median household
income, 1990

© RMcN.   DM-520500-3B-GD1- -1- 1-1

LIFETIME EXPECTANCE

Years
74
72
71
70
69
65

Average lifetime, both sexes
U.S. average 70.75 years

© RMcN.   DM-520500-1M-GD1- -1- 1-1

POVERTY

United States
Average 14.48%

25.01% and greater
20.01 - 25
15.01 - 20
10.01 - 15
0 - 10

Percentage of total county population
below 'poverty level' (as defined by
the U.S. Bureau of the Census) 1990

© RMcN.   DM-520500-3C-GD1- -1- -1

UNEMPLOYMENT

United States
Average 6.3%

12.0% and greater
8.0 - 11.99
6.0 - 7.99
4.0 - 5.99
0 - 3.99

Percentage of total civilian
labor force unemployed,
1990

© RMcN.   DM-520500-3D-GD1- -1- -1

Scale 1: 12 000 000; one inch to 190 miles.   Conic Projection

Elevations and depressions are given in feet

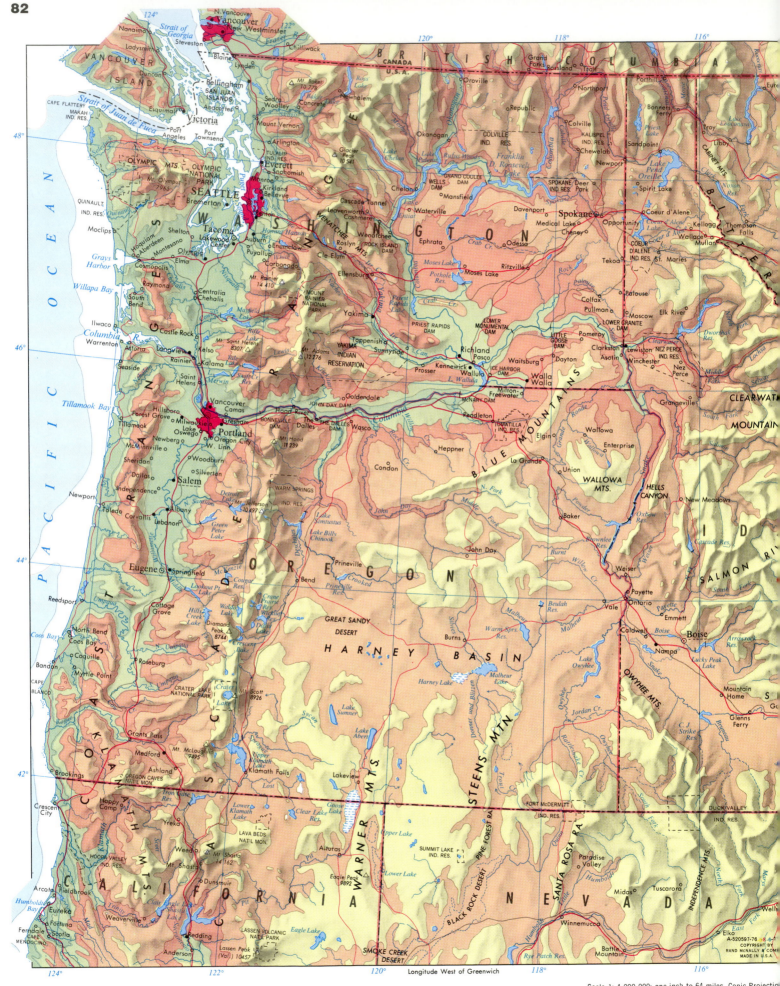

Longitude West of Greenwich

Scale 1: 4,000 000; one inch to 64 miles. Conic Projection
Elevations and depressions are given in feet

ALBERTA SASKATCHEWAN

CANADA
U.S.A.

WATERTON-GLACIER
INTERNATIONAL
PEACE PARK

BLACKFEET
IND. RES.

FORT PECK
IND. RES.

N. DAK.

FT. BELKNAP
IND. RES.

ROCKY BOYS
IND. RES.

Fort Peck
Lake

M O N T A N A

LEWIS RANGE

SWAN RANGE

R O C K Y

BIG BELT MTS.

LITTLE BELT MTS.

Great
Falls

CRAZY
MTS.

Missouri

M O U N T A I N S

PIONEER MTS.

BEAVERHEAD MTS.

LEMHI RANGE

LOST RIVER RA.

Homer
Youngs Peak
10,621

Borah Pk.
12,662

Hyndman Peak
12,009

CUSTER
BATTLEFIELD
NAT'L MON.

NORTHERN CHEYENNE
IND. RES.

CROW IND. RES.

DEVILS TOWER
NAT'L MON.

ABSAROKA RANGE

Electric Peak
10,992

Mt. Washburn
10,243

Granite Peak
12,799

BIGHORN MOUNTAINS

Cloud Peak
13,167

YELLOWSTONE

NATIONAL

PARK

Yellowstone Lake
7733 ft. above
sea level

Shoshone
Lake

GRAND TETON
NAT'L PARK

Grand Teton
13,770

CRATERS OF
THE MOON
NAT'L MON.

S N A K E

R I V E R   P L A I N

WYOMING RANGE

WIND RIVER RANGE

Gannett Peak
13,804

Fremont
Peak 13,745

W I N D   R I V E R

MOUNTAINS

WIND RIVER
IND. RES.

W Y O M I N G

FORT HALL
IND. RES.

American Falls
Res.

Blackfoot
Reservoir

Meade
Peak
9957

GREAT DIVIDE
BASIN

WASATCH RANGE

Great
Salt
Lake

GREAT

SALT LAKE

DESERT

U T A H

Salt Lake City

UINTA MTS.

Kings Peak
13,528

Mt. Emmons
13,440

UINTAH AND OURAY
IND. RES.

DINOSAUR
NAT'L MON.

COLO.

PARK RANGE

Flaming
Gorge
Res.

20   40   60   80   100   120 Miles
20   40   60   80   100   120   140   160   180   200 Kilometers

Relief

Meters		Feet
3050		10000
1525		5000
610		2000
305		1000
152.5		500
0	Sea Level	0
1525		500

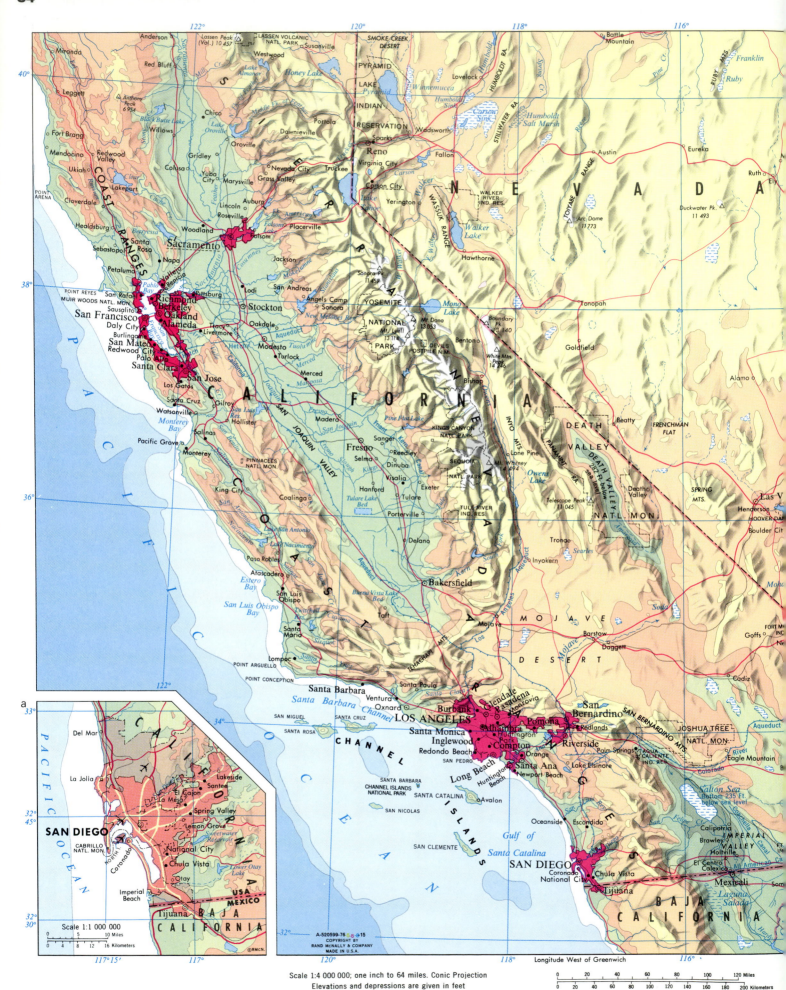

Scale 1:4 000 000; one inch to 64 miles. Conic Projection
Elevations and depressions are given in feet

Relief

Meters	Feet
3050	10000
1525	5000
610	2000
305	1000
152.5	500
0 Sea Level	0
	Below Sea Level
152.5	500
1525	5000
3050	10000

86

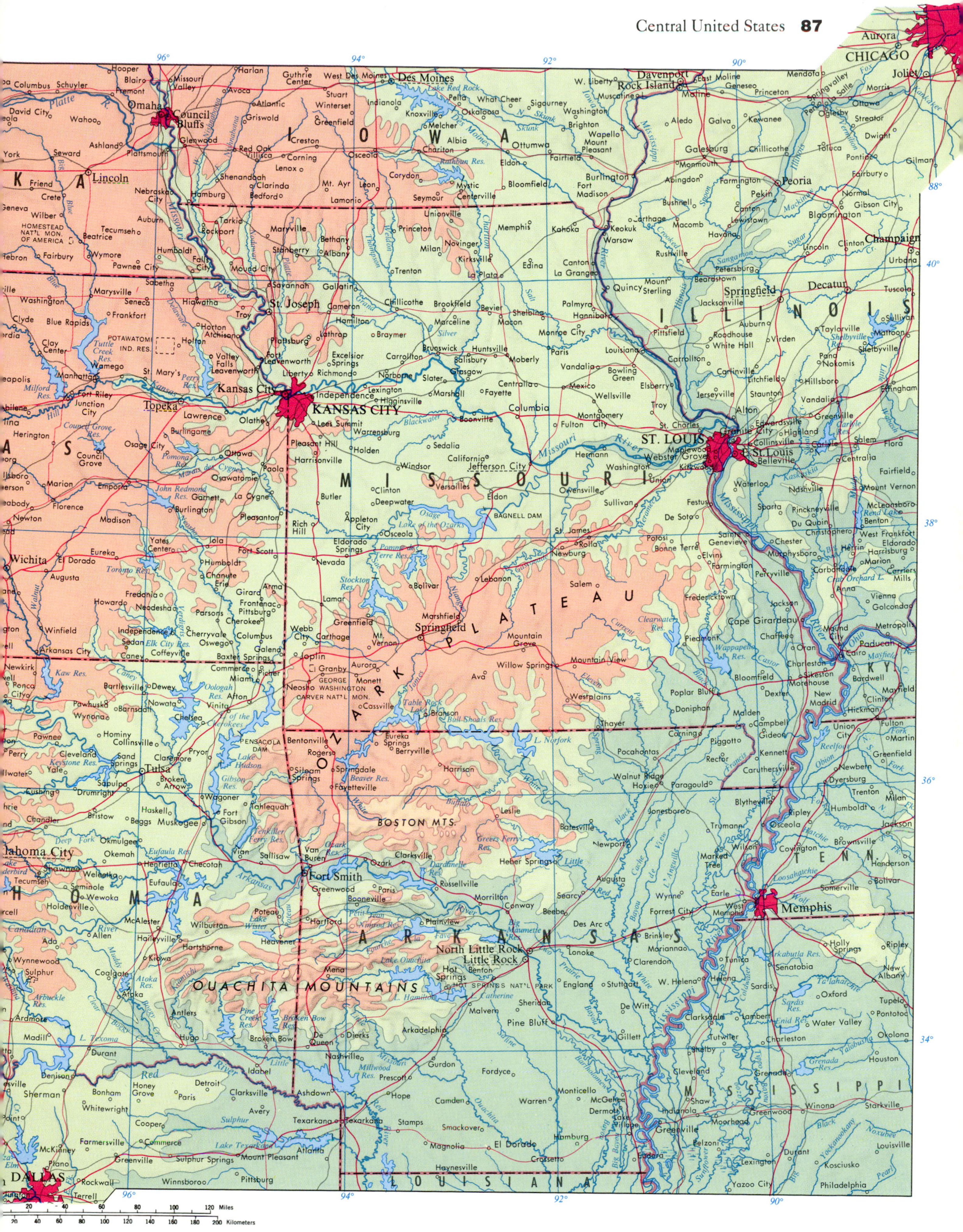

CHICAGO

IOWA

KANSAS

NEBRASKA

MISSOURI

ILLINOIS

OKLAHOMA

ARKANSAS

OZARK PLATEAU

BOSTON MTS.

OUACHITA MOUNTAINS

TENN.

MISSISSIPPI

LOUISIANA

KY.

Omaha · Council Bluffs · Lincoln · Des Moines · Kansas City · Topeka · St. Louis · Springfield · Wichita · Tulsa · Oklahoma City · Fort Smith · Little Rock · North Little Rock · Memphis · Dallas

20 40 60 80 100 120 Miles
20 40 60 80 100 120 140 160 180 200 Kilometers

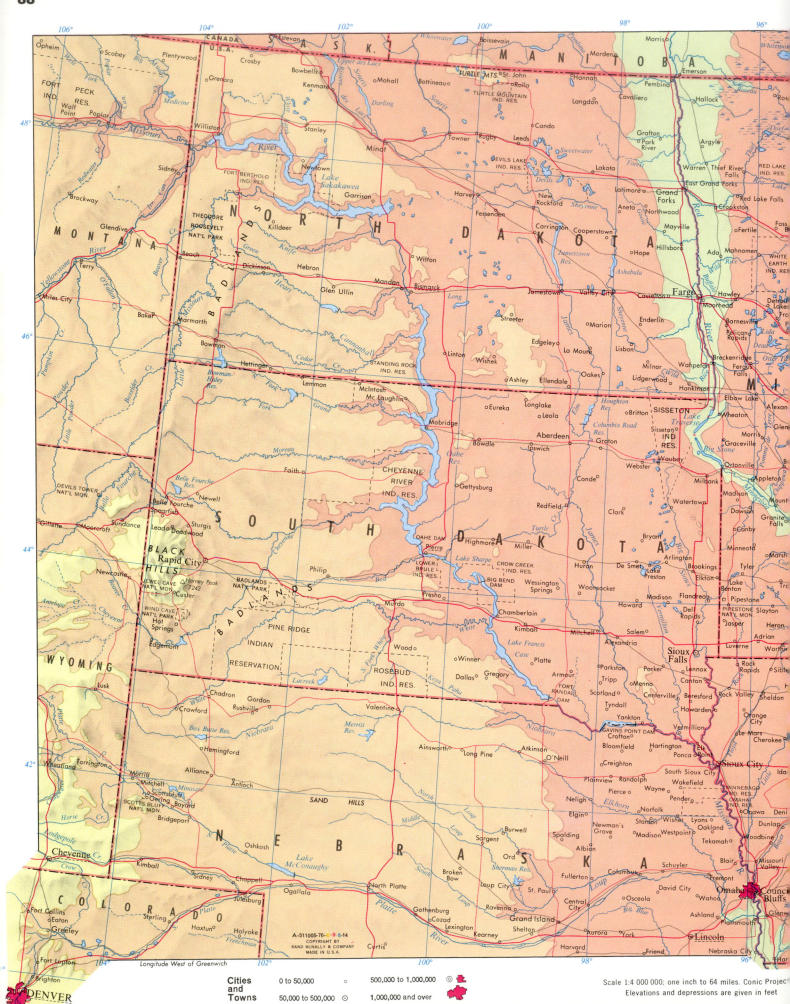

88

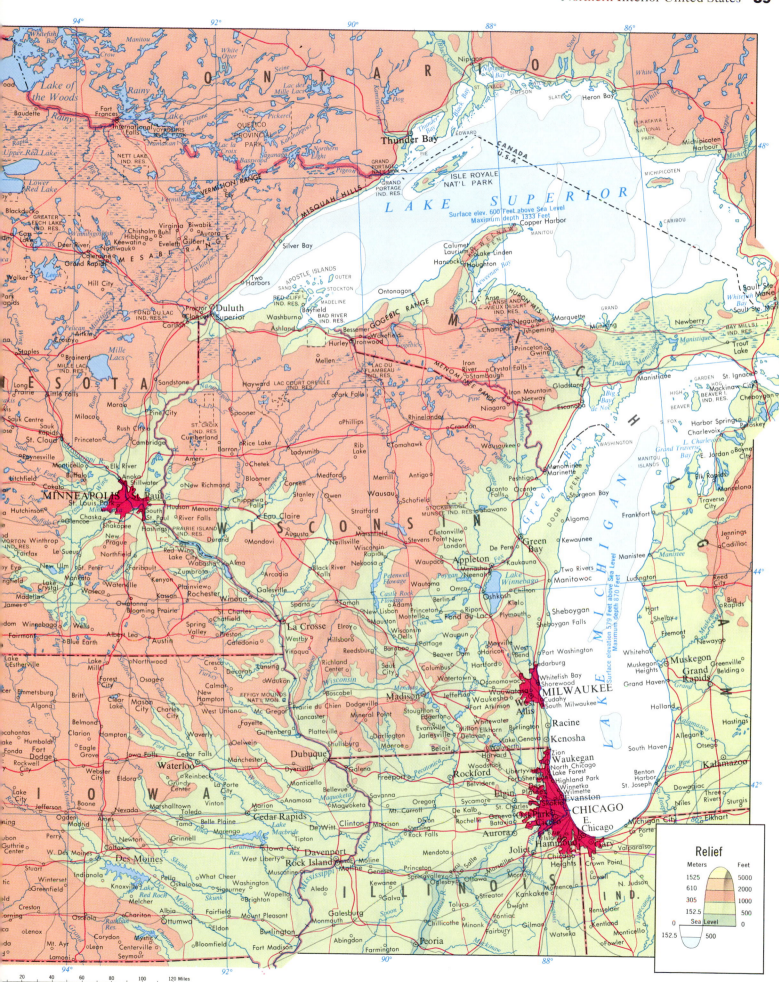

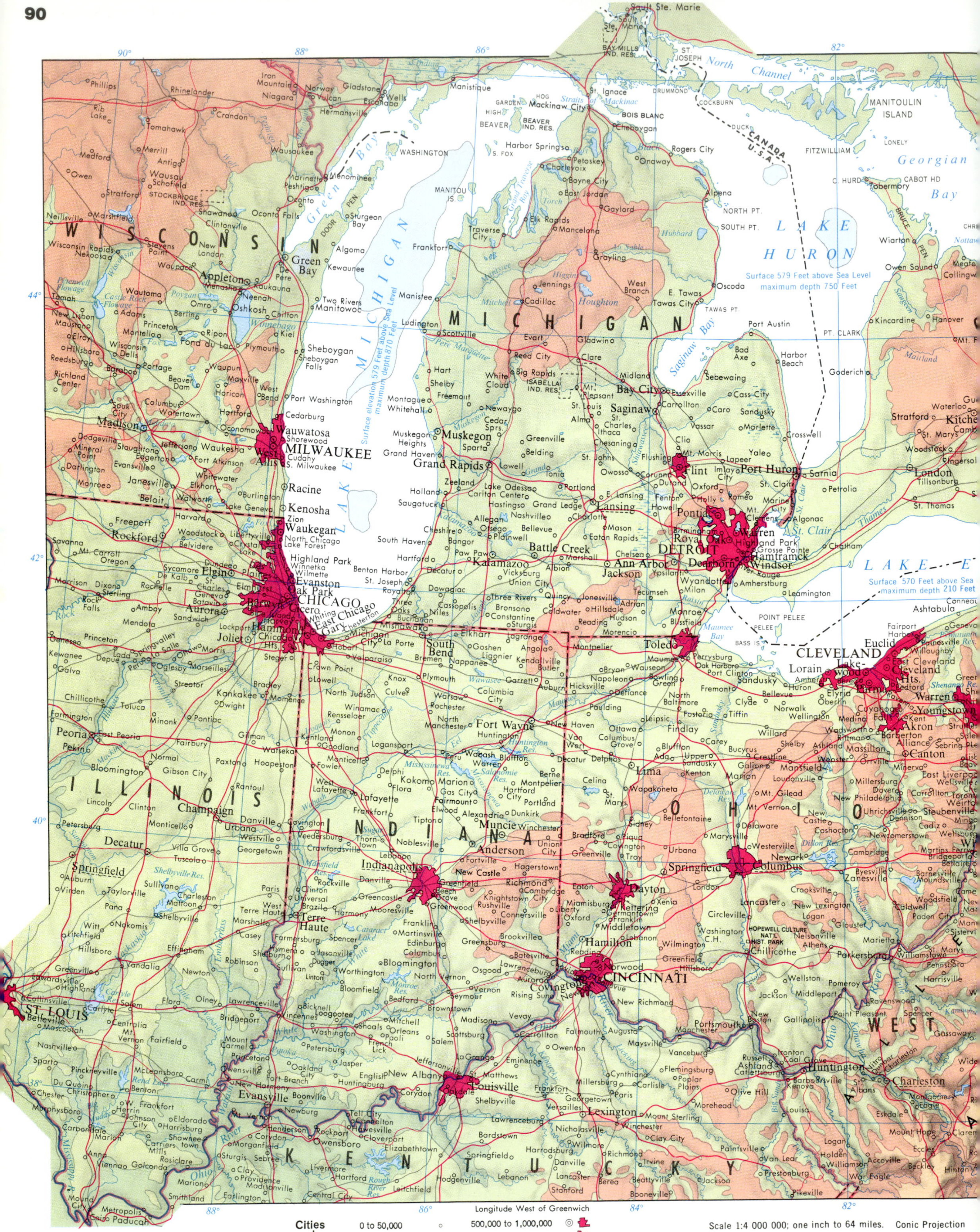

Cities
and
Towns

0 to 50,000

50,000 to 500,000

500,000 to 1,000,000

1,000,000 and over

Longitude West of Greenwich

Scale 1:4 000 000; one inch to 64 miles.   Conic Projection
Elevations and depressions are given in feet

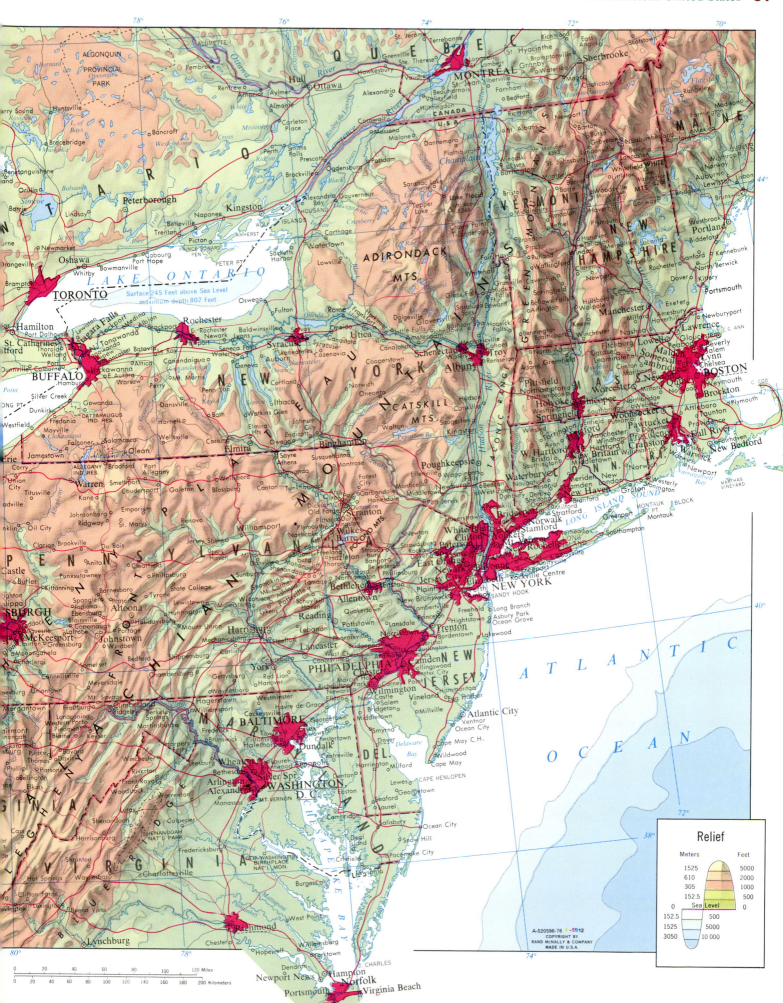

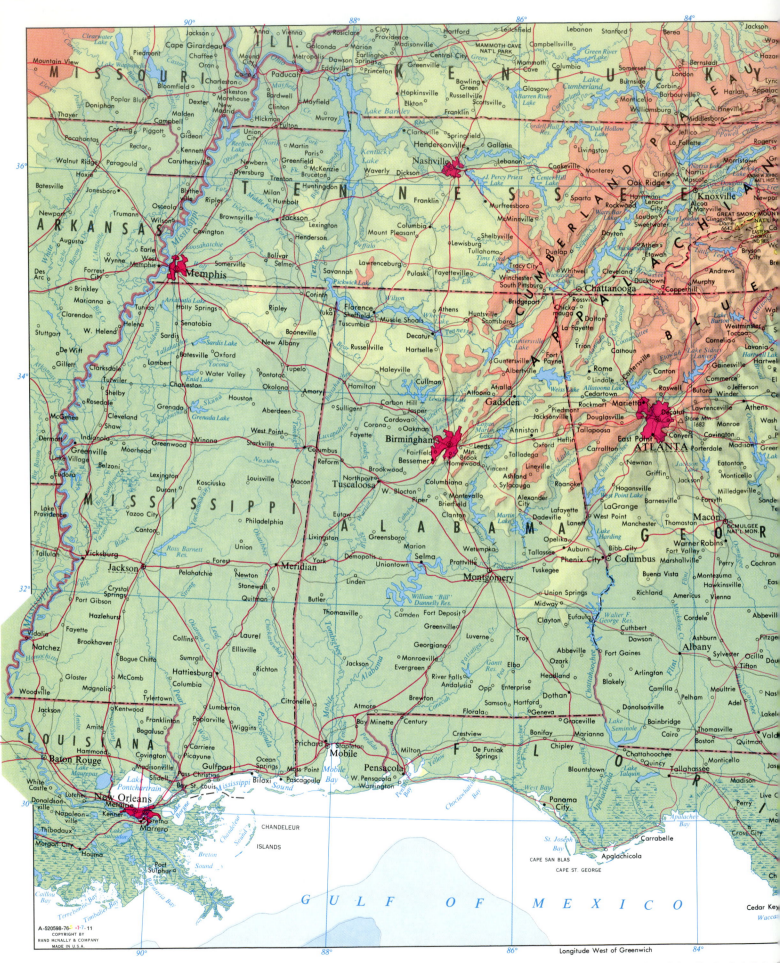

Longitude West of Greenwich

Scale 1:4 000 000; one inch to 64 miles. Conic Projecti
Elevations and depressions are given in feet

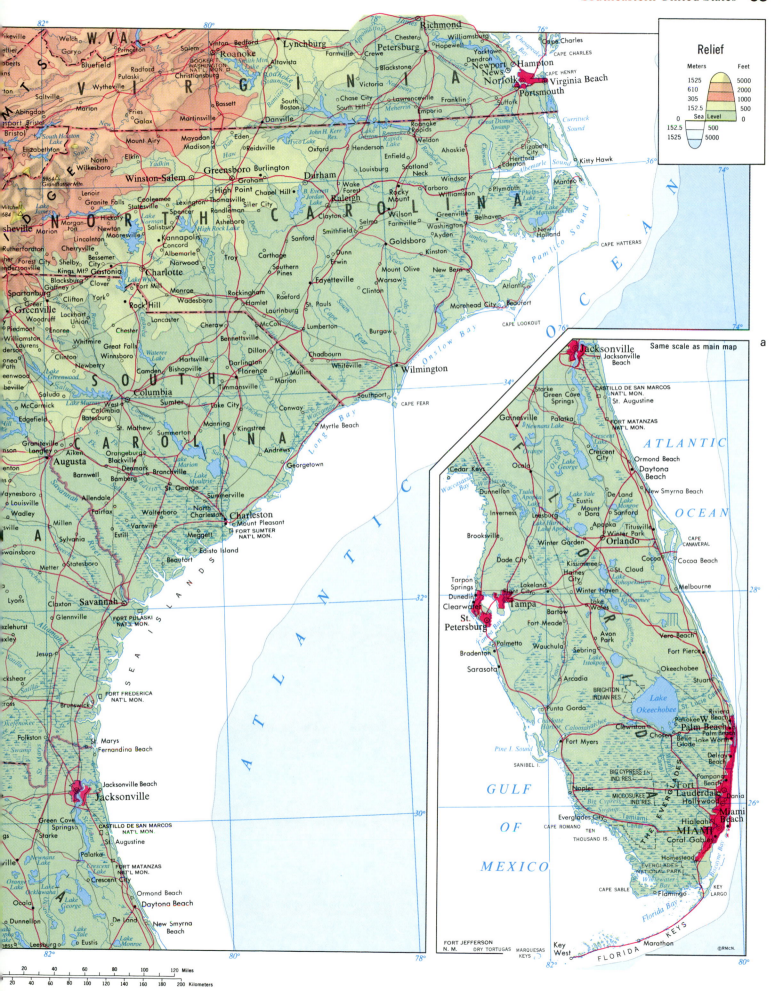

94

New Mexico · Texas · Chihuahua · Coahuila · Nuevo León · Durango

Relief

Meters	Feet
1525	5000
610	2000
305	1000
152.5	500
Sea Level	
152.5	500
1525	5000
3050	10000

Scale 1:4 000 000; one inch to 64 miles. Conic Projection
Elevations and depressions are given in feet

Longitude West of Greenwich

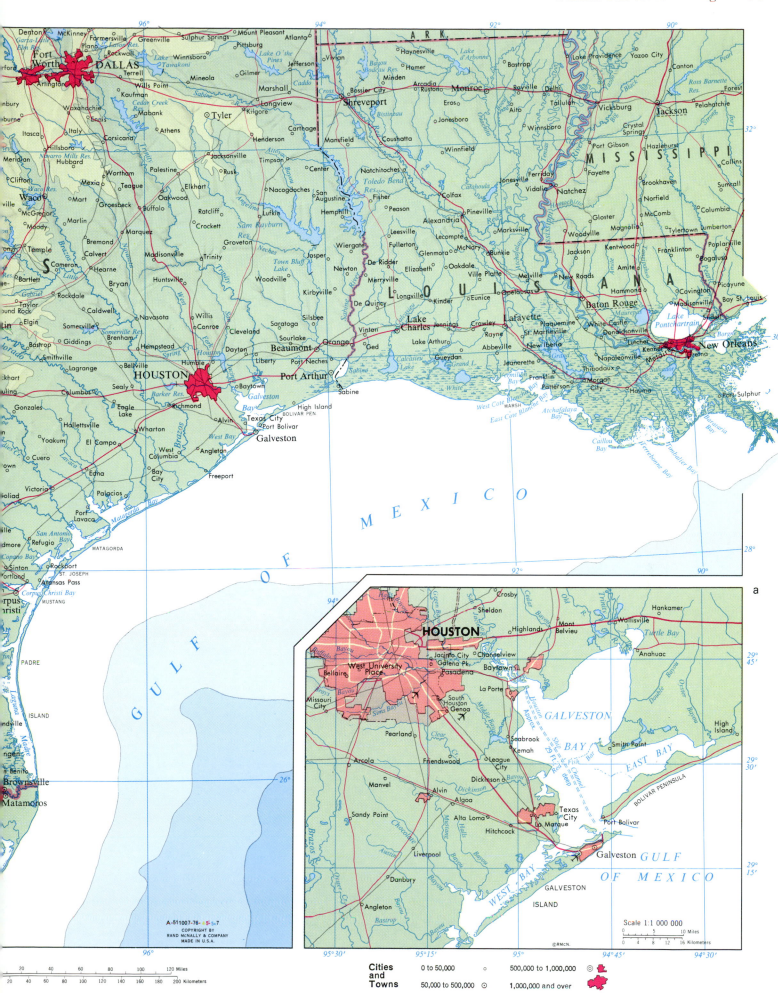

Scale 1:1 000 000

Cities
and
Towns

| | 0 to 50,000 | | 500,000 to 1,000,000 |
| | 50,000 to 500,000 | | 1,000,000 and over |

a

Scale 1:1 000 000

0   10 Miles
0 4   8 12   16 Kilometers

PANAMA

©RMcN.

A-530000-76.9 -6-25
COPYRIGHT BY
RAND McNALLY & COMPANY
MADE IN U.S.A.

Scale 1:16 000 000; one inch to 250 miles. Polyconic Project
Elevations and depressions are given in feet

b

ATLANTIC OCEAN

Arecibo · San Juan
Aguadilla · Bayamon
PTA. HIGUERO · Utuado · CABEZAS DE · ST. THOMAS · TORTOLA
SAN JUAN · (U.S.A.) · (Br.)
PUERTO RICO · Caguas · CULEBRA · Charlotte
Mayagüez · (U.S.A.) · Cayey · Humacao · Amalie · ST. JOHN
CABO ROJO · Vieques · (U.S.A.)
Ponce · Salinas · Guayama · VIEQUES
CARIBBEAN SEA · Christiansted
SAINT CROIX
(U.S.A.)
©RMcN. · Scale 1:4 000 000
0 10 20 30 40 Miles
0 10 20 30 40 50 60 Kilometers

c

65° · 64°50′
LITTLE · HANS LOLLICK
OUTER BRASS · HANS LOLLICK
INNER BRASS · PICARA PT
STORMY PT. · GRASS
THATCH CAY · CAY
ST. THOMAS
Crown Mt. (U.S.A.) · Charlotte Amalie
1558 · (St. Thomas)
WATER · Nadir
FLAMINGO PT. · St. Thomas
©RMcN. · Harbor · Scale 1:500 000

W. VIRGINIA
Roanoke · Richmond
VIRGINIA
·Norfolk
Raleigh
NORTH CAROLINA · CAPE HATTERAS
ANTA · Charlotte
SOUTH · Pamlico
CAROLINA · Wilmington
ORGIA · Columbia · CAPE FEAR
Augusta · Charleston
Savannah
·Jacksonville
allahassee · St. Augustine
Ocala
ampa · CAPE CANAVERAL
W. Palm
Beach
MIAMI
CAPE SABLE
Key West
FLORIDA KEYS
AVANA Guanabacoa
Matanzas
ianao· Cárdenas
del Río · Santa Clara
Cienfuegos · Sancti Spíritus
Ciego · Nuevitas
de Ávila · Camagüey
Holguín
Manzanillo · Guantánamo
Santiago
de Cuba
Montego Bay · Port Antonio
Spanish Town
JAMAICA · Kingston

ATLANTIC OCEAN

BERMUDA
(Br.)

NORTH AMERICAN
BASIN

GRAND
BAHAMA
GREAT ABACO
BAHAMAS
ELEUTHERA
Nassau
ANDROS
San Salvador (Watling)
LONG
ACKLINS
CAICOS
(Br.) TURKS
ST. INAGUA
PUERTO RICO TRENCH
CAYMAN

Cap-Haïtien · Puerto Plata
Santiago de los
Caballeros · SAMANA
HAITI · Sánchez
DOMINICAN
REPUBLIC · Mayagüez
ÎLE DE LA · Ponce · San Juan
GONAVE · Charlotte Amalie · ANGUILLA
Port-au-Prince · Santo Domingo · VIRGIN IS. (Br.)
PUERTO RICO · ST. THOMAS · BARBUDA
HISPANIOLA · (U.S.A.) · SAINT CROIX · ANTIGUA
(U.S.A.) · AND
ST. KITTS AND NEVIS · BARBUDA
MONTSERRAT · Pointe-à-Pitre
V. Soufrière · GUADELOUPE
4813 · (Fr.)
Basse Terre · DOMINICA

W E S T   I N D I E S
GREATER
ANTILLES
LESSER ANTILLES

MARTINIQUE (Fr.)
Fort-de-France
ST. LUCIA
ST. VINCENT
AND THE · BARBADOS
GRENADINES · Bridgetown
Kingstown
GRENADA

AMERICA
José· Limón
THMUS
Portobello
Panamá
David
CUBA

PUNTA DE GALLINAS
PENÍNSULA
DE GUAJIRA
ARUBA · CURAÇAO BONAIRE
(Neth.) · (Neth.) (Neth.)
SAN ROMAN
PEN. DE
PARAGUANA
Willemstad
Coro
Santa Marta · Maracaibo · Puerto
Barranquilla · Cabimas · La Guaira
Ciénaga · CARACAS
Cartagena · Soledad · Maracay
Maracaibo · Valencia
Barquisimeto
Lorica · Sincelejo · Mompós
Monteria · Magangue
Trujillo
Mérida · Guanare · Puerto de
Nutrias
San Fernando
de Apure
VENEZUELA
Ocaña
Cúcuta· San Cristóbal
Pamplona
Barrancabermeja
Bucaramanga
Medellín
Tunja
Manizales
Pereira · COLOMBIA
Armenia · SANTA FE DE
Ibagué · BOGOTÁ
Girardot · Villavicencio
San Fernando
de Atabapo
Buenaventura
Cali· Palmira

ISLA DE LA
TORTUGA
ISLA DE
MARGARITA
Carúpano
Puerto · Cumaná
Cabello · TRINIDAD AND TOBAGO
Puerto · Port of Spain
la Cruz · TRINIDAD
Maturín

Morawhanna

Calabozo
El Tigre
Ciudad Guayana
Ciudad Bolívar
Cerro Bolívar
Cerro Kula
7800 · GUYANA

SERRA PACARAIMA
BRAZIL

Relief

Meters		Feet
3050		10 000
1525		5000
610		2000
305		1000
152.5		500
0	Sea Level	0
152.5		500
1525		5000
3050		10 000
6100		20 000

50 100 200 300 400 500 Miles
100 200 400 600 800 Kilometers

**Cities
and
Towns**

0 to 50,000 ○ 500,000 to 1,000,000 ◎
50,000 to 500,000 ⊙ 1,000,000 and over

South America

Floodplain of the Amazon River, Brazil

With an area of 6.9 million square miles (17.8 million sq km), triangular-shaped South America is fourth among the continents in size. The Andes, which pass through seven of the continent's 13 mainland countries, are the longest mountain chain in the world. The mighty Amazon River carries a greater volume of water than any other river: 46 million gallons per second flow into the Atlantic Ocean. The Amazon basin contains an estimated one-fifth of the world's fresh water and is home to the world's largest rain forest with its countless plant and animal species. Angel Falls, in a remote Venezuelan forest, is the world's highest waterfall, dropping 3,212 feet (979 m), or almost the height of three Empire State Buildings.

One of South America's other great wonders is manmade. High in the Peruvian Andes lie the ruins of the sacred city of Machu Picchu, built centuries ago by the Incas. The city has an exquisite design and was built with remarkable skill. The Inca population, like most of South America's other native peoples, declined rapidly after the arrival of Europeans in the early 16th century.

South America at a glance

Land area: 6,900,000 square miles (17,800,000 sq km)

Estimated population (January 1, 1995): 313,900,000

Population density: 45/square mile (18/sq km)

Mean elevation: 1,800 feet (550 m)

Highest point: Aconcagua, Argentina, 22,831 feet (6,959 m)

Lowest point: Salinas Chicas, Argentina, 138 feet (42 m) below sea level

Longest river: Amazon-Ucayali, 4,000 mi (6,400 km)

Number of countries (incl. dependencies): 15

Largest independent country: Brazil, 3,286,500 square miles (8,511,996 sq km)

Smallest independent country: Suriname, 63,251 square miles (163,820 sq km)

Most populous independent country: Brazil, 159,690,000

Least populous independent country: Suriname, 426,000

Largest city: São Paulo, pop. 9,393,753 (1991)

The Andes, at the western edge of Argentina's Patagonia region.

Wettest place:
Quibdó, Colombia
354 inches (899 cm)/year

Driest place:
Arica, Chile
.03 inches (.08 cm)/year

Hottest place:
Rivadavia, Argentina
120°F (49°C)

Highest point:
Cerro Aconcagua, Argentina
22,831 ft (6,959 m)

Coldest place:
Sarmiento, Argentina
-27°F (-33°C)

Lowest point:
Salinas Chicas, Argentina
138 ft (42 m) below sea level

Landforms

- Mountains
- Widely spaced mountains
- High tablelands
- Hills and low tablelands
- Plains
- Depresssions, basins
- High tablelands and ice caps
- Mountains and ice caps

© Rand McNally & Co.
M-540000-7C-EL1-1-1- -1

Map labels: Orinoco, Llanos, Guiana Highlands, Equator, Amazon, Amazon Basin, Madeira, São Francisco, Mato Grosso, Brazilian Highlands, Lago Titicaca, Andes Mountains, Pacific Ocean, Atlantic Ocean, Gran Chaco, Paraná, Tropic of Capricorn, Paraguay, Pampas, Patagonia, Falkland Islands, Tierra del Fuego

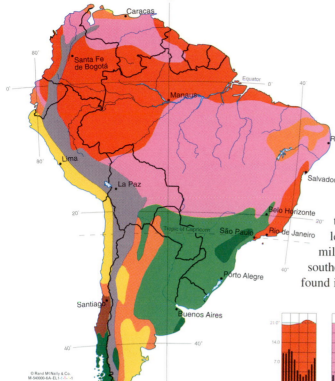

© Rand McNally & Co.
M-540000-6A-EL1-1-1- -1

Climate

South America's most predominant climate zones are the vast tropical rain forests and tropical savannas which cover most of the northern half of the continent. In the rain forests, rain falls throughout the year, averaging 60 to 80 inches (152 to 203 cm) annually. Daytime temperatures usually exceed 80° F (27° C). The tropical savanna regions experience the same high temperatures but less rainfall, with a dry season in winter. A temperate climate, with milder temperatures and moderate rainfall, prevails throughout much of southern South America, east of the Andes. Arid to semiarid conditions are found in the far south and at Brazil's eastern tip.

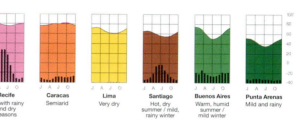

Tinted areas show temperature in degrees Fahrenheit. Vertical bars show precipitation in inches.

Manaus Hot and rainy

Recife Hot with rainy and dry seasons

Caracas Semiarid

Lima Very dry

Santiago Hot, dry summer / mild, rainy winter

Buenos Aires Warm, humid summer / mild winter

Punta Arenas Mild and rainy

Extensive uplands Climate varies with elevation and latitude

Population

South America is the fourth most-densely populated continent, with 45 people per square mile (18 per sq km). Despite this relatively low figure, the continent is intensely urban because the Andes and the Amazon rain forest render most of it either inaccessible or unsuitable for farming. More than 90% of South America's 314 million people live within 150 miles (240 km) of the coast. São Paulo, Brazil, with a metropolitan population of almost 17 million, is the world's third-largest metropolitan area. Most South Americans are *mestizo*—of mixed European and Indian descent. Spanish is the predominant language, followed by Portuguese. More than 90% of the people are Roman Catholics.

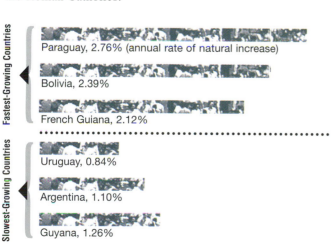

Fastest-Growing Countries

Paraguay, 2.76% (annual rate of natural increase)

Bolivia, 2.39%

French Guiana, 2.12%

Slowest-Growing Countries

Uruguay, 0.84%

Argentina, 1.10%

Guyana, 1.26%

Inhabitants per sq. km. (mi.)

Uninhabited

<1 (2)

1-10 (2-25)

10-25 (25-60)

25-50 (60-125)

50-100 (125-250)

>100 (250)

© Rand McNally & Co.
M-540000-1P-EL1-1-1- -1

Environments and Land Use

Land suitable for farming is very limited in South America, covering only about 6% of the continent. Small, family-run subsistence farms are common, and typical crops are maize, wheat, and potatoes. Despite the scarcity of arable land, commercial agriculture for export is a major part of the economies of several countries. Ecuador is the world's leading exporter of bananas, while Brazil and Colombia grow almost 40% of the world's coffee beans. Brazil is also a major exporter of sugar. Chile has developed a large trade in produce—such as tomatoes and grapes—that is exported to North America during its winter months (South America's summer months). Production of coca, the basis for illicit drugs, has become a part of the rural economies of Colombia, Bolivia and Peru.

Cattle ranching is centered on the vast, grassy Pampas region, which extends through northern Argentina, Uruguay, and southern Brazil. Sheep, raised both for meat and wool, are important throughout the Andes and southern Argentina. About 25% of the continent is suitable for grazing.

As South America's population grows, pressure builds to clear more land for farming. Much expansion has taken place in the Amazon basin at the cost of millions of acres of rain forest, which are cleared of trees and drained. Balancing the demands of the population with the need to preserve the rain forest is one of the continent's most pressing issues.

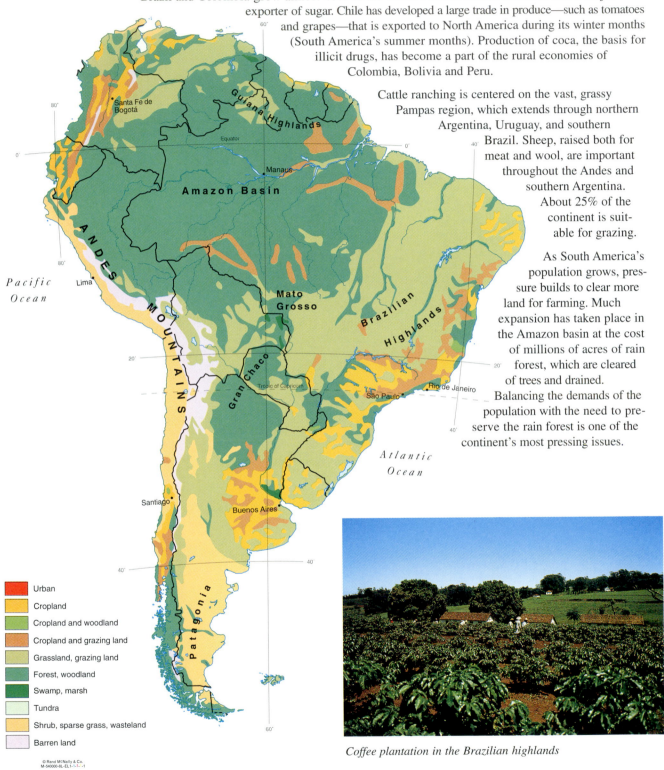

Urban

Cropland

Cropland and woodland

Cropland and grazing land

Grassland, grazing land

Forest, woodland

Swamp, marsh

Tundra

Shrub, sparse grass, wasteland

Barren land

© Rand McNally & Co.
M-540000-8L-EL1-1-1-1

| 0 | 200 | 400 | 600 | 800 | 1000 Miles |

| 0 | 300 | 600 | 900 | 1200 | 1500 Kilometers |

Coffee plantation in the Brazilian highlands

Destruction of the Rain Forest

The Amazonian rain forest contains an abundance and diversity of life that is matched by few places in the world. In fact, it has been estimated that the plant and animal species of Amazonia account for nearly one-half of those found on Earth. New plants and animals are constantly being discovered, and scientists have found in Amazonian plants a treasure trove of new substances, some of which are now being used to produce life-saving medicines. It is thought that cures for many more diseases could be found in the plants yet to be studied.

In recent decades, nearly 10% of the rain forest's original 1.58 million square miles (4.09 million sq km) has been cleared (see map below) for farming, cattle ranching, mining, and commercial logging. The most effective way to clear the land is the "slash-and-burn" method, which has been practiced by indigenous peoples on an insignificant scale for centuries. Today, widespread usage of this method is destroying vast areas of the rain forest, and smoke from the fires is polluting the atmosphere and possibly contributing to global warming. The destruction also imperils the Indians living within the forest; their numbers have shrunk by more than half in this century alone.

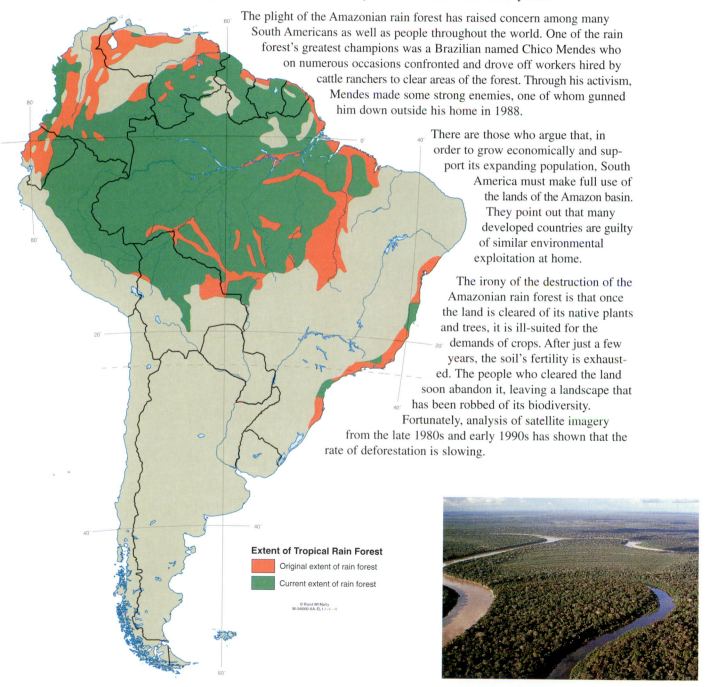

The plight of the Amazonian rain forest has raised concern among many South Americans as well as people throughout the world. One of the rain forest's greatest champions was a Brazilian named Chico Mendes who on numerous occasions confronted and drove off workers hired by cattle ranchers to clear areas of the forest. Through his activism, Mendes made some strong enemies, one of whom gunned him down outside his home in 1988.

There are those who argue that, in order to grow economically and support its expanding population, South America must make full use of the lands of the Amazon basin. They point out that many developed countries are guilty of similar environmental exploitation at home.

The irony of the destruction of the Amazonian rain forest is that once the land is cleared of its native plants and trees, it is ill-suited for the demands of crops. After just a few years, the soil's fertility is exhausted. The people who cleared the land soon abandon it, leaving a landscape that has been robbed of its biodiversity. Fortunately, analysis of satellite imagery from the late 1980s and early 1990s has shown that the rate of deforestation is slowing.

Extent of Tropical Rain Forest

Original extent of rain forest

Current extent of rain forest

© Rand McNally
M-540000-8A-EL1-1-1- -1

The Juruá River, at left, and a clearwater slough wind through the dense Amazon rain forest near Eirunepé, Brazil.

40,000 SQ MI
AREA

Scale 1:40 000 000; one inch to 630 miles. Lambert's Azimuthal, Equal Area Projection
Elevations and depressions are given in feet

A-540000-26
COPYRIGHT BY
RAND McNALLY & COMPANY
MADE IN U.S.A.

Relief

Meters		Feet
3050		10 000
1525		5000
610		2000
305		1000
0	Sea Level	0
152.5		500
1525		5000
3050		10 000
6100		20 000

Longitude West of Greenwich

Scale 1:40 000 000; one inch to 630 miles. Lambert's Azimuthal, Equal Area Projection
Elevations and depressions are given in feet

EL SALVADOR Golfo de Fonseca NICARAGUA

CARIBBEAN SEA

PENÍNSULA DE GUAJIRA ARUBA (Neth.) CURAÇAO (Neth.) BONAIRE ISLAS LOS ROQUES

Willemstad ISLA DE MARGARITA

Managua Bluefields

NICARAGUA

San Juan del Sur Lago de Nicaragua

San Juan del Norte (Greytown)

Puerto Colombia Santa Marta Ríohacha Golfo de Venezuela Coro Puerto Cabello La Guaira Maiquetía CARACAS Cumaná

Barranquilla Ciénaga Maracaibo CARACAS

Puntarenas Limón Bocas del Toro Golfo de los Mosquitos Colón Cartagena Valledupar Cabimas San Felipe Valencia Barcelona Puerto la Cruz

San José Irazú (Vol.) David Gulfo de Panamá Panamá PANAMÁ Sincelejo Maracaibo Trujillo Barquisimeto VENEZUELA

COSTA RICA Golfo Dulce Golfo de Chiriquí PENÍNSULA DE AZUERO Turbo Montería Mérida San Carlos Ciudad Guayana

ISLA DEL COCO (Costa Rica) CABO CORRIENTES Cúcuta Pamplona Bucaramanga Arauca San Fernando de Apure Ciudad Bolívar

Quibdó MEDELLÍN La Dorada Tunja SANTA FE DE BOGOTÁ Orocué

ISLA DE MALPELO (Colombia) Manizales Pereira Armenia Ibagué Girardot Villavicencio

Buenaventura Bahía de Buenaventura Cali Palmira Buga COLOMBIA

PACIFIC OCEAN Popayán Neiva MESA DE YAMBI

Tumaco Pasto Florencia

PINTA MARCHENA Esmeraldas Ibarra Mocoa

GENOVESA SAN SALVADOR Equator Quito ECUADOR

SANTA CRUZ ARCHIPIÉLAGO DE COLÓN (GALÁPAGOS ISLANDS) (Ecuador) Bahía de Caráquez Manta Portoviejo Ambato Riobamba

ISABELA SAN CRISTÓBAL Guayaquil Cuenca Macas

Golfo de Guayaquil Machala Loja

Tumbes Iquitos Leticia AMAZONAS SELVA

Talara Paita Sullana Chulucanas Piura Yurimaguas Moyobamba Lamas Tarapoto Eirunepé

Chiclayo Cajamarca Chachapoyas Cruzeiro do Sul ACRE

Chimbote Trujillo Huamachuco Tingo María Huánuco PERU Río Branco Porto Acre

Huaraz Cerro de Pasco Puerto Bermúdez Cobija Riberalta RONDÔNIA

Callao LIMA Huancayo Machu Picchu Puerto Maldonado MASSIÇO DE

Chincha Alta Ayacucho Cusco Sicuani Trinidad

Ica Abancay Ayaviri Juliaca BOLIVIA

Pisco Puquio Sicuani Lago Titicaca La Paz Cochabamba

Nazca Coracora Arequipa Puno Oruro Sucre Potosí

Camaná Mollendo ALTIPLANO Lago de Poopó

Ilo Tacna ATACAMA Iquique Uyuni ARGENTINA

Arica CHILE Tocopilla PUNA DE ATACAMA

Antofagasta

Tropic of Capricorn

A-549100-76 ©11 9-20 COPYRIGHT BY RAND McNALLY & COMPANY MADE IN U.S.A.

Scale 1:16 000 000; one inch to 250 miles. Sinusoidal Project Elevations and depressions are given in feet

Longitude

Inset map (a)

a

ANTIOQUIA CHOCÓ RISARALDA CALDAS QUINDÍO VALLE DEL CAUCA CORDILLERA OCCIDENTAL CORDILLERA CENTRAL CORDILLERA ORIENTAL

MEDELLÍN Manizales Pereira Armenia Ibagué SANTA FE DE BOGOTÁ

CUNDINAMARCA TOLIMA HUILA META

Cali Palmira Neiva

Scale 1:4 000 000

0 10 20 30 40 Miles
0 10 20 30 40 50 Kilometers

©R.McN.

Cities and Towns		
0 to 50,000	○	500,000 to 1,000,000
50,000 to 500,000	⊙	1,000,000 and over

BELO HORIZONTE

BOLIVIA
PARAGUAY
BRAZIL
URUGUAY
ARGENTINA
CHILE

PACIFIC OCEAN

ATLANTIC OCEAN

GRAN CHACO

PUNA DE ATACAMA

LA PAMPA

PATAGONIA

RIO NEGRO

CHUBUT

SANTA CRUZ

TIERRA DEL FUEGO

Antofagasta
Salta
Tucumán
Santiago del Estero
Córdoba
Rosario
Santa Fe
Paraná
BUENOS AIRES
La Plata
MONTEVIDEO
Mar del Plata
Bahía Blanca
SANTIAGO
Valparaíso
Mendoza
San Juan
Concepción
Temuco
Valdivia
Puerto Montt
ISLA DE CHILOÉ
Comodoro Rivadavia
Golfo San Jorge
Puerto Santa Cruz
Río Gallegos
Punta Arenas
Estrecho de Magallanes
CABO DE HORNOS (CAPE HORN)

Asunción
SÃO PAULO
RIO DE JANEIRO
Curitiba
Florianópolis
PORTO ALEGRE
Rio Grande
Pelotas

FALKLAND IS. (ISLAS MALVINAS) (Claimed by Argentina)
Stanley

Tropic of Capricorn

Longitude West of Greenwich

A-549200-76 -117-13
COPYRIGHT BY
RAND McNALLY & COMPANY
MADE IN U.S.A.

Relief

Meters		Feet
3050		10 000
1525		5000
610		2000
305		1000
152.5		500
0	Sea Level	Sea Level
152.5		500
		Below
1525		5000
3050		10 000
6100		20 000

Scale 1:16 000 000; one inch to 250 miles. Sinusoidal Projection
Elevations and depressions are given in feet

0 50 100 200 300 400 500 Miles
0 100 200 400 600 800 Kilometers

a — BUENOS AIRES

RÍO DE LA PLATA
San Fernando
San Isidro
Vicente López
Olivos
General Sarmiento
San Martín
Morón
San Justo
Lanús
Avellaneda
Quilmes
Lomas de Zamora
Banfield
Temperley
Almirante Brown
Longchamps
Ezeiza

Scale 1:1 000 000
0 4 8 12 16 Kilometers

b — RIO DE JANEIRO

SERRA DAS ARARAS
SERRA DO COULTO
Petrópolis
Teresópolis
Nova Iguaçu
Duque de Caxias
São João de Meriti
Nilópolis
Niterói
São Gonçalo
Baía de Guanabara
Copacabana
Campo Grande
Jacarepaguá
ATLANTIC OCEAN

Scale 1:1 000 000
0 4 8 12 16 Kilometers

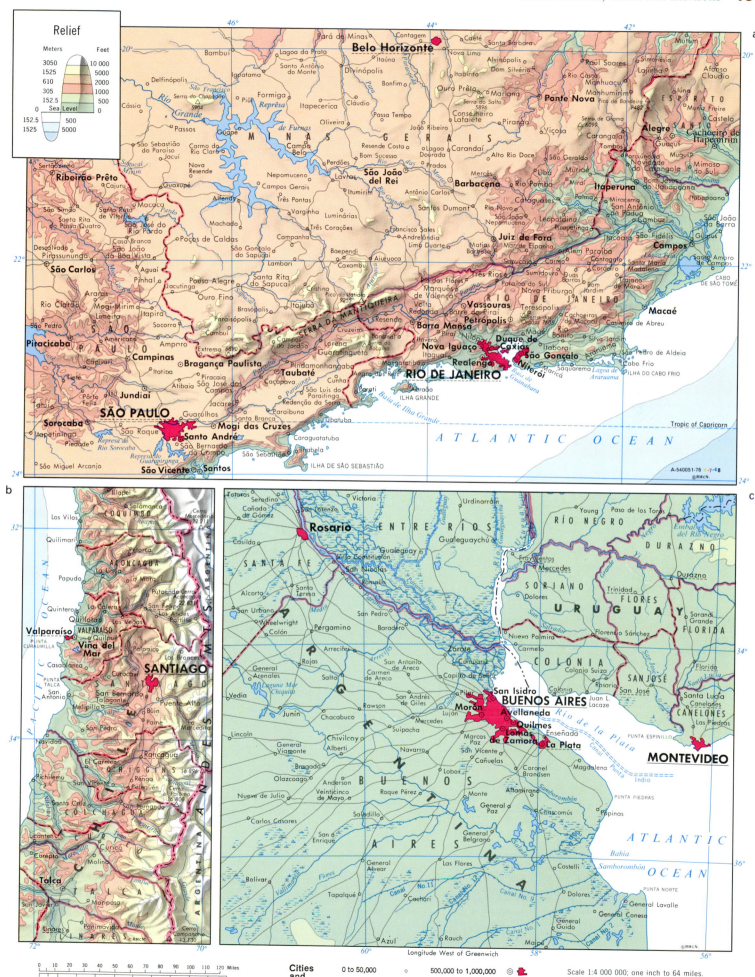

a

Relief

Meters	Feet
3050	10 000
1525	5000
610	2000
305	1000
152.5	500
0 Sea Level	0
152.5	500
1525	5000

b

c

Cities
and
Towns

0 to 50,000   ○   500,000 to 1,000,000 ◎

50,000 to 500,000 ⊙   1,000,000 and over

Scale 1:4 000 000; one inch to 64 miles.

Elevations and depressions are given in feet.

Europe

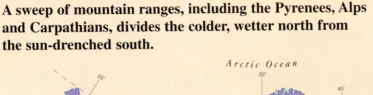

Europe is smaller than every other continent except Australia. In a sense, Europe is not really a continent at all, since it is part of the same vast landmass as Asia. Geographers sometimes refer to this landmass as a single continent, Eurasia. Europe occupies only about 18% of the land area of Eurasia.

Europe can be described as an enormous peninsula, stretching from the Ural Mountains, Ural River, and Caspian Sea in the east, to the Atlantic Ocean in the west; and from the Arctic Ocean in the north to the Mediterranean Sea, Black Sea, and Caucasus mountains in the south. The British Isles, Iceland, Corsica, Crete, and thousands of smaller islands that lie off the European mainland are usually considered as part of the continent.

A sweep of mountain ranges, including the Pyrenees, Alps and Carpathians, divides the colder, wetter north from the sun-drenched south.

Europe at a glance

Land area: 3,800,000 square miles (9,900,000 sq km)

Estimated population (January 1, 1995): 712,100,000

Population density: 187/square mile (72/sq km)

Mean elevation: 980 feet (300 m)

Highest point: Gora El' brus, Russia, 18,510 feet (5,642 m)

Lowest point: Caspian Sea, Asia-Europe, 92 feet (28 m) below sea level

Longest river: Volga, 2,194 mi (3,531 km)

Number of countries (incl. dependencies): 49

Largest independent country: Russia (Europe/Asia), 6,592,849 square miles (17,075,400 sq km)

Smallest independent country: Vatican City, 0.2 square miles (0.4 sq km)

Most populous independent country: Russia (Europe/Asia), 150,500,000

Least populous independent country: Vatican City, 1,000

Largest city: Moscow, pop. 8,801,500 (1991)

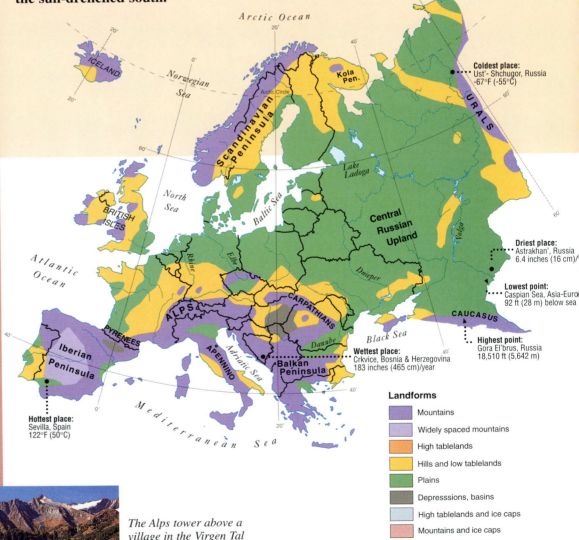

Coldest place: Ust'- Shchugor, Russia -67°F (-55°C)

Driest place: Astrakhan', Russia 6.4 inches (16 cm)

Lowest point: Caspian Sea, Asia-Euro 92 ft (28 m) below sea

Highest point: Gora El'brus, Russia 18,510 ft (5,642 m)

Wettest place: Crkvice, Bosnia & Herzegovina 183 inches (465 cm)/year

Hottest place: Sevilla, Spain 122°F (50°C)

Landforms

■	Mountains
■	Widely spaced mountains
■	High tablelands
■	Hills and low tablelands
■	Plains
■	Depresssions, basins
■	High tablelands and ice caps
■	Mountains and ice caps

© Rand McNally & Co.
M-550000-7C-EL1-1-1--1

The Alps tower above a village in the Virgen Tal valley of western Austria.

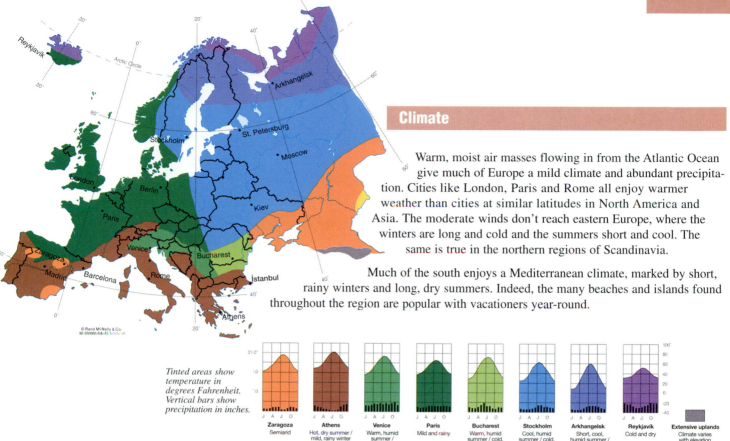

Climate

Warm, moist air masses flowing in from the Atlantic Ocean give much of Europe a mild climate and abundant precipitation. Cities like London, Paris and Rome all enjoy warmer weather than cities at similar latitudes in North America and Asia. The moderate winds don't reach eastern Europe, where the winters are long and cold and the summers short and cool. The same is true in the northern regions of Scandinavia.

Much of the south enjoys a Mediterranean climate, marked by short, rainy winters and long, dry summers. Indeed, the many beaches and islands found throughout the region are popular with vacationers year-round.

Tinted areas show temperature in degrees Fahrenheit. Vertical bars show precipitation in inches.

| **Zaragoza** Semiarid | **Athens** Hot, dry summer / mild, rainy winter | **Venice** Warm, humid summer / mild winter | **Paris** Mild and rainy | **Bucharest** Warm, humid summer / cold, snowy winter | **Stockholm** Cool, humid summer / cold, snowy winter | **Arkhangelsk** Short, cool, humid summer / very cold, snowy winter | **Reykjavik** Cold and dry | **Extensive uplands** Climate varies with elevation and latitude |

Population

With a population of 712 million, Europe is home to 13% of the world's people. Only one continent, Asia, has a larger population. Europe's population density—187 people per square mile (72 per sq km) is also second only to Asia. However, the continent's density varies dramatically from country to country. The Netherlands, for instance, has a density of 954 people per square mile (368 per sq km), making it one of the most densely populated countries in the world. In contrast, Norway has only 29 people per square mile (11 per sq km).

A vast array of ethnic groups and cultures can be found in Europe's relatively small area. Throughout the centuries, this diversity has enriched European culture while also leading to many hostilities. Of the 60 languages spoken, the majority are derived from Latin, Germanic or Slavic roots. Most Europeans are Christian, either Protestant or Roman Catholic.

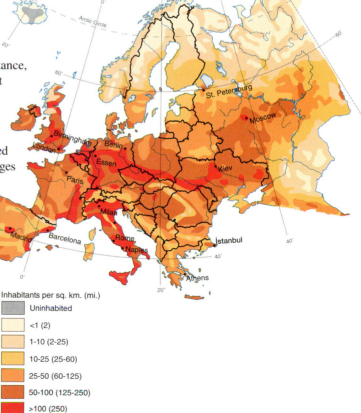

Inhabitants per sq. km. (mi.)

- Uninhabited
- <1 (2)
- 1-10 (2-25)
- 10-25 (25-60)
- 25-50 (60-125)
- 50-100 (125-250)
- >100 (250)

Fastest-Growing Countries

Albania, 1.71% (annual rate of natural increase)

Faeroe Islands, 1.04%

Iceland, 0.97%

Slowest-Growing Countries

Monaco, -0.15%

Ukraine, -0.03%

Hungary, -0.03%

Environments and Land Use

Given the high population density of Europe, it is not surprising that evidence of human development can be seen in every part of the continent, with the exception of the northern reaches of Scandinavia. In Western Europe, small farms are surrounded by towns, cities and industrial areas. Only in the east, in areas such as the vast rolling steppes of the Ukraine, can large farms and unbroken natural vistas be found.

Harvesting grapes from vineyards in Burgundy, France

The heavily industrialized countries of Western Europe boast rich economies and high standards of living. Switzerland has a per capita Gross Domestic Product (GDP) approaching U.S. $22,000, the highest in the world. The figures are generally much lower in Eastern Europe. One of the continent's poorest countries is the tiny former Communist state of Albania, which has a per capita GDP of only U.S. $998.

Pollution is an unfortunate by-product of the continent's industry. One example is the scenic Rhine River: in the 1980s, large stretches were found to be so polluted that they were devoid of life. These findings sparked a 20-year program to clean up the river. In general, the countries of Eastern Europe suffer from the worst pollution, as economic development has in the past taken precedence over environmental policies.

The vast forests of Scandinavia support a large paper and wood-products economy. Where forests survive in countries farther to the south, they are often used for recreation. Along the Mediterranean, the warm and dry lands support olive and fruit orchards. In many of these areas, agriculture is being supplemented and even replaced by tourism.

Over-fishing has depleted the seas and ocean around Europe. The fleets of countries such as Spain and Great Britain must sail far into the North Atlantic to find the ever-dwindling stocks of fish.

- Urban
- Cropland
- Cropland and woodland
- Cropland and grazing land
- Grassland, grazing land
- Forest, woodland
- Swamp, marsh
- Tundra
- Shrub, sparse grass, wasteland
- Barren land

Political Changes Since 1989

Much of Europe lay in economic and physical ruin after World War II ended in 1945. Germany's cities and industrial centers had been ravaged by aerial bombardment and assaults by the Allied armies. Many other countries, such as Russia, Poland, Belgium, and the Netherlands suffered gravely from Nazi invasions and occupation.

After 1945, tensions among the victorious Allies grew, specifically between the Western powers—the United States, Great Britain and France—and the Soviet Union. It became clear that the two sides had vastly different visions for post-war Europe. In 1946, former British prime minister Winston Churchill observed that an "Iron Curtain" had gone down across Europe. It was to stay in place for almost 45 years.

Germany and the city of Berlin were divided between the Western Allies and the Soviet Union. West Germany quickly joined the other countries of Western Europe in building a stable, affluent democratic society. East Germany became part of a bloc of Eastern European countries dominated by the Soviet Union. These included Poland, Czechoslovakia, Hungary, Romania, Albania, and Bulgaria (see map at right). The economies in these countries were tightly controlled and personal freedoms were severely limited by the Communist governments in power.

The two blocs faced each other in a tense, generally non-military standoff called "The Cold War," which lasted for four decades. However, in 1985 winds of reform began sweeping through Eastern Europe. In 1989, Hungary relaxed its borders with Austria, setting off a flow of refugees from the east who had been forbidden to travel to the West. Thus began a dizzying period of change: the next two years saw the collapse of the Soviet Union, the reunification of Germany, independence for the former Soviet republics, and freedom from Soviet influence for the former bloc countries.

Although much of the old east seems intent on adopting Western ideals of democracy and freedom, the process is not without problems. Switching from communism to market economies has meant hardship for millions. It has also led to ethnic tensions that resulted in the peaceful break-up of Czechoslovakia and the violent civil wars in the former Yugoslavia.

Still, most countries in the east seem intent on one day becoming a part of the European Union, the political and economic organization that currently has 15 member countries.

East Germany and West Germany reunited in 1990.

In 1991, the Soviet Union broke up into 15 independent states: Russia, Estonia, Latvia, Lithuania, Belarus, Ukraine, Moldova, Georgia, Armenia, Azerbaijan, Kazakhstan, Turkmenistan, Kyrgyzstan, Uzbekistan, and Tajikistan.

In 1991-92 the former Yugoslavia broke up when Slovenia, Croatia, Macedonia, and Bosnia and Herzegovina declared their independence, leaving Serbia and Montenegro as the remaining Yugoslav Republics.

In 1993, Czechoslovakia split into two separate countries: the Czech Republic and Slovakia.

Political Change Since 1989
- Former Soviet Union
- Former Czechoslovakia
- Former Yugoslavia
- Former East and West Germany
- Former Soviet-bloc countries

Berlin Wall memorial

40,000 SQ MI
AREA

0   100   200
Miles

Scale 1: 16 000 000; one inch to 250 miles. Conic Projection

Elevations and depressions are given in feet

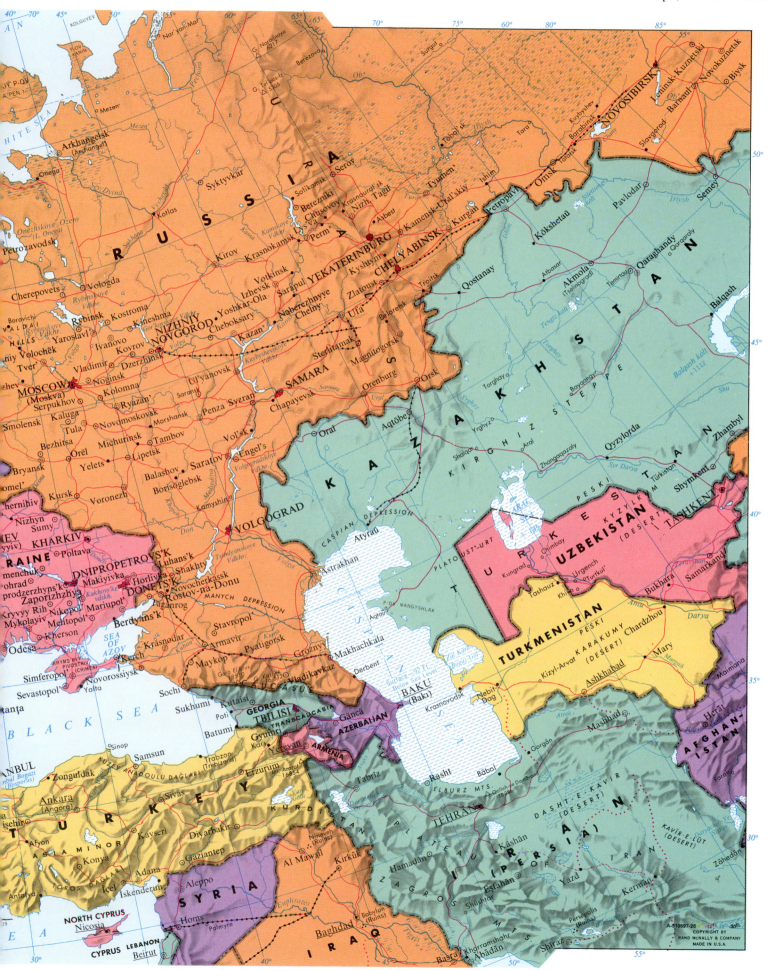

Relief

Meters	Feet
3050	10 000
1525	5000
610	2000
305	1000
152.5	500
0 Sea Level	0
152.5	500
1525	5000
3050	10 000 Below Sea Level

Scale 1: 16 000 000; one inch to 250 miles. Conic Projection
Elevations and depressions are given in feet

Longitude West of Greenwich   Longitude East of Greenwich

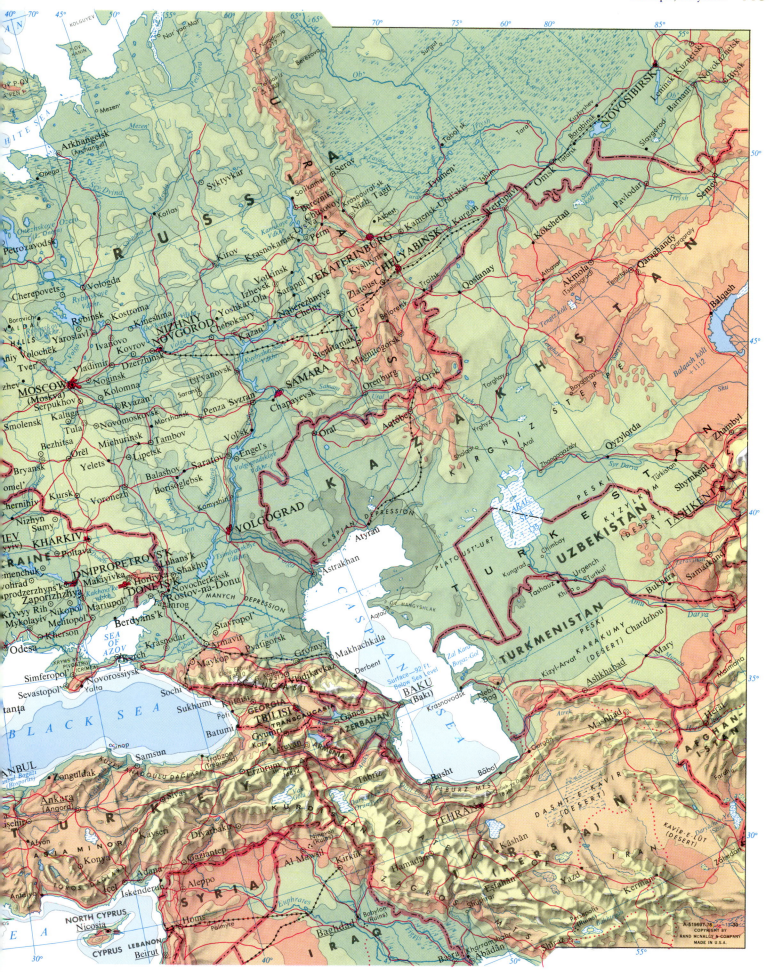

116

Relief

Meters	Feet	
3050	10 000	
1525	5000	
610	2000	
305	1000	
152.5	500	
0	Sea Level	Sea Level
152.5	500	Below Sea Level
1525	5000	
3050	10000	

Scale 1: 10 000 000; one inch to 160 miles. Conic Projec
Elevations and depressions are given in feet

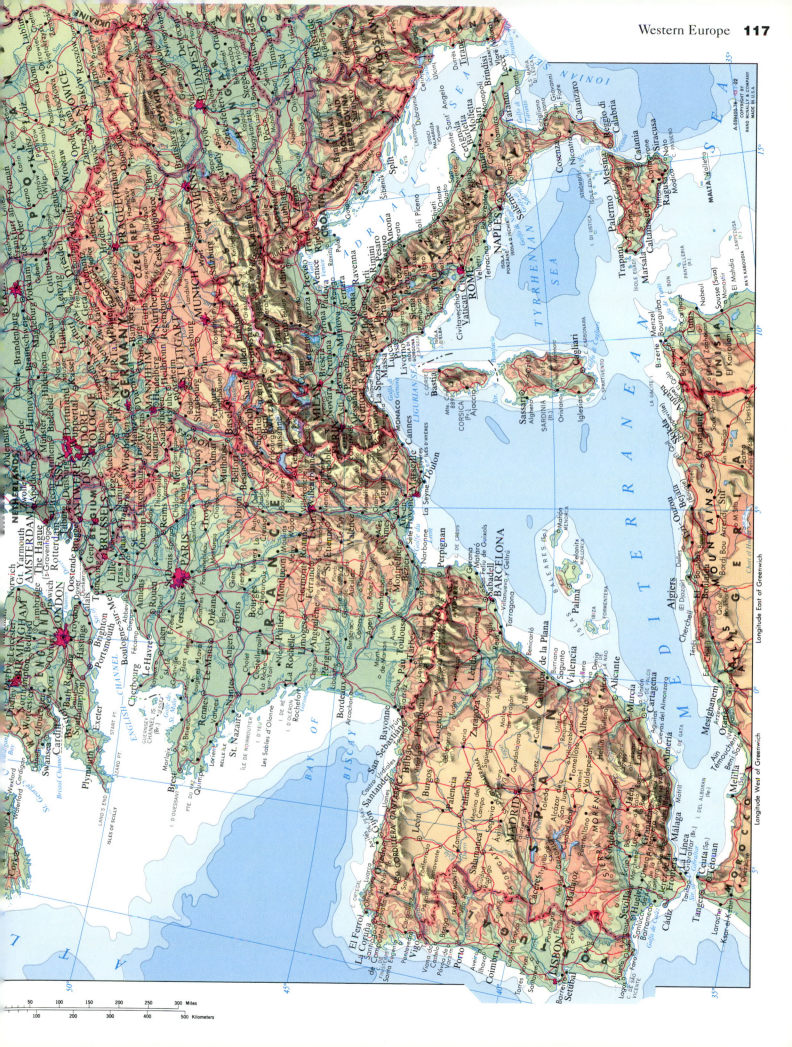

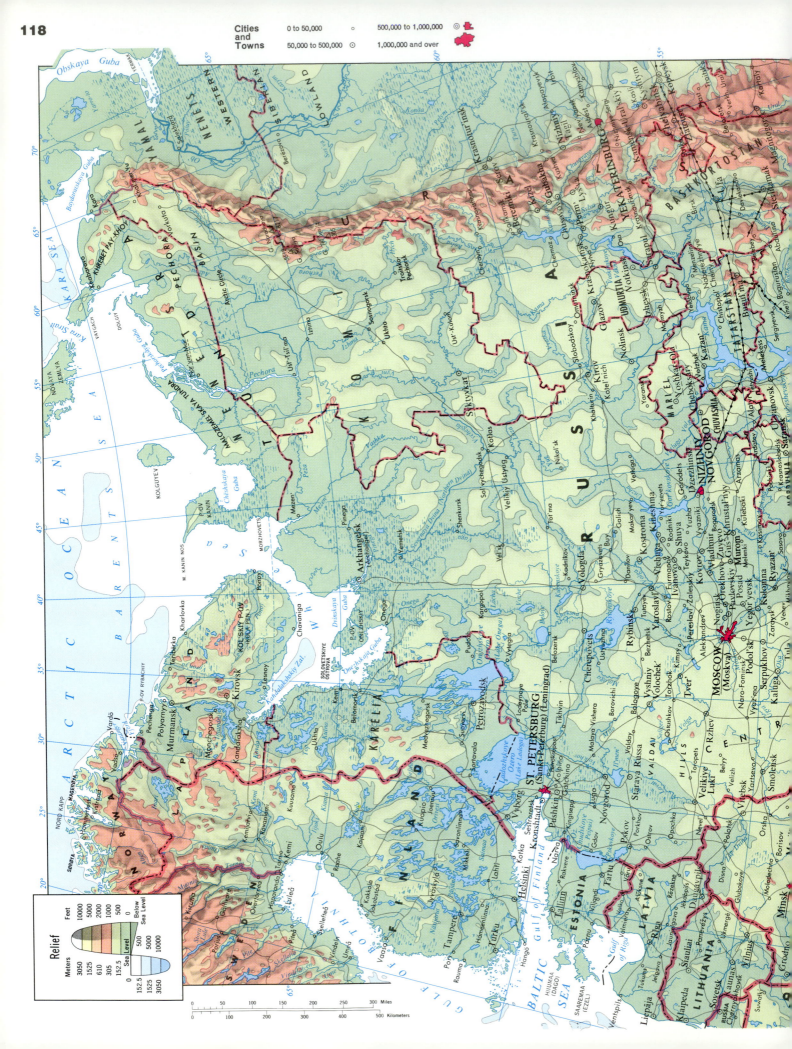

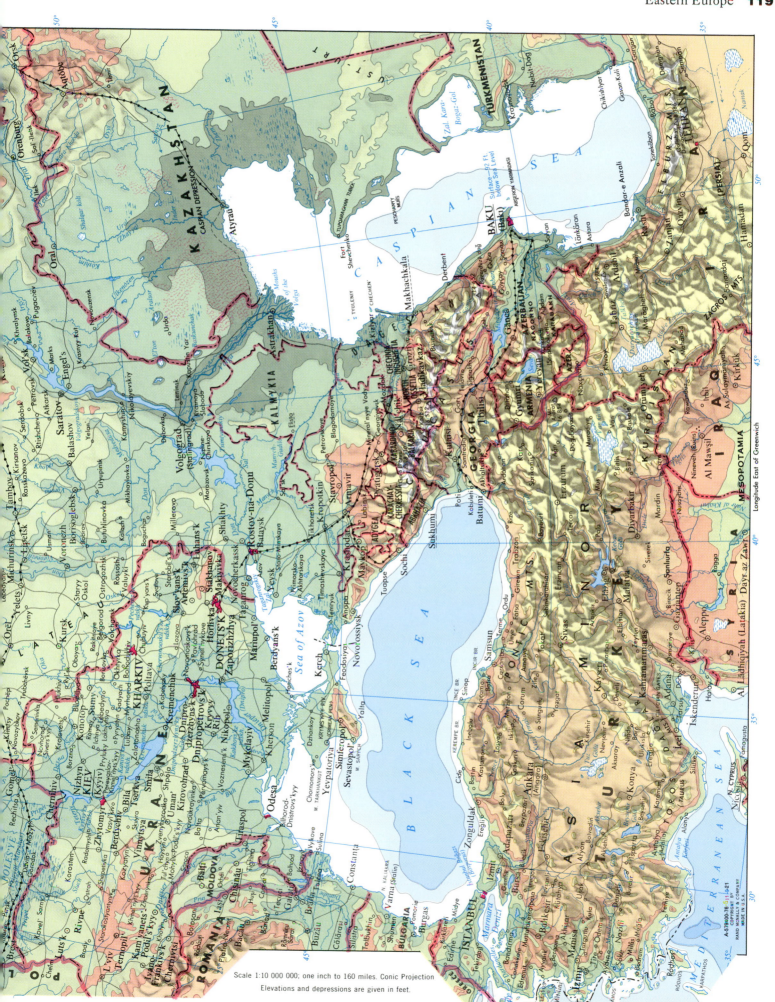

Scale 1:10 000 000; one inch to 160 miles. Conic Projection
Elevations and depressions are given in feet.

ATLANTIC
OCEAN

BAY
OF
BISCAY

GERMANY

FRANCE

SPAIN

PORTUGAL

LISBON

MADRID

BARCELONA

Valencia

PARIS

MILAN

TURIN

Genoa

ROME
(Roma)

VATICAN CITY

NAPLES
(Napoli)

CORSICA
(Fr.)

SARDINIA
(It.)

SICILY

LIGURIAN SEA

TYRRHENIAN
SEA

M E D I T E R R A N E A N

BALEARES (Sp.)

ISLAS

MALTA

MOROCCO

ALGERIA

TUNISIA

SAHARAN ATLAS MOUNTAINS

ATLAS

GRAND ERG OCCIDENTAL

GRAND ERG ORIENTAL

Tripoli (Tarābulus)

T A R Ā B U L U S
(TRIPOLITANIA)

Relief

Meters		Feet
3050		10000
1525		5000
610		2000
305		1000
152.5		500
0	Sea Level	0
		Below
		Sea Level
152.5		500
1525		5000
3050		10000

A-558300-76 18-12-33
COPYRIGHT BY
RAND McNALLY & COMPANY
MADE IN U.S.A.

Longitude West of Greenwich 0° Longitude East of Greenwich

Scale 1:10 000 000; one inch to 160 miles. Bonne's Projection
Elevations and depressions are given in feet

The Turkish Republic of Northern Cyprus unilaterally declared its independence on Nov. 15, 1983.

Areas occupied by Israel since 1967.

Africa

The Drakensberg Mountains mark the southern end of the African plateau.

Africa, the second-largest continent, comprises about one-fifth of the world's land area. From the Equator, Africa extends roughly the same distance to the north as it does to the south.

A high plateau covers much of the continent. The edges of the plateau are marked by steep slopes, called escarpments, where the land angles sharply downward onto narrow coastal plains or into the sea. Many of the continent's great rivers plunge over these escarpments in falls or rapids, and therefore cannot be used as transportation routes from the coast into the continent's interior.

Among Africa's most significant mountain systems are the Atlas range in the far north and the Drakensberg range in the far south. A long string of mountain ranges and highlands running north-south through eastern Africa marks the course of the Great Rift Valley.

Africa at a glance

Land area: 11,700,000 square miles (30,300,000 sq km)

Estimated population (January 1, 1995): 697,600,000

Population density: 60/ square mile (23/sq km)

Mean elevation: 1,900 feet (580 m)

Highest point: Kilimanjaro, Tanzania, 19,340 feet (5,895 m)

Lowest point: Lac Assal, Djibouti, 515 feet (157 m) below sea level

Longest river: Nile, 4,145 mi (6,671 km)

Number of countries (incl. dependencies): 61

Largest independent country: Sudan, 967,500 square miles (2,505,813 sq km)

Smallest independent country: Seychelles, 175 square miles (453 sq km)

Most populous independent country: Nigeria, 97,300,000

Least populous independent country: Seychelles, 75,000

Largest city: Cairo, pop. 6,068,695 (1990)

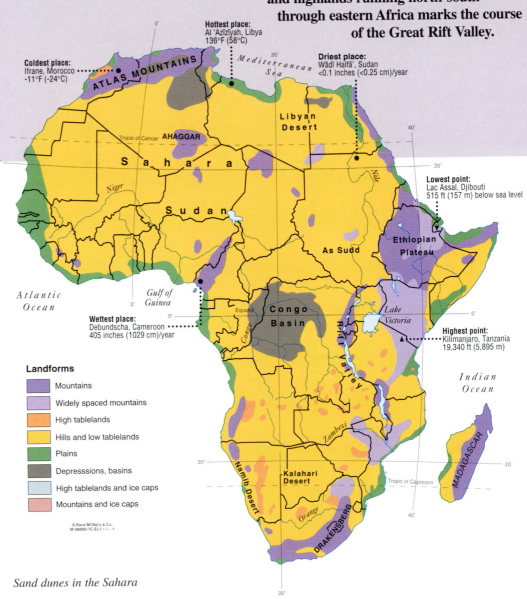

Coldest place:
Ifrane, Morocco
-11°F (-24°C)

Hottest place:
Al 'Azīzīyah, Libya
136°F (58°C)

Driest place:
Wādī Halfā', Sudan
<0.1 inches (<0.25 cm)/year

Lowest point:
Lac Assal, Djibouti
515 ft (157 m) below sea level

Wettest place:
Debundscha, Cameroon
405 inches (1029 cm)/year

Highest point:
Kilimanjaro, Tanzania
19,340 ft (5,895 m)

ATLAS MOUNTAINS
Mediterranean Sea
Libyan Desert
AHAGGAR
Tropic of Cancer
Sahara
Niger
Sudan
As Sudd
Nile
Ethiopian Plateau
Atlantic Ocean
Gulf of Guinea
Equator
Congo Basin
Congo
Rift Valley
Lake Victoria
Indian Ocean
Zambezi
Namib Desert
Kalahari Desert
Tropic of Capricorn
Orange
DRAKENSBERG
MADAGASCAR

Landforms

- Mountains
- Widely spaced mountains
- High tablelands
- Hills and low tablelands
- Plains
- Depressions, basins
- High tablelands and ice caps
- Mountains and ice caps

© Rand McNally & Co.
M-580000-7C-EL1-1-1-1--1

Sand dunes in the Sahara

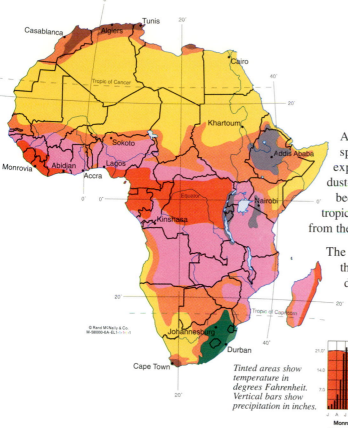

Climate

Africa's most prominent climatic region is the vast Sahara desert which spreads over much of the northern half of the continent. The Sahara experiences scorching daytime temperatures, minimal rainfall, and hot, dry, dust-laden winds that blow nearly continuously. South of the Sahara, the climate becomes increasingly humid, moving through zones of semiarid steppe and tropical savanna to the tropical rain forest that stretches across equatorial Africa from the Atlantic Ocean to the Rift Valley.

The climate patterns of northern Africa are repeated in reverse south of the Equator. The rain forest gives way to zones of decreasing humidity, and desert regions cover western South Africa and Namibia. Africa's mildest, most temperate climates are found along its Mediterranean coast, at its southwestern tip, and in eastern South Africa.

Tinted areas show temperature in degrees Fahrenheit. Vertical bars show precipitation in inches.

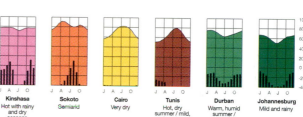

Monrovia	Kinshasa	Sokoto	Cairo	Tunis	Durban	Johannesburg	Extensive uplands
Hot and rainy	Hot with rainy and dry seasons	Semiarid	Very dry	Hot, dry summer / mild, rainy winter	Warm, humid summer / mild winter	Mild and rainy	Climate varies with elevation and latitude

Population

Approximately one-eighth of the world's people live in Africa. The population is almost evenly divided between the sub-Saharan countries and those bordering the Mediterranean. Large tracts of the Sahara are uninhabited. Despite recurring famines and warfare, the population is rapidly increasing. Twenty-two African countries have annual growth rates at or above 3%, which means that the number of inhabitants in each can double within 25 years.

The largest concentrations of people are generally found in regions in which one or more of the following conditions exist: moderate temperatures, ample water supply, and arable land. These regions include Egypt's fertile Nile Valley, the northern coast of the Gulf of Guinea, the highlands of East Africa, and the coastal regions of Morocco, Algeria, and Tunisia, north of the Atlas Mountains.

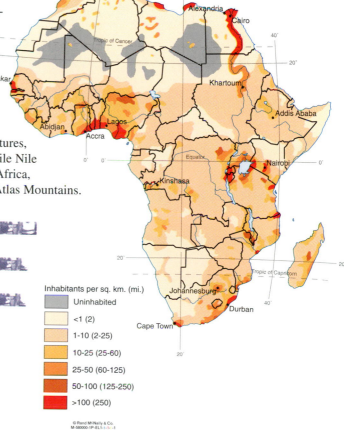

Inhabitants per sq. km. (mi.)

- Uninhabited
- <1 (2)
- 1-10 (2-25)
- 10-25 (25-60)
- 25-50 (60-125)
- 50-100 (125-250)
- >100 (250)

© Rand McNally & Co.
M-580000-1P-EL1-1-1- -1

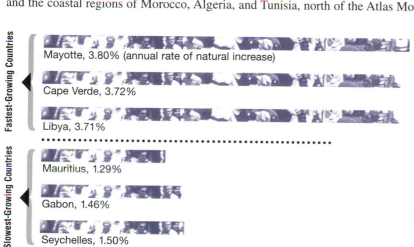

Fastest-Growing Countries

- Mayotte, 3.80% (annual rate of natural increase)
- Cape Verde, 3.72%
- Libya, 3.71%

Slowest-Growing Countries

- Mauritius, 1.29%
- Gabon, 1.46%
- Seychelles, 1.50%

Environments and Land Use

Deserts account for one-third of Africa's land area, and they claim new land every year. Drought, over-farming and over-grazing can quickly turn marginal land, such as that of the Sahel region, into barren wasteland. The huge Sahara desert has itself only existed a short time, in geological terms: cave paintings and other archeological evidence indicate that green pastureland covered the area just a few thousand years ago.

Shepherd with goats in the Sahel

Most Africans are subsistence farmers, growing sorghum, corn, millet, sweet potatoes, and other starchy foods. Commercial farms, most of which date from the colonial period, can be found throughout central and southern Africa, producing cash crops such as coffee, bananas, tobacco and cacao. One-quarter of the continent's land is suitable for grazing, but disease and drought have made raising animals difficult. Although three out of four Africans work in agriculture, Africa is the only continent that is not self-sufficient for food.

The great rain forests that cover much of equatorial Africa produce mahogany, ebony, and other valuable hardwoods. However, only limited areas of the forests are suitable for logging, and the lack of developed road networks makes it difficult and costly to transport the wood.

Vast mineral reserves are spread throughout the continent. Most are unexploited, but notable exceptions include the diamond mines of South Africa and Namibia, the copper mines of Zambia and Zaire, and the oil fields of Nigeria, Libya, and Algeria.

The great concentrations of wildlife for which Africa is famous can still be found in places such as Tanzania's Serengeti Plain and Botswana's Kalahari Desert. In many other parts of the continent, however, wildlife is quickly disappearing as humans encroach on habitat and poachers decimate entire species.

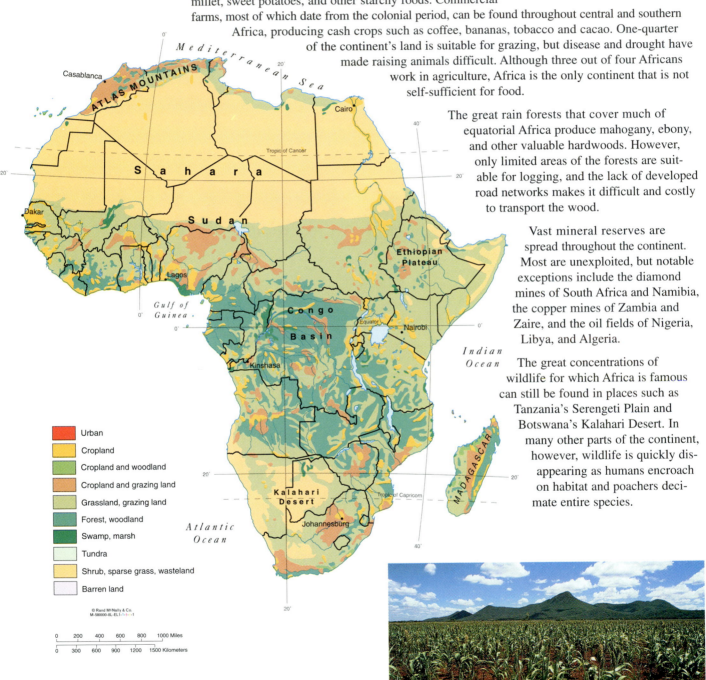

Legend:
- Urban
- Cropland
- Cropland and woodland
- Cropland and grazing land
- Grassland, grazing land
- Forest, woodland
- Swamp, marsh
- Tundra
- Shrub, sparse grass, wasteland
- Barren land

© Rand McNally & Co.
M-580000-8L-EL1-1-1- -1

0 200 400 600 800 1000 Miles
0 300 600 900 1200 1500 Kilometers

Field of sorghum in Zimbabwe

Africa: from Colonial Rule to Independence

The origins of Europe's colonization of Africa can be traced back to the 1500s, when a lucrative slave trade developed to supply European settlers in the New World with laborers. Africa became the primary source for slaves: between the mid-1500s and the mid-1800s, 11 million Africans were captured and sold into slavery.

When the slave trade was banned across Europe in the early 1800s, commercial trade with Africa continued. In the second half of the century, competition for Africa's minerals and other raw materials intensified, and between 1880 and 1914, France, Britain, Italy, Portugal, Belgium, Spain, and Germany annexed large areas of Africa. Colonial rule was often characterized by racial prejudice and segregation.

In the late 19th and early 20th centuries, Egypt, Ethiopia, and South Africa began to break free from colonial influence. For most or Africa, however, colonial rule persisted through the mid-1900s, although it faced growing bitterness and nationalist sentiment. As the colonial powers struggled through two world wars, and as their international dominance declined, it became increasingly difficult for them to maintain their empires.

In 1951, Libya gained its independence, following a UN resolution that ended British and French control. Sudan peacefully won independence from Britain and Egypt in 1956. A year later, Britain granted independence to the Gold Coast, which became the new country of Ghana. Guinea separated from France in 1958, followed by all of the other French colonies in 1960. Anti-colonial movements gathered strength across Africa, and by the end of the 1970s, a total of 43 countries had become independent.

The end of colonial rule, however, has not brought peace and prosperity. Many of the newly freed countries were ill-prepared for independence. Their economies were oriented to fit the needs of the now-departed colonists, few transportation networks existed, and dictators and rival despots fought for power in civil wars.

People of the Samburu tribe

Further, most Africans identify themselves primarily with the tribe to which they belong. The political delineations established by the European powers have little meaning and often conflict with traditional tribal boundaries. In some cases, enemy tribes found themselves pushed together in a single country; in others, single tribes were divided among several countries. These conditions have already brought much warfare and hardship. Still, Africa is a land of promise and opportunity. The rich diversity of its people and abundance of its resources should inevitably enable the continent to realize its potential.

Africa in 1950

- Independent
- British
- French
- Portuguese
- Spanish
- Belgian
- Italian
- Other

© Rand McNally & Co.
M-480045-2S-EL1-1-1- -1

Africa Today

- Independent
- Other

1960   Date of independence

© Rand McNally & Co.
M-580000-2S-EL1-1-1- -1

Ethno-linguistic Groups

- Semitic-Hamitic
- Mande
- Guinean
- Hausa
- Bantu
- Central Bantoid
- Eastern Bantoid
- Western Bantoid
- Indo-European
- Kanuri
- Songhai
- Khoisan
- Nilotic
- Malay-Polynesian
- Kanuri, Semitic-Hamitic
- Hausa, Western Bantoid
- Central/Eastern Sudanese, Bantu
- Indo-European, Semitic-Hamitic
- Central/Eastern Sudanese, Semitic-Hamitic
- Central/Eastern Sudanese

© Rand McNally & Co.
M-580000-1D-EL1-1-1- -1

40,000 SQ MI AREA

0   300   600
Miles

0   200   400   600   800   1000 Miles
0   400   800   1200   1600 Kilometers

Longitude West of Greenwich   Longitude East of Greenwich

Scale 1:40 000 000; one inch to 630 miles. Lambert's Azimuthal, Equal Area Projection

Elevations and depressions are given in feet.

A-580000-26   COPYRIGHT BY RAND McNALLY & COMPANY   MADE IN U.S.A.

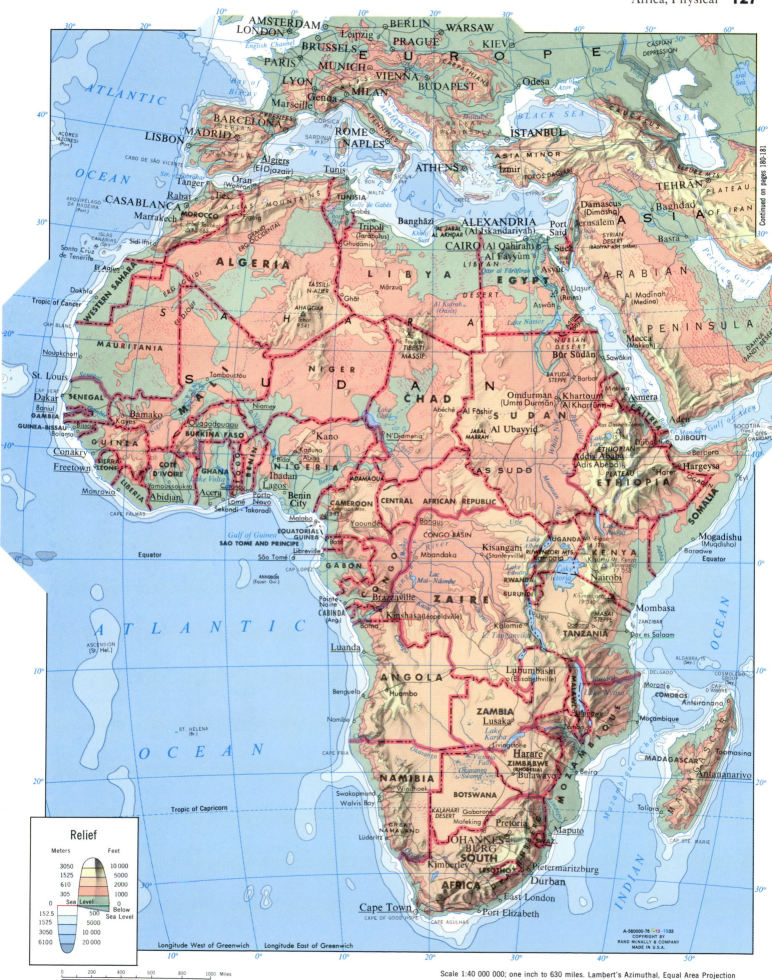

Scale 1:40 000 000; one inch to 630 miles. Lambert's Azimuthal, Equal Area Projection
Elevations and depressions are given in feet.

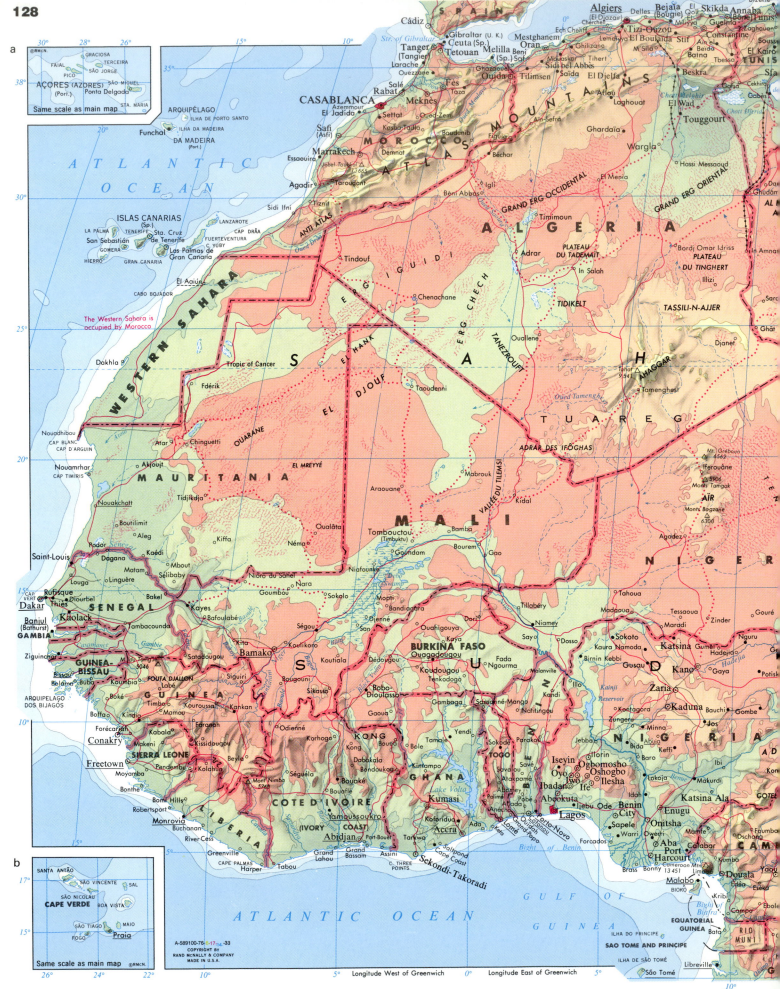

128

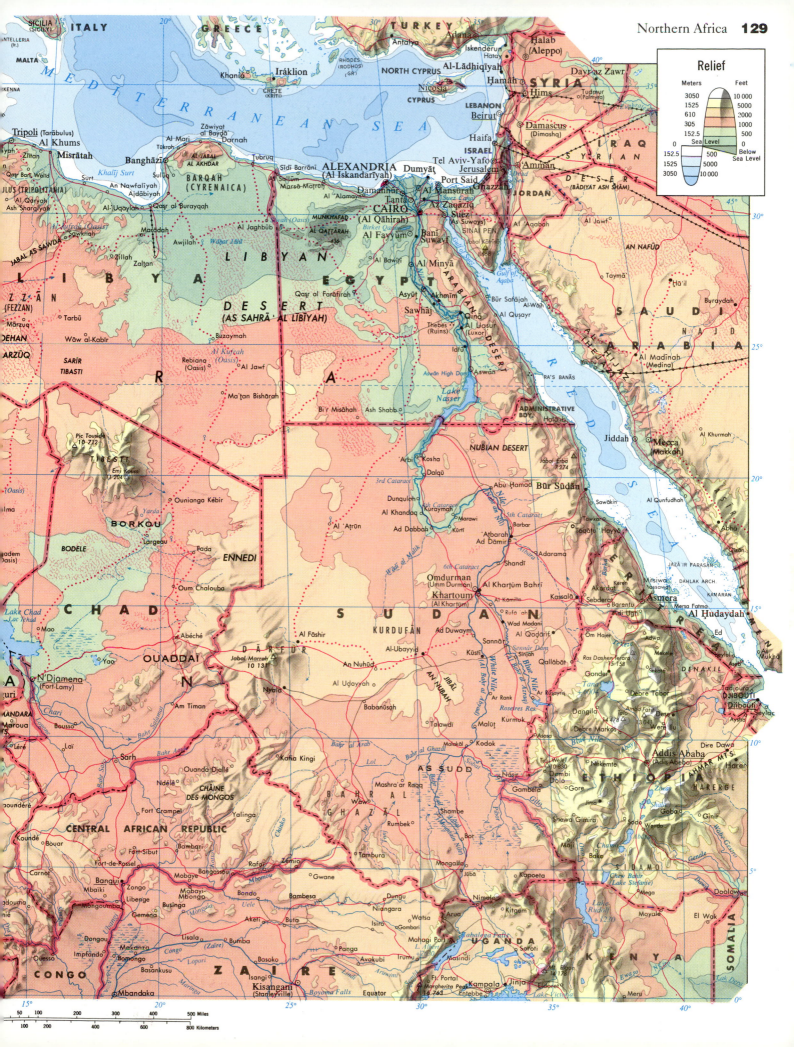

a

CAPE
TOWN

Scale 1:1 000 000

Scale 1:16 000 000; one inch to 250 miles. Sinusoidal Projection
Elevations and depressions are given in feet

SOMALIA

Nairobi

Mombasa

INDIAN

Dar es Salaam

COMOROS

MADAGASCAR

Antananarivo

Scale 1:16 000 000;
one inch to 250 miles

EUROPE
ASIA
AFRICA
Location
of area
shown
on the
map

YEMEN
Aden ('Adan)
Gulf of Aden
SOCOTRA (Yemen)
Hadibu

Djibouti

Hargeysa

ETHIOPIA

OGADEN

KENYA

Mogadishu
(Muqdisho)

c

LESOTHO

DRAKENSBERG

NATAL

Pietermaritzburg

Durban

SOUTH AFRICA

EASTERN CAPE

Umtata

East London

Port Elizabeth

INDIAN

OCEAN

Scale 1:4 000 000

Relief

Meters	Feet
3050	10 000
1525	5000
610	2000
305	1000
152.5	500
0	Sea Level
152.5	500
1525	5000
3050	10 000

Longitude East of Greenwich

Asia

Covering nearly one-third of the Earth's land surface, Asia is by far the largest of the seven continents. It is a land of extremes and dramatic physical contrasts, containing nearly every type of landform, and many of them on a vast scale. It boasts the world's lowest point (the Dead Sea), its highest point (Mt. Everest), its highest and largest plateau (the Plateau of Tibet), and its largest inland body of water (the Caspian Sea).

Wide belts of mountain systems cover much of Asia. The Himalayas, which form a great 1,500-mile (2,400-km) arc south of Tibet, are the highest mountains in the world: more than 90 Himalayan peaks rise above 24,000 feet (7,320 m).

The beginnings of civilization can be traced to three distinct areas of Asia: Mesopotamia, around 4000 BC; the Indus River valley, around 3000 BC; and China, around 2000 BC. Eight of the world's major religions—Buddhism, Christianity, Confucianism, Hinduism, Islam, Judaism, Shinto, and Taoism—originated in Asia.

Asia at a glance

Land area:
17,300,000 square miles
(44,900,000 sq km)

Estimated population
(January 1, 1995): 3,422,700,000

Population density:
198/square mile (76/sq km)

Mean elevation: 3,000 feet
(910 m)

Highest point: Mt. Everest, China (Tibet)-Nepal, 29,028 feet (8,848 m)

Lowest point: Dead Sea, Israel-Jordan, 1,339 feet (408 m) below sea level

Longest river: Yangtze (Chang), 3,900 mi (6,300 km)

Number of countries (incl. dependencies): 49

Largest independent country: Russia (Europe/Asia), 6,592,849 square miles (17,075,400 sq km)

Smallest independent country: Maldives, 115 square miles (298 sq km)

Most populous independent country: China, 1,196,980,000

Least populous independent country: Maldives, 251,000

Largest city: Seoul, South Korea, pop. 10,627,790 (1990)

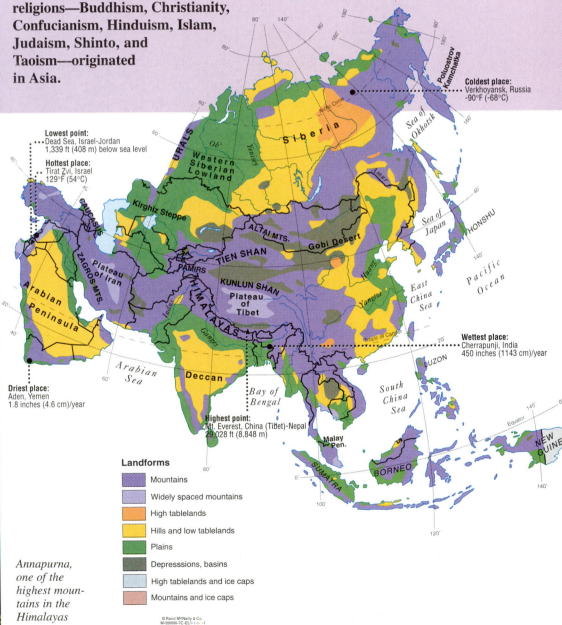

Landforms

- Mountains
- Widely spaced mountains
- High tablelands
- Hills and low tablelands
- Plains
- Depresssions, basins
- High tablelands and ice caps
- Mountains and ice caps

© Rand McNally & Co.
M-550000-7C-EL1-1-1---1

Annapurna, one of the highest mountains in the Himalayas

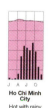
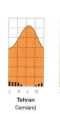
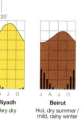

Climate

Climates vary greatly across Asia. In much of Siberia, temperatures average below -5°F (-20°C) in January, while the Persian Gulf region endures summer temperatures as high as 122°F (50°C). Monsoons interrupt hot dry spells with much-needed rain along the southeast and Indian Ocean coasts during the summer months. Between these extremes, almost every other type of climate on Earth can be found in Asia.

This climatic diversity can be explained by the continent's great expanse, from the Arctic to the tropics, and its great range in elevations.

Tinted areas show temperature in degrees Fahrenheit. Vertical bars show precipitation in inches.

Jakarta	Ho Chi Minh City	Tehran	Riyadh	Beirut	Shanghai	Shenyang	Novosibirsk	Tomsk	Chokurdakh	Extensive uplands
Hot and rainy	Hot with rainy and dry seasons	Semiarid	Very dry	Hot, dry summer / mild, rainy winter	Warm, humid summer / mild winter	Warm, humid summer / cold, snowy winter	Cool, humid summer / cold, snowy winter	Short, cool, humid summer / very cold, snowy winter	Cold and dry	Climate varies with elevation and latitude

Population

With 3.4 billion people, Asia is nearly five times as populous as any other continent and is home to six out of every ten people in the world. If its current 2% annual growth rate continues, Asia's population will double by the year 2030. The continent contains the two most populous countries in the world, China and India, as well as the most populous metropolitan area, Tōkyō-Yokohama, Japan.

Great concentrations of people are found in India, eastern China, Japan, Vietnam, and on the Indonesian island of Java. In contrast, vast stretches of northern Siberia, Mongolia, western China, and the Arabian Peninsula are only sparsely populated. Numerous desert regions, including Arabia's Rub' al Khālī and China's Takla Makān, are uninhabited.

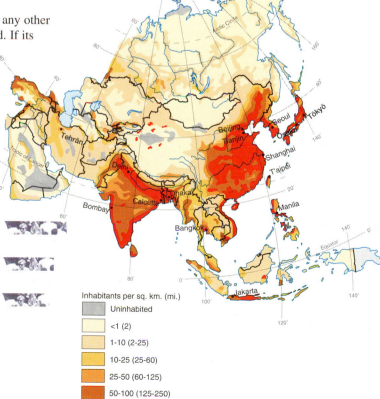

Inhabitants per sq. km. (mi.)

- Uninhabited
- <1 (2)
- 1-10 (2-25)
- 10-25 (25-60)
- 25-50 (60-125)
- 50-100 (125-250)
- >100 (250)

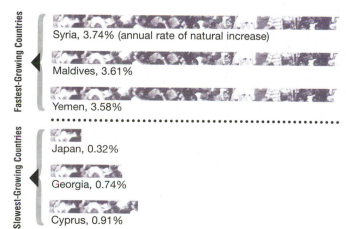

Fastest-Growing Countries

Syria, 3.74% (annual rate of natural increase)

Maldives, 3.61%

Yemen, 3.58%

Slowest-Growing Countries

Japan, 0.32%

Georgia, 0.74%

Cyprus, 0.91%

Environments and Land Use

Despite rapid industrialization in Japan, Korea, and Singapore, feeding the enormous and fast-growing population remains Asia's primary economic focus. In China, India, and Indonesia, two-thirds of the work force is engaged in farming. Where arable land exists, it is generally cultivated intensively. Rice is the most commonly grown crop: the continent produces more than 90% of the world's total. Other important crops include wheat, sorghum, millet, maize, and barley.

Asia's major agricultural regions are found in the fertile alluvial valleys, floodplains, and deltas of some of its greatest rivers, such as the Ganges and Brahmaputra in northern India, the Indus in Pakistan, the Huang (Yellow) and Yangtze in eastern China, the Irawaddy in Myanmar (Burma), the Mekong in Cambodia and Vietnam, and the Tigris and Euphrates in Iraq.

Tundra vegetation prevails across the arctic and subarctic regions of Siberia. Farther south, much of the land is densely forested. Deforestation, however, is rampant across the continent. In the colder central and northern areas, whole forests have been cut down to provide wood for heat and cooking. The tropical rain forests of the Indochina Peninsula, Malaysia, Indonesia, and the Philippines are rapidly being destroyed for their valuable hardwood, especially teak.

A wide sweep of semiarid grasslands across Central Asia covers one-quarter of the continent. These immense grazing lands are used by the people of many countries—notably Kazakhstan and Mongolia—for livestock that include almost one-third of the world's cattle, nearly three-fifths of its goats, and half of its pigs. In recent decades, the tremendous petroleum reserves located in the arid west, around the Persian Gulf, have been both a source of wealth and a cause of turmoil. The continent also has less exploited, but sizable reserves of natural gas in Siberia and coal in China.

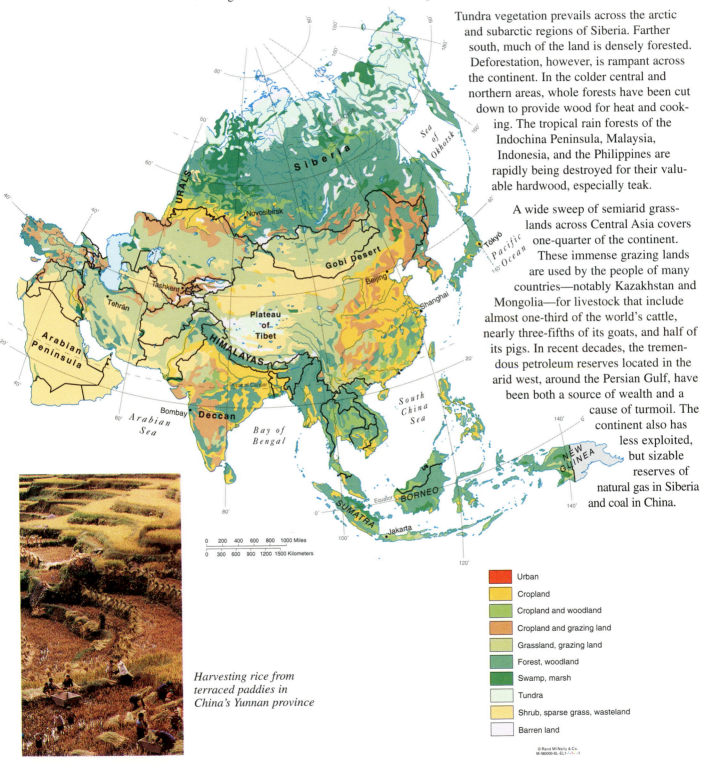

Harvesting rice from terraced paddies in China's Yunnan province

0 200 400 600 800 1000 Miles
0 300 600 900 1200 1500 Kilometers

- Urban
- Cropland
- Cropland and woodland
- Cropland and grazing land
- Grassland, grazing land
- Forest, woodland
- Swamp, marsh
- Tundra
- Shrub, sparse grass, wasteland
- Barren land

© Rand McNally & Co.
M-560000-8L-EL1-1-1-1

The Asian Tigers

Many people have predicted that the 21st century will be "the Asian Century"—a time when the countries of that continent will come of age internationally and will assert their economic, political, and cultural influence around the world. Indeed, Asia's power has been growing steadily since the end of World War II. Japan now boasts one of the world's most powerful economies, with an annual trade surplus of more than $100 billion.

Right behind Japan in economic development are a host of countries known collectively as "the Asian Tigers." Four of these "Tigers"—Hong Kong, Singapore, South Korea and Thailand—are challenging Japanese preeminence in manufacturing and finance. Each of the four has both a government providing strong support for economic growth and a population ready to exploit the opportunity. With an annual Gross Domestic Product (GDP) growth rate of over 10%, Singapore stands out from the others. It boasts a standard of living comparable to that of the U.S. or Western Europe.

Busy shopping district in Seoul, South Korea

In the next tier of economic development are Malaysia, Thailand, and Indonesia, which have been transformed in less than a generation by rapid economic growth. Primarily rural and agricultural 20 years ago, these countries now have vibrant urban areas that attract millions from the rural areas in search of greater opportunities. As a result of this influx of people, cities like Kuala Lumpur, Bangkok, and Jakarta have enormous problems with slums, traffic, and pollution.

China, as always, is a special case. Areas such as Guangdong Province, where the Communist government has loosened economic controls, boast "Asian Tiger" rates of growth, but other regions remain quite poor.

Asia's economic dominance in the next century is by no means assured. Presently, the new wealth is limited to the "Tigers," all of which lie along the continent's eastern and southeastern edges. Many other parts of the vast continent, including Russia and the Indian subcontinent, have no comparable rates of growth and are impoverished. Also, political upheaval could derail the economies of several countries, especially Taiwan, where the shadow of China is long, and Hong Kong.

GDP Growth Rate
- Under 5%
- 5% to 6.99%
- 7% to 10%
- Over 10%

© Rand McNally & Co.
M-569300-3G-EL1-1-1- -1

THE FASTEST–GROWING SOUTHEAST ASIAN ECONOMIES

GDP Growth Rate (12%, 10%, 8%, 6%, 4%, 2%, 0%)

China (excluding Taiwan), Singapore, Vietnam, Malaysia, Laos, South Korea, Thailand, Indonesia, Myanmar, Taiwan, Hong Kong, Cambodia, Philippines, Japan, United States, United Kingdom, Germany

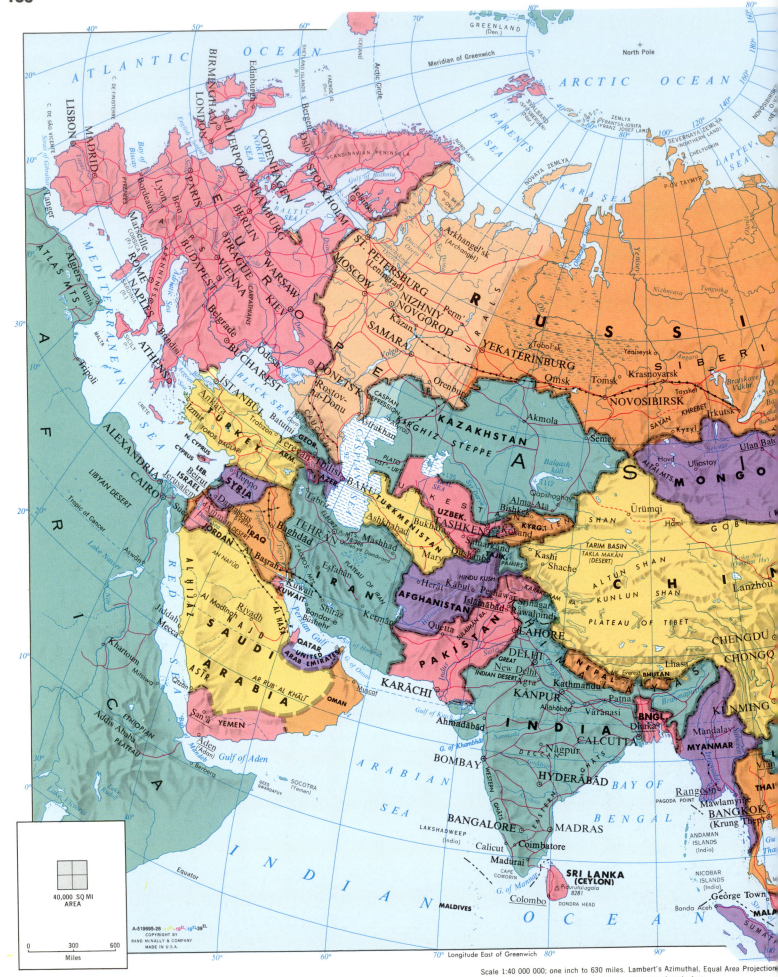

40,000 SQ MI
AREA

0   300   600
Miles

A-519695-26
COPYRIGHT BY
RAND McNALLY & COMPANY
MADE IN U.S.A.

Longitude East of Greenwich

Scale 1:40 000 000; one inch to 630 miles. Lambert's Azimuthal, Equal Area Projection
Elevations and depressions are given in feet

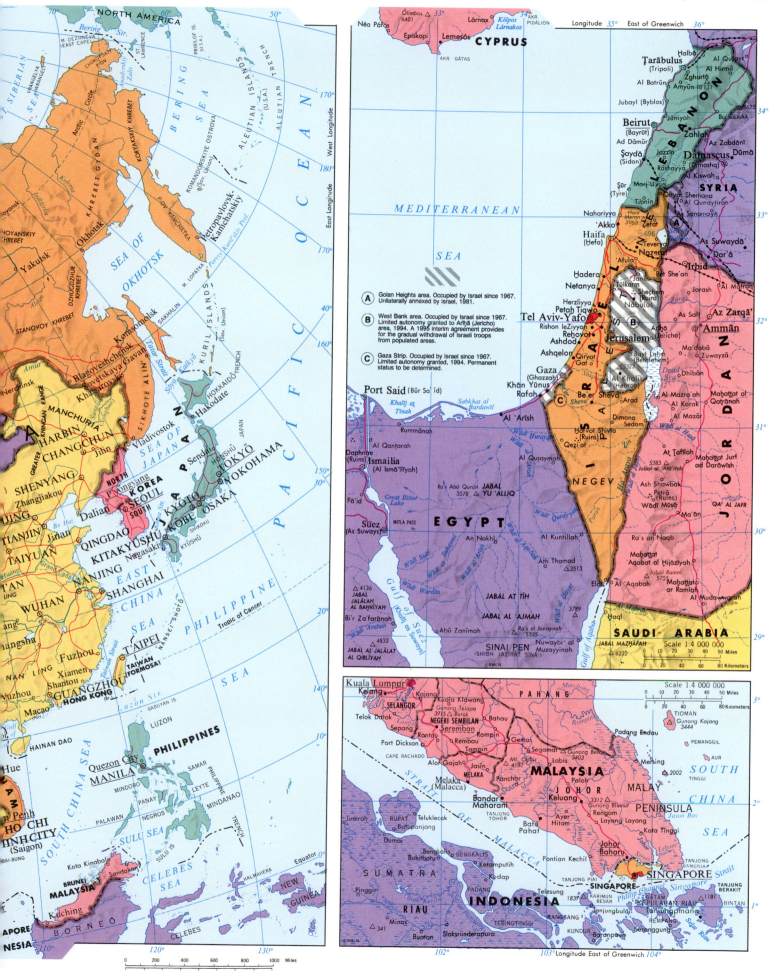

NORTH AMERICA

PACIFIC OCEAN

Arctic Circle

BERING SEA

SEA OF OKHOTSK

ALEUTIAN ISLANDS (U.S.A.)
ALEUTIAN TRENCH

West Longitude
East Longitude

SIBERIAN
SEA OF JAPAN
KURIL ISLANDS (Sov. Union)
SAKHALIN

Yakutsk
Okhotsk
Petropavlovsk-Kamchatskiy
Komsomolsk
Blagoveshchensk
Sovetskaya Gavan
Khabarovsk
Vladivostok
Hakodate
Sendai
TŌKYŌ
YOKOHAMA
KYŌTO
KŌBE
ŌSAKA
Nagasaki
KITAKYŪSHŪ
KYŪSHŪ
HONSHŪ
JAPAN
HOKKAIDŌ

MANCHURIA
HARBIN
CHANGCHUN
SHENYANG
Jilin
NORTH KOREA
Pyongyang
SEOUL
SOUTH KOREA

EAST CHINA SEA
Tropic of Cancer

TAIWAN (FORMOSA)
T'AIPEI

Zhangjiakou
BEIJING
TIANJIN
TAIYUAN
Jinan
QINGDAO
Dalian
NANJING
SHANGHAI
WUHAN
Changsha
Fuzhou
Xiamen
Shantou
GUANGZHOU
HONG KONG (Br.)
Macao

HAINAN DAO

PHILIPPINE SEA

LUZON
Quezon City
MANILA
PHILIPPINES
MINDORO
SAMAR
PANAY
LEYTE
NEGROS
PALAWAN
MINDANAO

SOUTH CHINA SEA

SULU SEA
CELEBES SEA

Kota Kinabalu
Sandakan
BRUNEI
MALAYSIA
Kuching
BORNEO
INDONESIA

Equator

HO CHI MINH CITY (Saigon)

SINGAPORE

CYPRUS
Néa Páfos
Ólimbos 6401
Lárnax
Kólpos Lárnakos
AKR PIDÁLION
Episkopi
Lemesós
AKR. GÁTAS

Longitude 35° East of Greenwich 36°

MEDITERRANEAN SEA

Ţarābulus (Tripoli)
Al Qusayr
Halbā
Al Hirmil
Ad Dāmūr
Zgharta
Amyūn 1013
Jubayl (Byblos)
Jūniyah
Ba'labakk
Beirut (Bayrūt)
Zahlah
Az Zabdānī
Ad Dāmūr
Şaydā (Sidon)
Jazzīn
Damascus (Dimashq)
Dūmā
Rāshayya
Marj 'Uyūn
Şūr (Tyre)
Al Kiswah
Tibnīn
Qiryat Shemona
Al Qunayţirah
As Sanamayn

SYRIA

Naharīyya
Hare Meron 3963
Zefat
696
As Suwaydā'
Akko (Acre)
Teverya
Dar'ā
Haifa (Hefa)
Nazerat
Irbid
Afula
Bet She'an
Jarash
Hadera
Jarash
Al Mafraq
Netanya
Ţūlkarm
Janīn
Shechem (Ruins)
Herzliyya
Nābulus
As Salt
Az Zarqā'
Petah Tiqwa
Tel Aviv-Yafo
Rishon leZiyyon
Arīhā (Jericho)
Amman
Rehovot
Jerusalem
Ma'dabā
Ashdod
Bayt Lahm (Bethlehem)
Zuwayzā'
Ashqelon
Qiryat Gat
3323
Gaza (Ghazzah)
Al Khalīl (Hebron)
Dead Sea
Dhībān
Khān Yūnus
Be'er Sheva
Al Mazra'ah
Rafah
Sheva
Arad
Al Karak
Port Said (Būr Sa'īd)
Dimona
Al Mazār
Khalīj aţ Ţīnah
Sedom
Horvot Shiva (Ruins)
Aţ Ţafīlah
Sabkhat al Bardawil
Qezi'ot
Maḩaţţat Jurf ad Darāwīsh
Al 'Arīsh
5383
Jabal al 'Aţā'itah
Rummānah
Ash Shawbak
Al Qantarah
Al Qusaymah
Petra (Ruins)
Ismailia (Al Ismā'īlīyah)
Wādī Mūsā
Ma'ān
Daphnae (Ruins)
An Nakhl
Fā'id
JABAL YU 'ALLIQ 3578
Al Kuntillah
Ra's an Naqb
Great Bitter Lake
Ath Thamad
3513
Suez (As Suways)
Maḩaţţat 'Aqabat al Hijāziyah
MITLA PASS
Jabal Ramm 3759
EGYPT
NEGEV
Elat
Al 'Aqabah
Maḩaţţat ar Ramlah
4136 JABAL JALĀLAH AL BAHRĪYAH
JABAL AT TĪH
3789
Al Mudawwarah
Bi'r Za'farānah
JABAL AL 'AJMAH
SAUDI ARABIA
4833
JABAL AL JALĀLAT AL QIBLĪYAH
Ra's al Junaynah 5335
JABAL MAZHAFAH
Abū Zanīmah
Nuwaybi' al Muzayyinah
6232
SINAI PEN. (SHIBH JAZĪRAT SĪNĀ')
Haql
Gulf of Suez (Khalīj as Suways)
Wādī 'Arābah
Gulf of Aqaba

LEBANON
ISRAEL
JORDAN

Scale 1:4 000 000
0 10 20 30 40 50 Miles
0 20 40 60 80 Kilometers

(A) Golan Heights area. Occupied by Israel since 1967. Unilaterally annexed by Israel, 1981.

(B) West Bank area. Occupied by Israel since 1967. Limited autonomy granted to Arīhā (Jericho) area, 1994. A 1995 interim agreement provides for the gradual withdrawal of Israeli troops from populated areas.

(C) Gaza Strip. Occupied by Israel since 1967. Limited autonomy granted, 1994. Permanent status to be determined.

Scale 1:4 000 000
0 10 20 30 40 50 Miles
0 20 40 60 80 Kilometers

Kuala Lumpur
Kelang
Kajang
PAHANG
Merchong
Gunung Telapa
Kuala Klawang
3915
Burak
Bahau
Rompin
TIOMAN
Gunong Kajang 3444
SELANGOR
Telok Datok
Sepang
Rantau
Rembau
Gemas
Padang Endau
Port Dickson
Tampin
A Segamat
Gunong Besar 3403
Mersing
PEMANGGIL
NEGERI SEMBILAN
Seremban
Jasin
Labis
AUR
CAPE RACHADO
Alor Gajah
Panchor
Gunong Blumut 3312
MALAYSIA
2002
SOUTH
Melaka (Malacca)
Mt. Ophir 4187
MELAKA
Palob
JOHOR
Keluang
Renggam
TINGGI
Bandar Maharani
Ayer Hitam
Layang Layang
MALAY PENINSULA
CHINA
Batu Pahat
Kota Tinggi
Jason Bay
TANJONG TOHOR
Pontian Kechil
Johor Baharu
SEA
Jumrah
RUPAT
Teluklecak
TANJONG PIAI
Lebam
Batupanjang
TANJONG RAMUNIA
Dumai
Pinggir
TANJUNG BERAKIT
SUMATRA
Bengkalis
BENGKALIS
Ketamputih
SINGAPORE
BATAM
Bukitbatu
SINGAPORE
Phillip Channel
Kudap
Singapore Strait
KEPULAUAN RIAU
Telesung 1837
KARIMUN BESAR
BINTAN
RIAU
Telesung
Bengkong
Sungai Guntung
REMPANG
INDONESIA
341 Minas
Slaksriinderapura
Tanjungbalai
Tanjungpinang
Buatan
TEBINGTINGGI
Baranghan
KUNDUR
Serangung

102° 103° Longitude East of Greenwich 104°

0 200 400 600 800 1000 Miles
0 400 800 1200 1600 Kilometers

Relief

Meters		Feet
3050		10 000
1525		5000
610		2000
305		1000
0	Sea Level	0
		Below Sea Level
152.5		500
1525		5000
3050		10 000
6100		20 000

A-519695-76 -1916-38
COPYRIGHT BY
RAND M°NALLY & COMPANY
MADE IN U.S.A.

Scale 1:40 000 000; one inch to 630 miles. Lambert's Azimuthal, Equal Area Projection
Elevations and depressions are given in feet

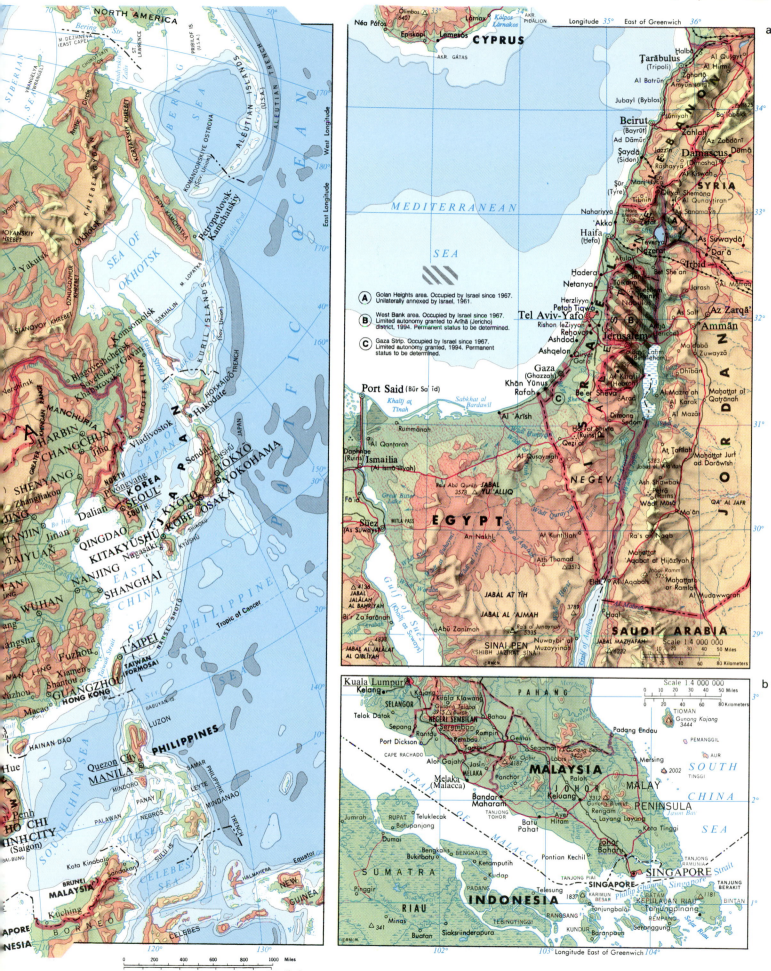

a

Longitude 35°   East of Greenwich   36°

NORTH AMERICA

CYPRUS

MEDITERRANEAN

SEA

Ⓐ Golan Heights area. Occupied by Israel since 1967.
   Unilaterally annexed by Israel, 1961.

Ⓑ West Bank area. Occupied by Israel since 1967.
   Limited autonomy granted to Arīḥā (Jericho)
   district, 1994. Permanent status to be determined.

Ⓒ Gaza Strip. Occupied by Israel since 1967.
   Limited autonomy granted, 1994. Permanent
   status to be determined.

Ṭarābulus (Tripoli)
Beirut (Bayrūt)
Damascus (Dimashq)
SYRIA
Tel Aviv-Yafo
Jerusalem
Amman
JORDAN
Port Said (Būr Saʿīd)
EGYPT
NEGEV
SAUDI ARABIA
SINAI PEN.
(SHIBH JAZĪRAT SĪNĀʾ)

Scale 1:4 000 000
0 10 20 30 40 50 Miles
0 20 40 60 80 Kilometers

SIBERIAN SEA
BERING SEA
SEA OF OKHOTSK
PACIFIC OCEAN
KURIL ISLANDS
ALEUTIAN ISLANDS (U.S.A.)
Petropavlovsk-Kamchatskiy
Komsomolsk
Khabarovsk
Vladivostok
SEA OF JAPAN
SAKHALIN
HOKKAIDO
Hakodate
Sendai
TŌKYŌ
YOKOHAMA
KYŌTO
KŌBE OSAKA
KITAKYŪSHŪ
Nagasaki
KYŪSHŪ
SHIKOKU
HONSHU
JAPAN
KOREA
SOUTH KOREA
SEOUL
Pyongyang
NORTH KOREA
MANCHURIA
HARBIN
CHANGCHUN
SHENYANG
Dalian
BEIJING
TIANJIN
Jinan
QINGDAO
TAIYUAN
NANJING
SHANGHAI
WUHAN
EAST CHINA SEA
Tropic of Cancer
Fuzhou
Xiamen
Shantou
GUANGZHOU
HONG KONG
Macao
TʼAIPEI
TAIWAN (FORMOSA)
HAINAN DAO
PHILIPPINES
MANILA
Quezon City
LUZON
MINDORO
PANAY
SAMAR
LEYTE
NEGROS
PALAWAN
MINDANAO
SULU SEA
CELEBES SEA
BRUNEI
MALAYSIA
Kuching
BORNEO
NEW GUINEA
CELEBES
HALMAHERA
SOUTH CHINA SEA
PHILIPPINE SEA
HO CHI MINH CITY (Saigon)

120°   130°

0 200 400 600 800 1000 Miles
0 400 800 1200 1600 Kilometers

b

Scale 1:4 000 000
0 10 20 30 40 50 Miles
0 20 40 60 80 Kilometers

Kuala Lumpur
Kelang
SELANGOR
PAHANG
NEGERI SEMBILAN
Seremban
Port Dickson
MALAYSIA
JOHOR
Keluang
MALAY PENINSULA
SINGAPORE
STRAIT OF MALACCA
SUMATRA
INDONESIA
RIAU
Dumai
SOUTH CHINA SEA
TIOMAN

102°   103°   Longitude East of Greenwich 104°

BLACK SEA

RUSSIA
Grozny
Fort Shevchenko
KAZA

GEORGIA
Tbilisi
ARMENIA AZERBAIJAN
Yerevan
Baku (Bakı)
CASPIAN SEA
Surface 92 feet below Sea Level

TURKMENISTAN
Krasnovodsk
Ashkhabad
KOPPEH DAGH
Mashhad
UZBEKISTAN
Nukus
Chardzhou
Mary
Kushka
HERAT

İstanbul Boğazı (Bosporus)
İstanbul
Bursa
İzmir
Ankara
TURKEY
Konya
Adana
CYPRUS
NORTH CYPRUS
Nicosia

Tabriz
Orūmiyeh
Rasht
Bandar-e Anzali
Bandar-e Torkeman
Gorgān
ELBURZ MTS
TEHRĀN
Dāmghān
Neyshābūr
Mashhad
AFGH

MEDITERRANEAN SEA

Areas occupied by Israel since 1967

Aleppo
Al Lādhiqīyah
Ḥimṣ
Ḥamāh
SYRIA
Damascus (Dimashq)
Beirut
LEBANON
Haifa
Tel Aviv-Yafo
Jerusalem
ISRAEL
Gaza
JORDAN
Ammān

Al Mawṣil
Irbīl
Kirkūk
As Sulaymānīyah
Tikrīt
BAGHDAD
Karbalā'
An Najaf
IRAQ

Hamadān
Bakhtarān
Qom
Arāk
Borūjerd
Eṣfahān
DASHT-E KAVĪR DESERT
PLATEAU OF IRAN
Yazd
Kermān
Zāhedān

ALEXANDRIA (Al Iskandarīyah)
CAIRO (Al Qāhirah)
Suez (As Suways)
SINAI
EGYPT
Al 'Aqabah

SYRIAN DESERT
Ar Ramādī
Babylon (Ruins)

IRAN
ZAGROS
Dezfūl
Ahvāz
Khorramshahr
Ābādān
Bandar-e Khomeynī
Shīrāz
Persepolis (Ruins)
Rafsanjān

RED SEA
GULF OF SUEZ
GULF OF AQABA

AL ḤIJĀZ
AN NAFŪD
Taymā'
JABAL SHAMMAR
Ḥā'il
SAUDI ARABIA
NAJD
Al Qayṣūmah
KUWAIT
Kuwait (Al Kuwayt)

PERSIAN GULF
Bandar-e Būshehr
RA'S AT TANNŪRAH
Ad Dammām
BAHRAIN
Al Manāmah
QATAR
Ad Dawḥah
Abū Ẓaby
UNITED ARAB EMIRATES
Dubayy
OMAN
Muscat
Matraḥ

GULF OF OMAN
Jāsk
Bandar 'Abbās
Bandar-e Lengeh
Qeshm

Al Jawf
Sakākah
Rafḥā
Badanah
Tabūk

Al Madīnah (Medina)
Buraydah
'Unayzah
Ash Shaqrā'
Riyadh (Ar Riyāḍ)
AL AFLĀJ

Jiddah
Mecca (Makkah)
Aṭ Ṭā'if
Tropic of Cancer
NAFŪD
AD DAHNĀ'
Al Kharmah

SUDAN
Būr Sūdān
Sawākin
Ṭawkar
Al Qunfudhah

A R A B I A
AR RUB' AL KHĀLĪ
OMAN
RA'S AL ḤADD

Abhā
NAJRAN
JABAL AL AKHDAR
Jabal ash Sham 9957
Al Buraymī

ERITREA
Kassalā
Keren
Mitsiwa (Massawa)
Asmera
ETHIOPIA

ṢANʻĀ'
SaʻDah
Ḥajjah
Shibām
Tarīm
Say'ūn
Al Ḥawṭah
HADRAMAWT
RA'S FARTAK

YEMEN
Al Ḥudaydah
Al Mukhā (Mocha)
Ta'izz
Aden ('Adan)
Al Mukallā
Ash Shiḥr
Say'ūn

GULF OF ADEN
DJIBOUTI
Djibouti
SOMALIA
Berbera
SUQUTRA (SOCOTRA) (Yemen)

ARABIAN SEA

Relief

Meters	Feet
3050	10 000
1525	5000
610	2000
305	1000
152.5	500
0 Sea Level	0 Sea Level
152.5	500 Below Sea Level
1525	5000
3050	10 000

A-569400-76 -21 -37
COPYRIGHT BY
RAND McNALLY & COMPANY
MADE IN U.S.A.

Longitude East of Greenwich

Scale 1:16 000 000; one inch to 250 miles. Polyconic Projection
Elevations and depressions are given in feet

a

AFGHANISTAN
PAKISTAN
Dargai
Jalālābād
KHYBER PASS
MORGA RA.
Chārsadda
930
Peshāwar

Scale 1:4 000 000
0 10 20 30 40 Miles
0 20 40 60 Kilometers

b

Scale 1:40 000 000

AFGHANISTAN
JAMMU AND KASHMIR
CHINA
HIMACHAL PRADESH
PUNJAB
XIZAGN (TIBET)
PAKISTAN
HARYANA
UTTAR PRADESH
NEPAL
SIKKIM
BHUTAN
ARUNACHAL PRADESH
NAGALAND
RĀJASTHĀN
BIHAR
ASSAM
MEGHALAYA
BANGLADESH
MIZORAM
Tropic of Cancer
GUJARAT
MADHYA PRADESH
WEST BENGAL
MYANMAR
MAHĀRĀSHTRA
ORISSA
ARABIAN SEA
KARNATAKA
ANDHRA PRADESH
BAY OF BENGAL
KERALA
TAMIL NADU

1 - TRIPURA
2 - MANIPUR
3 - LAKSHADWEEP
4 - DELHI
5 - DĀDRA AND NAGAR HAVELI
6 - PONDICHERRY
7 - GOA, DAMĀN, AND DIU

SRI LANKA (CEYLON)

INDIA · POLITICAL

Continued on pages 188-189

c

Tiruchchirāppalli
Ernākulam
Thanjāvūr
Nāgappattinam
KERALA
TAMIL NADU
Alleppey
Madurai
Jaffna
Quilon
Tuticorin
Trincomalee
Trivandrum
Tirunelveli
CAPE COMORIN
Puttalam
Anurādhapura
Kandy
SRI LANKA (CEYLON)
Colombo
INDIAN OCEAN
Galle
DONDRA HEAD
Matara

Same scale as main map

Area occupied by Pakistan and claimed by India.
Area claimed and occupied by India; status disputed by Pakistan.
Area occupied by China and claimed by India.
Area occupied by India and claimed by China.

0 50 100 200 300 400 500 Miles
0 100 200 400 600 800 Kilometers

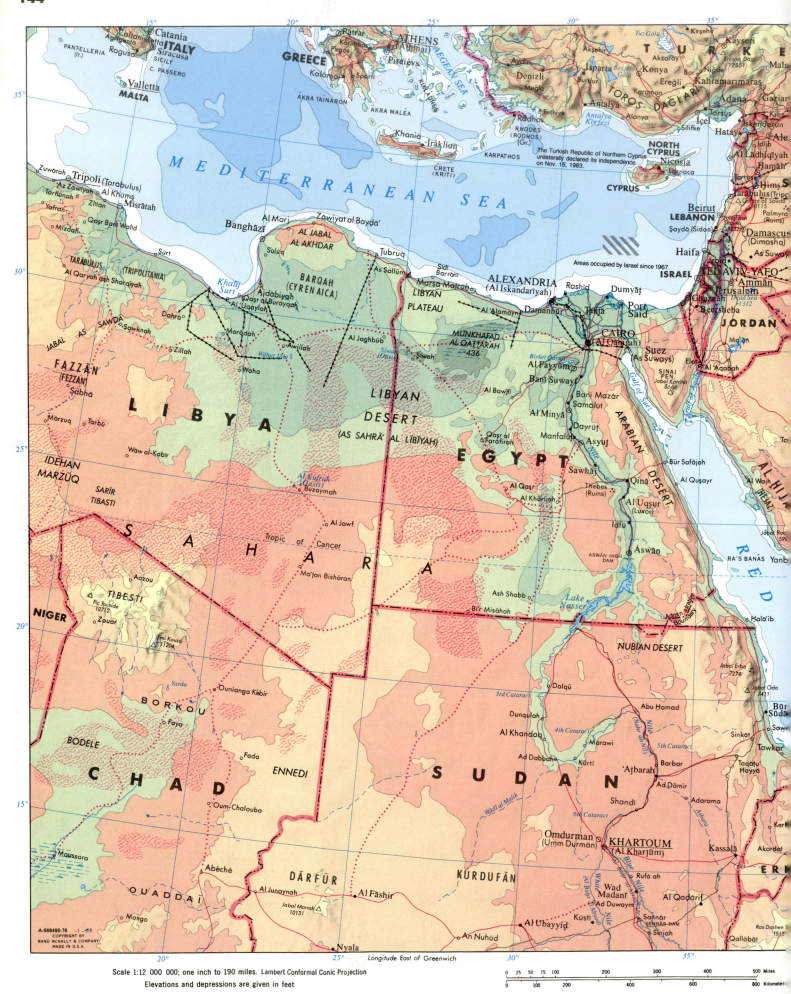

144

Relief

Meters	Feet
3050	10 000
1525	5000
610	2000
305	1000
152.5	500
0 Sea Level	0
	Below
152.5	500 Sea Level
1525	5 000
3050	10 000
6100	20 000

Scale 1:16 000 000; one inch to 250 miles. Polyconic Projection
Elevations and depressions are given in feet

115° 120° 125° 130° 135° 140° 145° 150°

Chinese Provinces, Autonomous Regions (AR) and Municipalities (M)

Conventional Form	—	Pinyin Form
Anhwei	—	Anhui
Chekiang	—	Zhejiang
Fukien	—	Fujian
Heilungkiang	—	Heilongjiang
Honan	—	Henan
Hopeh	—	Hebei
Hunan	—	Hunan
Hupeh	—	Hubei
Inner Mongolia (AR)	—	Nei Monggol
Kansu	—	Gansu
Kiangsi	—	Jiangxi
Kiangsu	—	Jiangsu
Kirin	—	Jilin
Kwangsi (AR)	—	Guangxi Zhuangzú
Kwangtung	—	Guangdong
Kweichow	—	Guizhou
Liaoning	—	Liaoning
Ningsia Hui (AR)	—	Ningxia Huizu
Peking (M)	—	Beijing
Shanghai (M)	—	Shanghai
Shansi	—	Shanxi
Shantung	—	Shandong
Shensi	—	Shaanxi
Sinkiang (AR)	—	Xinjiang Uygur
Szechwan	—	Sichuan
Tibet (AR)	—	Xizang
Tientsin (M)	—	Tianjin
Tsinghai	—	Qinghai
Yunnan	—	Yunnan

(A) Area occupied by Pakistan and claimed by India.
(B) Area claimed by India; status disputed by Pakistan.
(C) Area occupied by China and claimed by India.
(D) Area occupied by India and claimed by China.

Habomai, Shikotan, Kunashiri, and Etorofu, occupied by Russia since 1945 are claimed by Japan pending a final peace treaty.

Relief

Meters	Feet
3050	10 000
1525	5000
610	2000
305	1000
152.5	500
Sea Level	Sea Level
152.5	500
1525	5000
3050	10 000
6100	20 000
	Below Sea Level

A-569700-76   15-11-27
COPYRIGHT BY
RAND MCNALLY & COMPANY
MADE IN U.S.A.

Continued on pages 196-197

Longitude East of Greenwich

0   50   100   200   300   400   500 Miles
0   100   200   400   600   800 Kilometers

Cities and Towns
0 to 50,000 ·
50,000 to 500,000 ○
500,000 to 1,000,000 ◉
1,000,000 and over ◎

SEA OF OKHOTSK

PACIFIC OCEAN

SEA OF JAPAN

YELLOW SEA

EAST CHINA SEA

SOUTH CHINA SEA

PHILIPPINE SEA

Tropic of Cancer

Southeastern Asia

a

Oceania (including Australia and New Zealand)

Bay of Islands, North Island, New Zealand

Oceania is comprised of Australia, New Zealand, eastern New Guinea, and approximately 25,000 other islands in the South Pacific, most of which are uninhabited. Many of the islands are coral atolls, formed by microscopic creatures over scores of centuries, while others are the result of volcanic action.

Oceania's largest landmass is Australia, which at three million square miles (7.7 million sq km) is the world's smallest continent. In fact, it is smaller than five countries—Russia, Canada, China, Brazil, and the United States. Australia is generally flat and dry. The interior is sparsely populated, with most people living in coastal cities such as Sydney.

The next-largest part of Oceania is Papua New Guinea, the country occupying the eastern half of the island of New Guinea, which has some of the most forbidding and remote terrain in the world. New Zealand, Oceania's third-largest country, is known for its natural beauty and its huge herds of sheep.

Oceania at a glance

Land area: 3,300,000 square miles (8,500,000 sq km)

Estimated population (January 1, 1995): 28,400,000

Population density: 8.6/square mile (3.3/sq km)

Mean elevation: 1,000 feet (305 m)

Highest point: Mt. Wilhelm, Papua New Guinea, 14,793 feet (4,509 m)

Lowest point: Lake Eyre, South Australia, 52 feet (16 m) below sea level

Longest river: Murray-Darling, 2,330 mi (3,750 km)

Number of countries (incl. dependencies): 33

Largest independent country: Australia, 2,966,155 square miles (7,682,300 sq km)

Smallest independent country: Nauru, 8.1 square miles (21 sq km)

Most populous independent country: Australia, 18,205,000

Least populous independent country: Tuvalu, 10,000

Largest city: Brisbane, pop. 1,334,017 (1991)

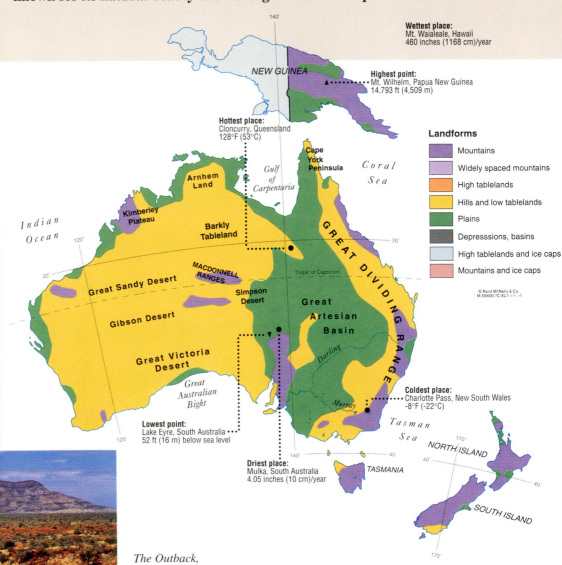

The Outback, Australia

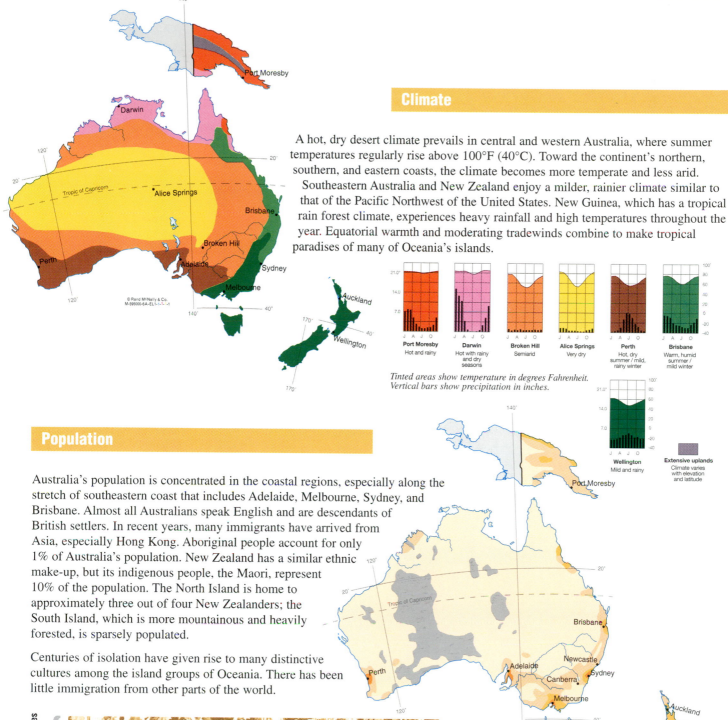

Climate

A hot, dry desert climate prevails in central and western Australia, where summer temperatures regularly rise above 100°F (40°C). Toward the continent's northern, southern, and eastern coasts, the climate becomes more temperate and less arid. Southeastern Australia and New Zealand enjoy a milder, rainier climate similar to that of the Pacific Northwest of the United States. New Guinea, which has a tropical rain forest climate, experiences heavy rainfall and high temperatures throughout the year. Equatorial warmth and moderating tradewinds combine to make tropical paradises of many of Oceania's islands.

Port Moresby — Hot and rainy
Darwin — Hot with rainy and dry seasons
Broken Hill — Semiarid
Alice Springs — Very dry
Perth — Hot, dry summer / mild, rainy winter
Brisbane — Warm, humid summer / mild winter

Tinted areas show temperature in degrees Fahrenheit. Vertical bars show precipitation in inches.

Wellington — Mild and rainy

Extensive uplands — Climate varies with elevation and latitude

Population

Australia's population is concentrated in the coastal regions, especially along the stretch of southeastern coast that includes Adelaide, Melbourne, Sydney, and Brisbane. Almost all Australians speak English and are descendants of British settlers. In recent years, many immigrants have arrived from Asia, especially Hong Kong. Aboriginal people account for only 1% of Australia's population. New Zealand has a similar ethnic make-up, but its indigenous people, the Maori, represent 10% of the population. The North Island is home to approximately three out of four New Zealanders; the South Island, which is more mountainous and heavily forested, is sparsely populated.

Centuries of isolation have given rise to many distinctive cultures among the island groups of Oceania. There has been little immigration from other parts of the world.

Inhabitants per sq. km. (mi.)

- Uninhabited
- <1 (2)
- 1-10 (2-25)
- 10-25 (25-60)
- 25-50 (60-125)
- 50-100 (125-250)
- >100 (250)

© Rand McNally & Co.
M-595000-1P-EL1-·1-·1-

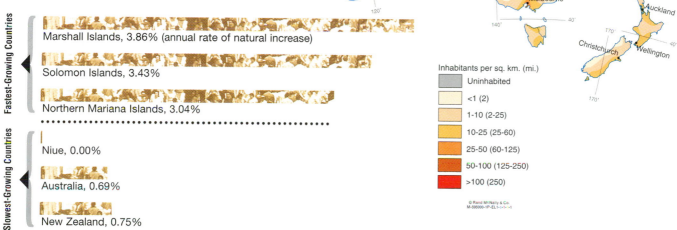

Fastest-Growing Countries

Marshall Islands, 3.86% (annual rate of natural increase)

Solomon Islands, 3.43%

Northern Mariana Islands, 3.04%

Slowest-Growing Countries

Niue, 0.00%

Australia, 0.69%

New Zealand, 0.75%

Environments and Land Use

Much of central and western Australia is a dry, inhospitable land of sand, rocks, and scrub vegetation. Surrounding this desert region is a broad band of semiarid grassland that covers more than half of the continent and supports a huge livestock industry. Australia has more sheep—132 million—than any other country in the world, as well as sizable herds of cattle. The dry climate and sparse plant life, however, mean that each animal requires a dozen or more acres to survive. Six percent of the continent is suitable for crops; most of the arable land is found on fertile plains in the southeast. Major crops include wheat, sugar cane, oats, barley, sorghum, and rice.

Farmland on North Island, New Zealand

Tourism plays an important role in Australia's economy. Among the continent's major attractions are its unusual wildlife, such as kangaroos, koalas, wombats, and platypuses; the Great Barrier Reef, which stretches for 1,250 miles (2,100 km) along the northeastern coast; and the ruggedly beautiful Outback, with its dramatic rock formations such as Ayers Rock (Uluru) and the Olga Rocks.

Thanks to its fertile land and temperate climate, New Zealand has a thriving livestock industry and is a leading world exporter of dairy products and lamb. Thinly populated and with little industry, it is one of the world's least polluted countries. Its pristine beauty encompasses a variety of scenery, including mountains, fjords, glaciers, rain forests, beaches and geysers. Only the country's relative isolation restrains its growing tourism industry.

Dense tropical rain forests blanket much of Papua New Guinea. These forests have thus far escaped the large-scale deforestation that is taking place in other tropical forests around the world.

Tourism is central to the economies of many of the islands throughout Oceania. Abundant sunshine, pleasant temperatures, and beautiful beaches draw millions of visitors each year to islands such as Tahiti and Fiji. For islands with little or no tourism, the economic scene is less promising: many islanders rely on subsistence fishing and foreign aid from former colonial powers.

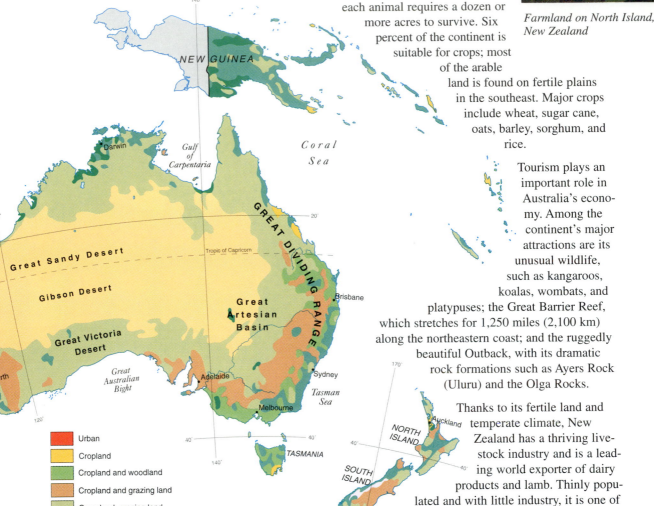

■	Urban
■	Cropland
■	Cropland and woodland
■	Cropland and grazing land
■	Grassland, grazing land
■	Forest, woodland
■	Swamp, marsh
■	Tundra
■	Shrub, sparse grass, wasteland
■	Barren land

© Rand McNally & Co.
M-590200-8L-EL1-

0 100 200 300 400 500 Miles
0 200 400 600 800 Kilometers

Herding sheep near Goulburn, New South Wales

The Original Australians and New Zealanders

Many anthropologists believe that Australia's Aborigines are the oldest race of people on Earth. During the 40,000 years since they migrated to the island continent from Asia, they have developed a rich culture with an intricate spiritual and social life.

The original New Zealanders, the Maoris, arrived from other Polynesian islands in the 10th century. At the beginning of large-scale immigration from Britain in the 1800s, the British government signed a treaty with the Maoris which granted them full rights as citizens. With the exception of some disputes over land, this agreement has paved the way for the historically harmonious relations between the races in New Zealand.

Aboriginal boy with elders, Western Australia

Relations between the Aborigines and whites in Australia have been less harmonious. The arrival of the first European colonists in 1788 set in motion a chain of events that decimated the Aborigines and threatened their unique culture. Disease and skirmishes killed Aborigines along the coast, and thousands of others were forced from their lands by settlers. Some sought refuge with Aborigines already living in Australia's interior, the Outback. Alcoholism and other social problems became common among the Aborigines as they found themselves confronted by a society they did not understand.

Australia was slow to recognize the rights of its first inhabitants. In the early 1960s, official attitudes began to change as public embarrassment grew over the decades of discrimination. A significant step occurred in 1962 when full rights of citizenship were extended to the Aborigines.

Questions of land ownership, however, remain problematic for both

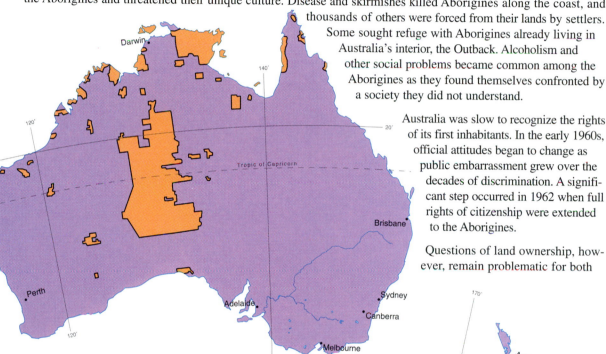

Lands of Australia's Aborigines

Aboriginal reserves

sides. The government has set aside large reserves for the Aborigines, but much of the land is in the continent's hostile interior (see map above). Only in the past two decades has an agreement been reached allowing Aborigines to share in the vast mineral wealth of their northern lands. Recent court decisions have awarded individual Aborigines rights to ancestral lands which were seized by settlers, but many local governments continue to fight these decisions.

In the face of indifference and hostility, there has recently been an upsurge of interest in cultural traditions among the 240,000 Australians of aboriginal descent. Still, many of the traditions of the 500 different tribes that were present 200 years ago have been lost.

I N D O N E S I A

SELARU   TANJUNG VALS

Pasuruan 10932
Singaraja   Rinjani 12225   Lombok Selat   ALOR
Go. Mahameru 12060   Besar   Sumbawa   Bena   LOMBLEN PANTAR   Dili
LOMBOK   FLORES   SUMBAWA   Waingapu   SAVU   TIMOR

A R A F U R A   S E A

SUMBA   SAWU   ROTI   Kupang   SEA

SUMBA   SAWU   ROTI   Kupang

S U N D A

S U N D A   I S L A N D S

SUNDA TRENCH

TIMOR   SEA

CAPE   VAN DIEMEN   CROKER
Dundas   Van Diemen   BUCKLING PEN.   WESSEL IS.
BATHURST   Gulf   Clarence Str.   CAPE ARNHEM
MELVILLE
Darwin   Blue Mud Bay   GROOTE
Anson Bay   Daly   ARNHEM LAND   EYLANDT   GULF O
Pine Creek   Limmen   SIR EDWARD PELLEW
Katherine   Bight   GROUP
Roper   CARPENTAR

I N D I A N

CAPE LONDONDERRY   Joseph
Bonaparte Gulf
Collier Bay   WELLESLE
Buccaneer   Queens   BURKETOWN
O C E A N   Sunday Str.   ARCH.   Wyndham   Ch'n   Leichhar

KING   Mt Hann   Ord   Victoria River   Birdum   Borroloola   QU
CAPE LEVEQUE   King Sd.   2800   Downs   Daly Waters
DAMPIER   Derby   GEIKIE   LEOPOLD   RANGES   NORTHERN   Newcastle Waters
BROOME   RANGE   Fitzroy   Halls Creek
LAND   Fitzroy   Crossing   Woods   Burketown
Roebuck Bay   LaGrange   Tanami   TERRITORY   Tennant Creek   Camooweal

EIGHTY MILE BEACH   GREAT SANDY DESERT   Mackay   Mount Isa   Ma
LARREY POINT   Barrow Creek   Dajari
RIPON   MacDonald
MONTE BELLO IS.   DAMPIER   Port Hedland   DeGrey   Mt. Ziel   RANGES   Arltunga   Birdville
BARROW   ARCH.   Roebourne   Forteseue   4955   Alice Springs   SIMPSON   QI
NORTH WEST CAPE   Marble Bar   HAMERSLEY   RANGE   JAMES RANGE   Dobb
Millstream   Nullagine   MACDONNELL   Finke   Charlotte   DESERT
Onslow   Mt. Bruce   Jiggalong   Amadeus   Ayers Rock   Waters   Birdsville
Ashburton   4052   Disappointment   2844   MUSGRAVE RANGES
POINT CLOATES   Carey   GIBSON DESERT   Mt. Woodroffe   4724   Oodnadatta
Tropic of Capricorn   W E S T E R N   EVERARD RANGES   The Alberga
CAPE FARQUHAR   Gascoyne   Peak Hill   Carnegie   Gillen   Cooper

Geographe Chan.   Carnarvon   Nabberu   Wells   S O U T H   A U S T R A L I A   William Creek   39
BERNIER   Austin   Wiluna   Stuart Range   Marree
DORRE   Meekatharra   GREAT VICTORIA DESERT   Oodnadatta
Shark Bay   Nannine   A U S T R A L I A   Everard   Pimba   FLINDERS RANGES
DIRK HARTOG   Cue   Sandstone   Yeo   Hughes   Ooldea Station   Woomera   Farina
STEEP POINT   Mount   Laverton   Penong   Pimba
Ajana   Magnet   Ballard   Menzies   NULLARBOR   Ceduna   Pt. Augu
Northampton   Carey   GREAT VICTORIA DESERT   Whyalla   Port Pirie
HOUTMAN ROCKS   Mingenew   Barlee   Rawlinna   PLAIN   Moonta   Gladsto
Geraldton   Moore   Kalgoorlie-Boulder   POINT FOWLER   EYRE   Wallaroo
Dongara   Pithara   Coolgardie   Goddards Soak   Eucla   PENINSULA   Port Wa
Miling   Lake Brown   Lefroy   Rawlinna   Eyre   Port Lincoln   Pete
Moora   Southern Cross   Cowan   Norseman   GREAT AUSTRALIAN BIGHT   Gaw
Northam   SWANLAND   Dundas   Salmon Gums   KANGAROO   Ad
Perth   York   Norseman   Kings
Fremantle   Narrogin   Ravensthorpe   CAPE JAFF
Collie   Esperance   Mt.
Geographe Bay   Bunbury   Katanning   Hopetoun
CAPE NATURALISTE   Busselton   ARCHIPELAGO
Nornalup   OF THE RECHERCHE
CAPE LEEUWIN   Albany
PT. D'ENTRECASTEAUX   King George Sd.
WEST CAPE HOWE

I N D I A N   O C E A N

40,000 SQ MI
AREA

0   100   200
Miles

A-590200-26   -5EL -5EL-15EL
COPYRIGHT BY
RAND McNALLY & COMPANY
MADE IN U.S.A.

Longitude 115° East of Greenwich   120°   125°   130°   135°

Scale 1:16 000 000; one inch to 250 miles. Lambert's Azimuthal, Equal Area Project
Elevations and depressions are given in feet

PAPUA NEW GUINEA
NEW GUINEA
Port Moresby
Buna
Port Edward
OWEN STANLEY MTS.
Victoria 13363
Torres Strait
Samarai
SOUTH CAPE
TROBRIAND IS.
WOODLARK
D'ENTRECASTEAUX ISLANDS
LOUISIADE ARCHIPELAGO
TAGULA
ROSSEL
BANKS
HORN
GRAVE
CE OF
les

CHOISEUL
VELLA LAVELLA
NEW GEORGIA
RENDOVA
FLORIDA
RUSSELL IS.
GUADALCANAL
HONIARA
TULAGI
SANTA ISABEL
MALAITA
SOLOMON ISLANDS
SAN CRISTÓBAL
RENNELL
SANTA CRUZ ISLANDS

CAPE YORK PENINSULA
CAPE MELVILLE
OSPREY REEF

CORAL SEA

TORRES IS.
BANKS ISLANDS
ESPÍRITU SANTO
NEW HEBRIDES
MAEWO
PENTECOST
MALEKULA
AMBRIM
EPI
VANUATU
EFATE
Port Vila
EROMANGA
TANA
ANEITYUM

CAPE
YORK
PENINSULA

ATHERTON
Cooktown
Laura
Palmerville
Mungana
PLATEAU
Croydon
Forsayth
Cairns
Mt. Bartle Frere 5322
Ingham
HINCHINBROOK I.
Halifax Bay
Townsville
GREAT BARRIER REEF
HOLMES REEFS
WILLIS IS.
FLINDERS REEFS
LIHOU REEF
TREGROSSE IS.
MARION REEF

GREGORY RANGE
GREAT DIVIDING RANGE
Richmond
Kynuna
Hughenden
Charters Towers
Bowen
Mt. Dalrymple 4190
Mackay
WHITSUNDAY I.
CUMBERLAND IS.
REPULSE BAY
NORTHUMBERLAND IS.
SWAIN REEFS
WRECK REEFS

PACIFIC OCEAN

ÎLES CHESTERFIELD (Fr.)
ÎLES BÉLEP
OUVÉA
LIFOU
ÎLES LOYAUTÉ (French)
MARÉ
NEW CALEDONIA (Fr.)
Nouméa
ÎLE DES PINS
Tropic of Capricorn

QUEENSLAND
GREAT DIVIDING RANGE
Winton
Longreach
Barcaldine
Jericho
Clermont
Emerald
Dingo
Mount Morgan
Rockhampton
CURTIS
Gladstone
Yaraka
Blackall
Tambo
BUCKLAND TABLELAND
Capricorn Chan.
Thargomindah
Quilpie
Charleville
Roma
Bundaberg
Hervey Bay
SANDY CAPE
FRASER
Maryborough
Gympie
Windorah
Yamma
Hungerford
Cunnamulla
St. George
DARLING DOWNS
Dalby
Toowoomba
Ipswich
Brisbane
N. STRADBROKE I.
Southport
Warwick
Dirranbandi
Mungindi
Goondiwindi

NEW SOUTH WALES
Bourke
Brewarrina
Walgett
Moree
Inverell
Glen Innes
Tenterfield
Lismore
Grafton
NEW ENGLAND RANGE
The Round Mountain 5300
Wilcannia
Cobar
Nyngan
Coonamble
Narrabri
Tamworth
Armidale
WARRUMBUNGLE RA.
Kempsey
Port Macquarie
Nymagee
Dubbo
LIVERPOOL RA.
Forbes
Maitland
Newcastle
West Wyalong
Bathurst
Orange
Cessnock
BLUE MTS.
SYDNEY
Wollongong
Narrandera
Wagga Wagga
Canberra
AUSTL. CAP. TER.
Jervis Bay
Albury
Cooma
SNOWY MTS.
Kosciusko 7316
Bega
Bombala
CAPE HOWE

LORD HOWE (NEW S. WALES)

BARRIER RANGE
en Hill
RIVERINA
REGION
MURRAY
Wentworth
Swan Hill
Kerang
Echuca
Deniliquin

VICTORIA
Bendigo
Ballarat
Maryborough
Benalla
731
GREAT DIVIDING RANGE
Geelong
MELBOURNE
Port Phillip Bay
Warrnambool
CAPE OTWAY
Wonthaggi
Sale
NINETY MILE BEACH
WILSON'S PROMONTORY
Bairnsdale

TASMANIA
Burnie
Ulverstone
Devonport
Strahan
Mt. Ossa 5305
Launceston
New Norfolk
Hobart
SOUTH EAST CAPE
BRUNY
KING
FLINDERS
FURNEAUX GROUP
CAPE BARREN
HUNTER IS.
BASS STRAIT

TASMAN SEA

New Zealand inset

a

PACIFIC OCEAN

NORTH CAPE
Kaitaia
Russell
GREAT BARRIER
Hauraki Gulf
Devonport
Auckland
NORTH ISLAND
Hamilton
Bay of Plenty
EAST CAPE
North Taranaki Bight
New Plymouth
C. EGMONT
Gisborne
NEW ZEALAND
Lake Ruapehu 9177
Napier
South Taranaki Bight
Wanganui
Hastings
Palmerston North
CAPE FAREWELL
Tasman Bay
Nelson
Lower Hutt
Wellington
Cook Strait
Karamea Bight
CAPE FOULWIND
Greymouth
Hokitika
Pegasus Bay
SOUTH ISLAND
SOUTHERN ALPS
Mt. Cook 12316
Christchurch
Canterbury Bight
Timaru
CASCADE PT.
RESOLUTION ISLAND
Dunedin
CAPE SAUNDERS
Invercargill
Foveaux Strait
STEWART ISLAND
SOUTHWEST CAPE

TASMAN SEA

PACIFIC OCEAN

Same scale as main map

Cities and Towns		
0 to 50,000	500,000 to 1,000,000	
50,000 to 500,000	1,000,000 and over	

0 50 100 200 300 500 Miles
0 100 200 400 600 800 Kilometers

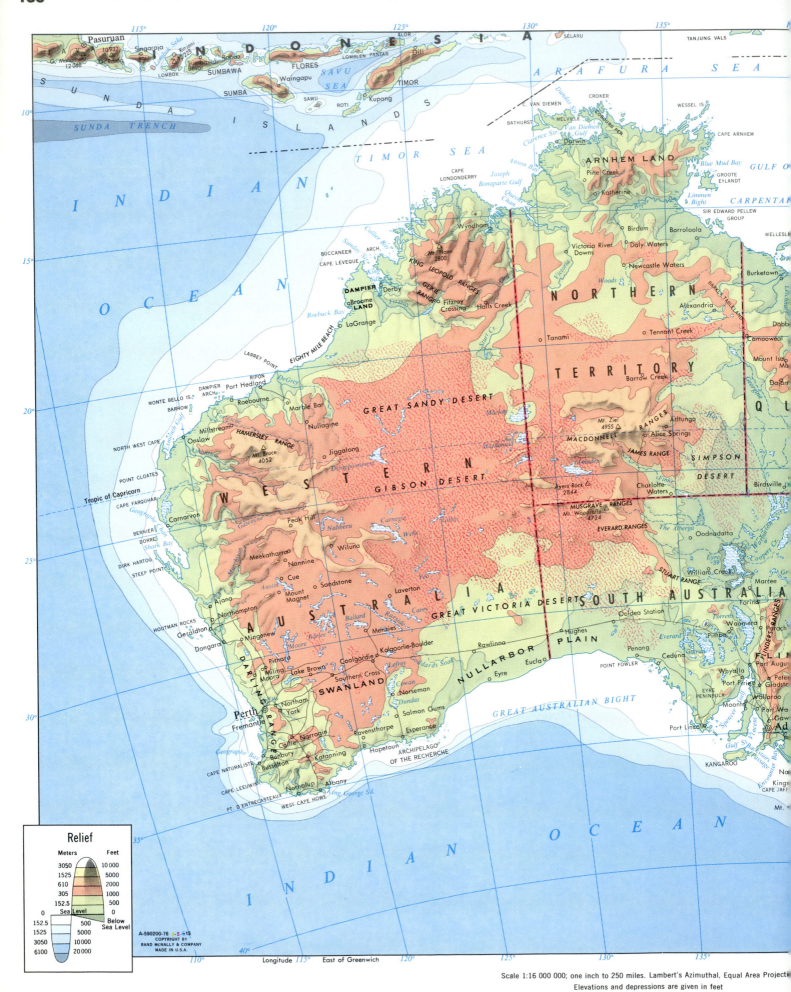

Relief

Meters		Feet
3050		10 000
1525		5000
610		2000
305		1000
152.5		500
0	Sea Level	0
		Below Sea Level
152.5		500
1525		5000
3050		10 000
6100		20 000

A-590200-76
COPYRIGHT BY
RAND McNALLY & COMPANY
MADE IN U.S.A.

Scale 1:16 000 000; one inch to 250 miles. Lambert's Azimuthal, Equal Area Projection
Elevations and depressions are given in feet

Cities and Towns		
0 to 50,000	○	500,000 to 1,000,000 ◎
50,000 to 500,000 ⊙		1,000,000 and over

Same scale as main map

Scale bars: 0 50 100 200 300 400 500 Miles / 0 100 200 400 600 800 Kilometers

RUSSIA

KAZAKHSTAN

MONGOLIA

Irkutsk
Ulan Bator
GOBI DESERT

MANCHURIA
CHANGCHUN
HARBIN
SHENYANG
BEIJING
TIANJIN
Dalian
KOREA
SEOUL (Sŏul)
Vladivostok
HOKKAIDO
TOKYO
YOKOHAMA
KŌBE
KITAKYUSHU
Nagasaki
KYUSHU

CHINA
KUNLUN SHAN
NANJING
WUHAN
SHANGHAI
Fuzhou
T'AIPEI
TAIWAN (FORMOSA)
GUANGZHOU
Hanoi
HONG KONG (Br.)
HAINAN DAO
Hue

SEA OF OKHOTSK
Petropavlovsk-Kamchatskiy
KAMCHATKA
KURIL IS.
SEA OF JAPAN
BERING SEA
KOMANDORSKIYE OSTROVA
ALEUTIAN IS.
Unalaska
Nome
ST. LAWRENCE
ALASKA (U.S.)

JAPAN CURRENT

BONIN IS. (Japan)
MARCUS (Japan)
MIDWAY IS. (U.S.A)
WAKE (U.S.A.)
INTERNATIONAL DATE LINE

Tropic of Cancer

PHILIPPINE SEA
MANILA
PHILIPPINES
LUZON
SAMAR
MINDANAO
PALAU

SOUTH CHINA SEA
THAILAND
BANGKOK
CAMBODIA
VIETNAM
HO CHI MINH CITY (Saigon)
Gulf of Thailand
MALAY PENINSULA
MALAYSIA
Bandar Seri Begawan
BRUNEI
MALAYSIA
SINGAPORE
SUMATRA
INDONESIA
JAKARTA
JAVA SEA
CELEBES SEA
CELEBES
BORNEO
MOLUCCAS
CERAM
HALMAHERA
Manokwari
Jayapura (Sukarnapura)

NORTH EQUATORIAL CURRENT
MICRONESIA
NORTHERN MARIANA ISLANDS (U.S.A.)
MARIANA IS.
GUAM (U.S.A.)
CAROLINE IS.
FEDERATED STATES OF MICRONESIA
MARSHALL IS.
MARSHALL ISLANDS
NAURU
GILBERT IS.
HOWLAND (U.S.A.)
BAKER (U.S.A.)
KANTON
PHOENIX IS.
KIRIBATI

Equator

MELANESIA
PAPUA NEW GUINEA
NEW IRELAND
NEW BRITAIN
BISMARCK ARCH.
BOUGAINVILLE
Port Moresby
SOUTH CAPE
SOLOMON ISLANDS
TUVALU
TOKELAU
WALLIS AND FUTUNA
WESTERN SAMOA

ARAFURA SEA
TIMOR SEA
TIMOR
Darwin
Gulf of Carpentaria
THURSDAY CAPE YORK
CORAL SEA
NEW HEBRIDES
VANUATU
FIJI
NEW CALEDONIA
TONGA

CHRISTMAS (Austl.)
NORTH WEST CAPE
GREAT SANDY DESERT
Tropic of Capricorn
MACDONNELL RANGES
AUSTRALIA
GREAT DIVIDING RANGE
EAST AUSTRALIAN CURRENT
Brisbane
NORFOLK (Austl.)
KERMADEC (N.Z.)

Perth
Fremantle
Great Australian Bight
Albany
Torrens
Murray
Adelaide
Canberra
SYDNEY
MELBOURNE
TASMAN SEA
NORTH CAPE
NORTH ISLAND
Auckland
NEW ZEALAND
Wellington

INDIAN OCEAN
Hobart
TASMANIA
SOUTH EAST CAPE
BASS STRAIT
SOUTH ISLAND
STEWART
SOUTHWEST CAPE
Dunedin

Relief

Meters	Feet
3050	10 000
1525	5000
610	2000
305	1000
152.5	500
Sea Level	0
0	0
152.5	500
1525	5000
3050	10 000
6100	20 000

A-598500-76 40 G-25
COPYRIGHT BY
RAND McNALLY & COMPANY
MADE IN U.S.A.

→ Warm ocean currents
→ Cold ocean currents

Longitude East of Greenwich

Scale 1:50 000 000; one inch to 800 miles. Goode's Homolosine Equal Area Projection
Elevations and depressions are given in feet

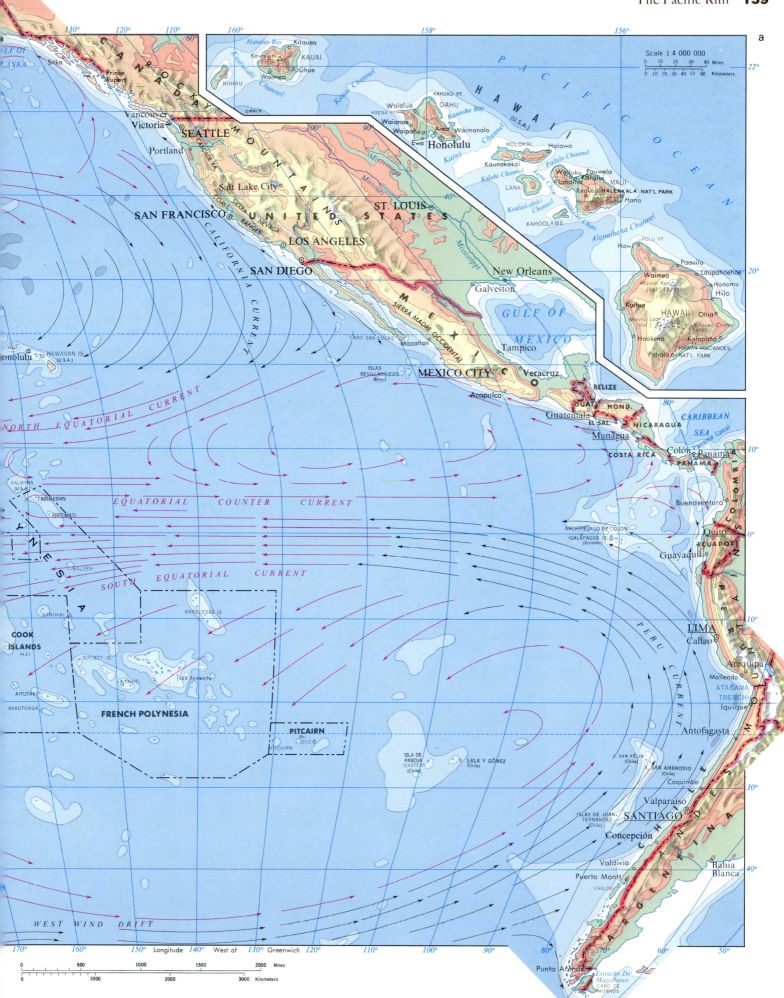

Relief

Meters		Feet
3050		10 000
1525		5000
610		2000
305		1000
0	Sea Level	0
	500	Below
152.5	5000	Sea Level
1525		
3050	10 000	
6100	20 000	

A-594000-76 4-7-17
COPYRIGHT BY
RAND McNALLY & COMPANY
MADE IN U.S.A.

ANTARCTICA IN PROFILE

SECTION ALONG LINE AB

			South Pole			Framnes	
15000						Mts.	15000
10000		Horlick Mts.					10000
5000							5000
Feet (A)	Byrd Basin		Polar Basin		Sea Level		(B) Feet
5000							5000

Scale 1: 60 000 000; (approximate)
Lambert's Azimuthal, Equal Area Projection
Elevations and depressions are given in feet

Glossary

Foreign Geographical Terms

- Afk. — Afrikaans
- Ara. — Arabic
- Ber. — Berber
- Blg. — Bulgarian
- Bur. — Burmese
- Cbd. — Cambodian
- Ch. — Chinese
- Czech — Czech
- Dan. — Danish
- Du. — Dutch
- Est. — Estonian
- Finn. — Finnish
- Fr. — French
- Gae. — Gaelic
- Ger. — German
- Gr. — Greek
- Heb. — Hebrew
- Ice. — Icelandic
- Indon. — Indonesian
- It. — Italian
- Jpn. — Japanese
- Kor. — Korean
- Lao. — Laotian
- Lapp. — Lappish
- Mal. — Malay
- Mong. — Mongolian
- Nor. — Norwegian
- Pas. — Pashto
- Per. — Persian
- Pol. — Polish
- Port. — Portuguese
- Rom. — mountains
- Rus. — Russian
- S./C. — Serbo-Croatian
- Slo. — Slovak
- Sp. — Spanish
- Swe. — Swedish
- Thai — Thai
- Tib. — Tibetan
- Tur. — Turkish
- Ukr. — Ukranian
- Viet. — Vietnamese
- Viet. — Vietnamese

- **-å,** Dan., Nor., Swe. — river
- **āb,** Per. — river
- **ada(lar),** Tur. — island(s)
- **adrar,** Ber. — mountains
- **ákra, akrotírion,** Gr. — cape
- **altos,** Sp. — mountains, hills
- **-älv,-älven,** Swe. — river
- **-ån,** Swe. — river
- **archipel,** Fr. — archipelago
- **archipiélago,** Sp. — archipelago
- **arquipélago,** Port. — archipelago
- **arroyo,** Sp. — brook
- **-ås,-åsen,** Swe. — hills
- **baai,** Du. — bay
- **bab,** Ara. — strait
- **Bach,** Ger. — brook, creek
- **-backen,** Swe. — hill
- **bælt,** Dan. — strait
- **bahía,** Sp. — bay
- **bahr, baḩr,** Ara. — river, sea
- **baía,** Port. — bay
- **baie,** Fr. — bay
- **-bana,** Jpn. — cape
- **banco,** Sp. — bank
- **bandao,** Ch. — peninsula
- **bassin,** Fr. — basin
- **batang,** Indon. — river
- **bātlāq,** Per. — marsh
- **ben,** Gae. — mountain
- **Berg,** Ger. — mountain, hill
- **-berg,** Afk. — mountains
- **Berge,** Ger. — mountains
- **bi'r,** Ara. — well
- **birkat,** Ara. — lake
- **bocca,** It. — river mouth, pass
- **boğazı,** Tur. — strait
- **bogd,** Mong. — range
- **bolsón,** Sp. — enclosed basin
- **-breen,** Nor. — glacier
- **Brücke,** Ger. — bridge
- **Bucht,** Ger. — bay
- **bugt,** Dan. — bay
- **bukit,** Indon., Mal. — mountain, hill
- **-bukten,** Swe. — bay
- **bulu,** Indon. — mountain
- **Burg,** Ger. — castle
- **burn,** Gae. — brook
- **burnu, burun,** Tur. — cape
- **cabezas,** Sp. — peaks
- **cabo,** Port., Sp. — cape
- **campo,** It. — plain
- **cap,** Fr., Cat. — cape
- **capo,** It. — cape
- **catena,** Sp. — range
- **cayo(s),** Sp. — cay(s), islet(s)
- **cerro(s),** Sp. — mountain(s), hill(s)
- **chaîne,** Fr. — range
- **château,** Fr. — castle
- **chiang,** Ch. — harbor, harbour
- **chott,** Ara. — intermittent lake, salt marsh
- **cima,** It., Sp. — peak
- **città,** It. — city
- **ciudad,** Sp. — city
- **co,** Tib. — lake
- **co., cerro,** Sp. — mountain, hill
- **col,** Fr. — pass
- **colina(s),** Sp. — hill(s)
- **colline,** It. — hills
- **collines,** Fr. — hills
- **con,** Viet. — islands
- **cord., cordillera,** Sp. — range
- **costa,** Sp. — coast
- **côte,** Fr. — coast, hills
- **cuchilla,** Sp. — hills, ridge
- **dağ, dağı,** Tur. — mountain
- **dāgh,** Per. — mountains
- **-dake,** Jpn. — mountain
- **-dal, -dalen,** Nor., Swe. — valley
- **danau,** Indon. — lake
- **dao,** Ch., Viet. — island
- **daryācheh,** Per. — lake
- **dasht,** Per. — desert
- **deniz, denizi,** Tur. — sea
- **desierto,** Sp. — desert
- **détroit,** Fr. — strait
- **dijk,** Du. — dike
- **distrito,** Sp. — district
- **djebel,** Ara. — mountain(s)
- **-do,** Kor. — island
- **-elv,-elva,** Nor. — river
- **embalse,** Sp. — reservoir
- **erg,** Ara. — sand desert
- **estrecho,** Sp. — strait
- **étang,** Fr. — pond
- **-ey,** Ice. — island
- **fjäll(en),** Swe. — mountain(s)
- **fjället,** Swe. — mountain
- **fjärden,** Swe. — fjord
- **-fjell, -fjellet,** Nor. — mountain
- **-fjord,** Nor. — fjord
- **-fjorden,** Nor., Swe. — fjord, lake
- **-fjörur,** Ice. — fjord, bay
- **-flói,** Ice. — bay
- **foce,** It. — river mouth, pass
- **forêt,** Fr. — forest
- **-forsen,** Swe. — waterfall
- **Forst,** Ger. — forest
- **-foss,** Ice. — waterfall
- **-fossen,** Nor. — waterfall
- **g., gora,** Rus. — mountain, hill
- **g., gunong,** Mal. — mountain
- **gang,** Ch. — bay
- **-gang,** Kor. — river
- **gave,** Fr. — mountain torrent
- **gebergte,** Du. — range
- **Gebirge,** Ger. — range
- **Gipfel,** Ger. — peak
- **göl,** Tur. — lake
- **golfe,** Fr. — gulf
- **golfete,** Sp. — bay
- **golfo,** It., Sp. — gulf
- **gölü,** Tur. — lake
- **gora,** Rus. — mountain, hill
- **gora,** S./C. — mountains
- **góra,** Pol. — mountain
- **gory,** Rus. — mountains, hills
- **góry,** Pol. — mountains
- **gr'ada,** Rus. — ridge
- **guba,** Rus. — bay
- **gunong,** Mal. — mountain
- **gunung,** Indon. — mountain
- **-guntō,** Jpn. — islands
- **Haff,** Ger. — lagoon
- **hai,** Ch. — sea, lake
- **-hama,** Jpn. — beach
- **hamada,** Ara. — desert
- **hāmūn,** Per. — lake, marsh
- **-hantō,** Jpn. — peninsula
- **hare,** Heb. — mountains, hills
- **-hav,** Swe. — sea, bay
- **havre,** Fr. — harbor, harbour
- **he,** Ch. — river
- **ho,** Ch. — river
- **-ho,** Kor. — reservoir
- **-holm,** Dan. — island
- **hora,** Czech, Slo. — mountain
- **Horn,** Ger. — point, peak
- **hu,** Ch. — lake, reservoir
- **Hügel,** Ger. — hill
- **-huk,** Swe. — cape
- **ig., igarapé,** Port. — river
- **île(s),** Fr. — island(s)
- **îlet(s),** Fr. — islet(s)
- **ilha(s),** Port. — island(s)
- **ilhéu(s),** Port. — islet(s)
- **Insel(n),** Ger. — island(s)
- **isla(s),** Sp. — island(s)
- **isola,** It. — island
- **isole,** It. — islands
- **istmo,** Sp. — isthmus
- **jabal,** Ara. — mountain(s)
- **järv,** Est. — lake
- **-järvi,** Finn. — lake
- **jazā'ir,** Ara. — islands
- **jazirah,** Indon. — peninsula
- **jiang,** Ch. — river
- **-jima,** Jpn. — island
- **-joki,** Finn. — river
- **-jökull,** Ice. — glacier
- **-kai,** Jpn. — sea
- **-kaikyō,** Jpn. — strait
- **-kaise,** Lapp. — mountain
- **kali,** Indon. — brook
- **kandao,** Pas. — pass
- **-kang,** Kor. — river
- **-kapp,** Nor. — cape
- **kepulauan,** Indon. — islands
- **khalīj,** Ara. — gulf
- **khrebet,** Russ., Ukr. — range
- **-ko,** Jpn. — lake, lagoon
- **-kō,** Jpn. — harbor, harbour
- **kólpos,** Gr. — bay
- **Kopf,** Ger. — peak
- **körfezi,** Tur. — gulf, bay
- **kosa,** Rus., Ukr. — spit
- **kou,** Ch. — bay, pass
- **kuala,** Mal. — bay
- **kūh(ha),** Per. — mountain(s)
- **la,** Tib. — pass
- **lac(s),** Fr. — lake(s)
- **lag., laguna,** Sp. — lagoon, lake
- **lago,** It., Port., Sp. — lake
- **lagoa,** Port. — lake, lagoon
- **laguna,** Sp. — lagoon, lake
- **lagune,** Fr. — lagoon
- **laht,** Est. — bay
- **-lahti,** Finn. — gulf
- **län,** Swe. — county
- **laut,** Indon. — sea
- **liedao,** Ch. — islands
- **liman,** Rus. — estuary
- **ling,** Ch. — mountain(s), peak
- **llano(s),** Sp. — plain(s)
- **loch,** Gae. — lake, inlet
- **lomas,** Sp. — hills
- **lough,** Gae. — lake
- **lyman,** Ukr. — estuary
- **-maa,** Est. — island
- **-man,** Kor. — bay
- **mar,** Sp., It. — sea
- **marais,** Fr. — marsh
- **mare,** It. — sea
- **massif,** Eng., Fr. — massif
- **Meer,** Ger. — sea, lake
- **mer,** Fr. — sea
- **mesa,** Sp. — mesa
- **meseta,** Sp. — plateau
- **-misaki,** Jpn. — cape
- **mont,** Fr. — mount
- **montagna,** It. — mountain
- **montagne(s),** Fr. — mountain(s)
- **montaña(s),** Sp. — mountain(s)
- **monte,** It., Port., Sp. — mount
- **montes,** Port., Sp. — mountains
- **monti,** It. — mountains
- **monts,** Fr. — mountains
- **more,** Rus., Ukr. — sea
- **morne,** Fr. — mountain
- **morro,** Port., Sp. — hill, mountain
- **mui,** Viet. — point
- **munkhafad,** Ara. — depression
- **munţii,** Rom. — mountains
- **-nada,** Jpn. — sea, gulf
- **nafūd,** Ara. — desert
- **nagor'ye,** Rus. — plateau, mountains
- **-näs,** Swe. — peninsula
- **ness,** Gae. — promontory
- **nos,** Blg. — cape
- **nuruu,** Mong. — mountains
- **nuur,** Mong. — lake
- **-ø,** Dan., Nor. — island
- **-ö,** Swe. — island
- **o., ostrov,** Rus. — island
- **óros,** Gr. — mountain(s)
- **ostriv,** Ukr. — island
- **ostrov(a),** Rus. — island(s)
- **otok,** S./C. — island
- **ouadi,** Ara. — wadi
- **oued,** Ara. — wadi
- **-øy, -øya,** Nor. — island
- **oz., ozero,** Rus., Ukr. — lake
- **pampa,** Sp. — plain
- **pas,** Fr. — strait
- **paso,** Sp. — pass
- **Pass,** Ger. — pass
- **passe,** Fr. — passage
- **passo,** It. — pass
- **peg., pegunungan,** Indon. — mountains
- **pélagos,** Gr. — sea
- **peña,** Sp. — peak, rock
- **península,** Sp. — peninsula
- **pertuis,** Fr. — strait
- **peski,** Rus. — sand desert
- **phnum,** Cbd. — mountain
- **phou,** Lao. — mountain
- **pic,** Fr. — peak
- **pico(s),** Port., Sp. — peak(s)
- **-piggen,** Nor. — mountain
- **pik,** Rus. — peak
- **pique,** Fr. — peak
- **piton(s),** Fr. — peak(s)
- **pivostriv,** Ukr. — peninsula
- **planalto,** Port. — plateau
- **planina,** S./C. — mountain, range
- **plato,** Afk., Blg., Rus. — plateau
- **playa,** Sp. — beach
- **pointe,** Fr. — point
- **polje,** S./C. — plain, basin
- **poluostrov,** Rus. — peninsula
- **pont,** Fr. — bridge
- **ponta, pontal,** Port. — point
- **porto,** It. — port
- **presa,** Sp. — reservoir, dam
- **presqu'île,** Fr. — peninsula
- **proliv,** Rus. — strait
- **puerto,** Sp. — port
- **pulau,** Indon., Mal. — island
- **puncak,** Indon. — peak
- **punta,** It., Sp. — point, peak
- **qundao,** Ch. — islands
- **rão., ribeirão,** Port. — river
- **ras, ra's,** Ara. — cape
- **rās,** Per. — cape
- **récif,** Fr. — reef
- **represa,** Port. — dam, reservoir
- **-retto,** Jpn. — islands
- **ría,** Sp. — ria (inlet)
- **rib., ribeira,** Port. — brook
- **ribeirão,** Port. — river
- **rio,** Port. — river
- **río,** Sp. — river
- **riviera,** It. — coast
- **rivière,** Fr. — river
- **roca,** Sp. — rock
- **rocca,** It. — rock, mountain
- **rt,** S./C. — cape
- **sa., serra,** Port. — range
- **sahrā',** Ara. — desert
- **-saki,** Jpn. — cape
- **salar,** Sp. — salt flat
- **salina(s),** Sp. — salt marsh, salt flat
- **salto(s),** Port., Sp. — waterfall
- **-sammyaku,** Jpn. — range
- **-san,** Jpn., Kor. — mountain
- **-sanmaek,** Kor. — mountains
- **Schloss,** Ger. — castle
- **sebkha,** Ara. — salt flat
- **See(n),** Ger. — lake(s)
- **selat,** Indon. — strait
- **seno,** Sp. — sound
- **serra,** Port. — range, mountain
- **serranía(s),** Sp. — ridge(s)
- **shan,** Ch. — mountain(s), island
- **shanmo,** Ch. — mountains
- **-shima,** Jpn. — island
- **-shotō,** Jpn. — islands
- **sierra,** Sp. — range, ridge
- **-sjø,** Nor. — lake
- **-sjön,** Swe. — lake, bay
- **-sø,** Dan. — lake
- **Spitze,** Ger. — peak
- **sta., santa,** Port., Sp. — saint
- **ste., sainte,** Fr. — saint
- **step',** Rus. — steppe
- **štít,** Slo. — peak
- **sto., santo,** Port., Sp. — saint
- **stretto,** It. — strait
- **Strom,** Ger. — stream
- **-ström, -strömmen,** Swe. — stream
- **-su,** Kor. — river
- **-suidō,** Jpn. — channel
- **Sund,** Ger. — sound
- **-sund,** Swe. — sound
- **-take,** Jpn. — mountain
- **Tal,** Ger. — valley
- **tanjong,** Mal. — cape
- **tanjung,** Indon. — cape
- **tao,** Ch. — island
- **teluk,** Indon. — bay
- **thale,** Thai — lagoon
- **-tō,** Jpn. — island
- **tônlé,** Cbd. — lake
- **-tunturi,** Finn. — hill, mountain
- **ujung,** Indon. — cape
- **-umi,** Jpn. — lagoon
- **-ura,** Jpn. — lake
- **valle,** It., Sp. — valley
- **vallée,** Fr. — valley
- **vârful,** Rom. — mountain
- **-vatn,** Ice., Nor. — lake
- **vdkhr., vodokhranilishche,** Rus. — reservoir
- **-vesi,** Finn. — lake
- **-viken,** Swe. — gulf
- **vodokhranilishche,** Rus. — reservoir
- **vodoskhovyshche,** Ukr. — reservoir
- **vol., volcán,** Sp. — volcano
- **wādī,** Ara. — wadi
- **wāhat, wāḩāt,** Ara. — oasis
- **wan,** Ch., Jpn. — bay
- **-yama,** Jpn. — mountain
- **yarımadası,** Tur. — peninsula
- **yoma,** Bur. — mountains
- **yumco,** Tib. — lake
- **yunhe,** Ch. — canal
- **-zaki,** Jpn. — point
- **zaliv,** Rus. — gulf, bay
- **zatoka,** Ukr. — gulf, bay
- **zee,** Du. — sea, lake

Abbreviations of Geographical Names and Terms

Ab., Can..... Alberta, Can.
Afg. ....Afghanistan
Afr. ....Africa
Ak., U.S. .... Alaska, U.S.
Al., U.S. ....Alabama, U.S.
Alb. ....Albania
Alg. ....Algeria
Ang. ....Angola
Ant. ....Antarctica
Ar., U.S.... Arkansas, U.S.
Arg. ....Argentina
Arm. ....Armenia
Aus. ....Austria
Austl. ....Australia
Az., U.S. .....Arizona, U.S.
Azer............. Azerbaijan
B. ....Bay
Bah. ....Bahamas
Bahr. ....Bahrain
Barb. ....Barbados
B.C., Can. ....British
        Columbia, Can.
Bdi. ....Burundi
Bel. ....Belgium
Bela. ....Belarus
Bhu. ....Bhutan
Bngl. ....Bangladesh
Bol. ....Bolivia
Bos. ....Bosnia
        and Hercegovina
Bots. ....Botswana
Braz. ....Brazil
Bul. ....Bulgaria
Burkina ...... Burkina Faso
C. ....Cape
Ca., U.S. .....California, U.S.
Camb. ....Cambodia
Can. ....Canada
C.A.R..............Central
        African Republic
Cay. Is. ..... Cayman Islands
C. Iv. .... Cote d'Ivoire
Co., U.S. .. Colorado, U.S.
Col. ....Colombia
C.R. .... Costa Rica
Cro. ....Croatia
Ct., U.S. ....
        Connecticut, U.S.

Ctry. ....Country
C.V. ....Cape Verde
Cyp. ....Cyprus
Czech Rep......... Czech
        Republic
D.C., U.S. ......District of
        Columbia, U.S.
De., U.S. .. Delaware, U.S.
Den............Denmark
Dep. ....Dependency
Des....................Desert
Dji. ....Djibouti
Ec. ....Ecuador
El Sal. ....El Salvador
Eng., U.K. .England, U.K.
Eq. Gui.........Equatorial
        Guinea
Erit. ....Eritrea
Est. ....Estonia
Eth. ....Ethiopia
Eur....................Europe
Falk. Is....Falkland Islands
Fin. ....Finland
Fl., U.S. ......Florida, U.S.
Fr. ....France
Fr. Gu. ..... French Guiana
G. ....Gulf
Ga., U.S. .....Georgia, U.S.
Gam. ....Gambia
Gaza Str. .... Gaza Strip
Geor. ....Georgia
Ger. ....Germany
Grc. ....Greece
Guad. ....Guadeloupe
Guat. ....Guatemala
Gui. ....Guinea
Gui.-B. ..... Guinea-Bissau
Guy. ....Guyana
Hi., U.S. ......Hawaii, U.S.
H.K. ....Hong Kong
Hond............Honduras
Hung. ....Hungary
I. ....Island
Ia., U.S. ......Iowa, U.S.
Ice. ....Iceland
Id., U.S. .... Idaho, U.S.
Il., U.S. ......Illinois, U.S.

In., U.S. ...... Indiana, U.S.
Indon. ....Indonesia
Ire. ....Ireland
Is. ....Islands
Isr. ....Israel
Jam. ....Jamaica
Jord. ....Jordan
Kaz. ....Kazakhstan
Ks., U.S. .....Kansas, U.S.
Kuw. ....Kuwait
Ky., U.S. ..Kentucky, U.S.
Kyrg............Kyrgyzstan
L. ....Lake
La., U.S....Louisiana, U.S.
Lat. ....Latvia
Leb. ....Lebanon
Leso. ....Lesotho
Lib. ....Liberia
Lith. ....Lithuania
Lux. ....Luxembourg
Ma., U.S. .. Massachusetts,
        U.S.
Mac. ....Macedonia
Madag. ....Madagascar
Malay. ....Malaysia
Mart............Martinique
Maur............Mauritania
Mb., Can...................
        Manitoba, Can.
Md., U.S...Maryland, U.S.
Me., U.S. ....Maine, U.S.
Mex. ....Mexico
Mi., U.S. ..Michigan, U.S.
Mn., U.S..Minnesota, U.S.
Mo., U.S....Missouri, U.S.
Mol. ....Moldova
Mong. ....Mongolia
Monts. ....Montserrat
Mor. ....Morocco
Moz. ....Mozambique
Ms., U.S....................
        Mississippi, U.S.
Mt. ....Mountain
Mt., U.S. .. Montana, U.S.
Mts. ....Mountains
Mwi. ....Malawi
Myan............Myanmar

N.A. ....North America
N.B., Can. ....New
        Brunswick, Can.
N.C., U.S. ....North
        Carolina, U.S.
N. Cal. ....New Caledonia
N.D., U.S. .... North
        Dakota, U.S.
Ne., U.S. ..Nebraska, U.S.
Neth. ....Netherlands
Neth. Ant. ...Netherlands
        Antilles
Nf, Can... Newfoundland,
        Can.
N.H., U.S. ....New
        Hampshire, U.S.
Nic. ....Nicaragua
Nig. ....Nigeria
N. Ire., U.K....Northern
        Ireland, U.K.
N.J., U.S. ....
        New Jersey, U.S.
N. Kor. ...... Korea, North
N.M., U.S. ......New
        Mexico, U.S.
Nmb............Namibia
Nor. ....Norway
N.S., Can. ....Nova
        Scotia, Can.
N.T., Can......Northwest
        Territories, Can.
Nv., U.S. .... Nevada, U.S.
N.Y., U.S. ....
        New York, U.S.
N.Z............ New Zealand
Oc. .... Oceania
Oh., U.S. ...... Ohio, U.S.
Ok., U.S. .Oklahoma, U.S.
On., Can... Ontario, Can.
Or., U.S...... Oregon, U.S.
Pa., U.S. ....
        Pennsylvania, U.S.
Pak. ....Pakistan
Pan. ....Panama
Pap. N. Gui........ Papua
        New Guinea

Para. .... Paraguay
P.E., Can. .Prince Edward
        Island, Can.
Pen. ....Peninsula
Phil. ....Philippines
Pk. ....Peak
Plat. ....Plateau
Pol. ....Poland
Polit. Reg. ..Political Region
Port. ....Portugal
P.Q., Can. ..Quebec, Can.
P.R. ....Puerto Rico
Prov. ....Province
R. ....River
Ra. ....Range
Region ....Reg.
Res. ....Reservoir
R.I., U.S. ....Rhode
        Island, U.S.
Rom. ....Romania
Rw............Rwanda
S.A. ....South America
S. Afr. ....South Africa
Sau. Ar.........Saudi Arabia
S.C., U.S. ....South
        Carolina, U.S.
Scot., U.K. ....
        Scotland, U.K.
S.D., U.S. ....South
        Dakota, U.S.
Sen............Senegal
Sk., Can.... Saskatchewan,
        Can.
S. Kor. ...... Korea, South
S.L. ....Sierra Leone
Slvk. ....Slovakia
Slvn. ....Slovenia
Som. ....Somalia
Sp. N. Afr. .... Spanish
        North Africa
Sri L. ....Sri Lanka
Str. ....Strait
St. Vin. .... St. Vincent
        and the Grenadines
Sur. ....Suriname
Swaz. ....Swaziland

Swe............Sweden
Switz............Switzerland
Tai. ....Taiwan
Taj. ....Tajikistan
Tan. ....Tanzania
Ter. ....Territory
Thai............Thailand
Tn., U.S. .Tennessee, U.S.
Trin. ....Trinidad
        and Tobago
Tun. ....Tunisia
Tur. ....Turkey
Turk............Turkmenistan
Tx., U.S. .....Texas, U.S.
U.A.E. ....United
        Arab Emirates
Ug. ....Uganda
U.K.............United Kingdom
Ukr............Ukraine
Ur. ....Uruguay
U.S. ....United States
Ut., U.S. ......Utah, U.S.
Uzb............Uzbekistan
Va., U.S....Virginia, U.S.
Ven. ....Venezuela
Viet. ....Vietnam
V.I.U.S. ....Virgin
        Islands (U.S.)
Vol. ....Volcano
Vt., U.S. .....Vermont, U.S.
Wa., U.S. ....
        Washington, U.S.
Wales, U.K. . Wales, U.K.
Wal./F. ..Wallis and Futuna
W.B. ....West Bank
Wi., U.S. .Wisconsin, U.S.
W. Sah. .... Western Sahara
W. Sam. .....Western Samoa
W.V., U.S. ....West
        Virginia, U.S.
Wy., U.S...Wyoming, U.S.
Yk., Can. ....Yukon
        Territory, Can.
Yugo. ....Yugoslavia
Zam. ....Zambia
Zimb............Zimbabwe

Index

This universal index includes in a single alphabetical list approximately 4,100 names of features that appear on the reference maps. Each name is followed by geographical coordinates and a page reference.

Abbreviation and Capitalization
Abbreviations of names on the maps have been standardized as much as possible. Names that are abbreviated on the maps are generally spelled out in full in the index. Periods are used after all abbreviations regardless of local practice. The abbreviation "St." is used only for "Saint". "Sankt" and other forms of this term are spelled out.

Most initial letters of names are capitalized, except for a few Dutch names, such as "'s-Gravenhage." Capitalization of non-initial words in a name generally follows local practice.

Alphabetization
Names are alphabetized in the order of the letters of the English alphabet. Spanish *ll* and *ch*, for example, are not treated as distinct letters. Furthermore, diacritical marks are disregarded in alphabetization. German or Scandinavian *ä* or *ö* are treated as *a* or *o*.

The names of physical features may appear inverted, since they are always alphabetized under the proper, not the generic, part of the name, thus: "Gibraltar, Strait of." Otherwise every entry, whether consisting of one word or more, is alphabetized as a single continuous entity. "Lakeland," for example, appears after "Lake Forest" and before "La Línea." Names beginning with articles (Le Havre, Al Manāmah, Ad Dawhah) are not inverted. Names beginning "St.," "Ste." and "Sainte" are alphabetized as though spelled "Saint."

In the case of identical names, towns are listed first, then political divisions, then physical features.

Generic Terms
Except for cities, the names of all features are followed by terms that represent broad classes of features, for example, *Mississippi, R.* or *Alabama, State.*

Country names and names of features that extend beyond the boundaries of one country are followed by the name of the continent in which each is located. Country designations follow the names of all other places in the index. The locations of places in the United States and the United Kingdom are further defined by abbreviations that indicate the state or political division in which each is located.

Page References and Geographical Coordinates

The geographical coordinates and page references are found in the last columns of each entry.

Latitude and longitude coordinates for point features, such as cities and mountain peaks, indicate the locations of the symbols. For extensive areal features, such as countries or mountain ranges, or linear features, such as canals and rivers, locations are given for the position of the type as it appears on the map.

Index

Santa Fe de Bogotá, Col. 5N 74W 104
Santa Lucia, Ur. 34S 56W 106
Santa Maria, Braz. 30S 54W 106
Santa Marta, Col. 11N 74W 104
Santa Monica, Ca., U.S. 34N 118W 84
Santa Rosa, Arg. 37S 64W 106
Santander, Spain 43N 4W 120
Santa Rosa, Ca., U.S. 38N 123W 84
Santiago, Chile 33S 71W 106
Santiago de Campostela, Spain 43N 9W 120
Santiago de Cuba, Cuba 20N 76W 97
Santiago del Estero, Arg. 28S 64W 106
Santo Domingo, Dom. Rep. 18N 70W 97
Santos, Braz. 24S 46W 106
São Carlos, Braz. 22S 48W 105
São Francisco, R., Braz. 9S 40W 105
São Gonçalo, Braz. 23S 43W 106
São João del Rei, Braz. 21S 44W 106
São João de Meriti, Braz. 23S 43W 106
São Luis (Maranhão), Braz. 3S 43W 105
Saone, R., Fr. 46N 5E 117
São Paulo, Braz. 24S 47W 106
São Vicente, Braz. 24S 46W 106
Sapele, Nig. 6N 5E 128
Sapporo, Japan 43N 141E 147
Sarajevo, Bos. 43N 18E 121
Sarandi, Arg. 34S 58W 106
Saransk, Russia 54N 45E 115
Sarapul, Russia 56N 54E 115
Sarasota, Fl., U.S. 27N 83W 93
Saratov, Russia 52N 45E 115
Sarawak, Polit. Reg., Malay. 3N 113E 148
Sardinia, I., Italy 40N 9E 117
Sarnia, On., Can. 43N 82W 73
Sasarām, India 25N 84E 143
Sasebo, Japan 33N 130E 147
Saskatchewan, Prov., Can. 55N 108W 72
Saskatchewan, R., Can. 54N 103W 72
Saskatoon, Sk., Can. 52N 107W 72
Sassari, Italy 41N 9E 117
Satu Mare, Rom. 48N 23E 121
Saudarkrokur, Ice. 66N 20W 116
Saudi Arabia, Ctry., Asia 27N 42E 142
Savannah, Ga., U.S. 32N 81W 93
Savannah, R., U.S. 33N 82W 93
Savona, Italy 44N 8E 117
Sawhāj, Egypt 27N 32E 129
Sayḩūt, Yemen 15N 51E 142
Sayr Usa, Mong. 45N 107E 146
Say'un, Yemen 16N 49E 142
Schaffhausen, Switz. 48N 9E 117
Schenectady, N.Y., U.S. 43N 74W 91
Schleswig, Ger. 55N 10E 116
Scotland, Polit. Reg., U.K. 57N 3W 116
Scottsbluff, Ne., U.S. 42N 104W 88
Scranton, Pa., U.S. 42N 76W 91
Seattle, Wa., U.S. 48N 122W 82
Sedalia, Mo., U.S. 39N 93W 87
Segovia, Spain 41N 4W 120
Seine, R., Fr. 49N 1E 117
Sekondi-Takoradi, Ghana 5N 2W 128
Selkirk Mts., B.C., Can. 51N 117W 72
Selma, Al., U.S. 32N 87W 92
Selvas, Reg., Braz. 5S 64W 104
Semarang, Indon. 7S 110E 148
Semey, Kaz. 50N 80E 140
Semipalatinsk, see Semey, Kaz. 50N 80E 140
Sendai, Japan 38N 141E 147
Senegal, Ctry., Afr. 15N 15W 128
Seoul (Sŏul), S. Kor. 38N 127E 147
Sept-Îles, P.Q., Can. 50N 66W 73
Serov, Russia 60N 60E 115
Serpukhov, Russia 55N 37E 115
Sérrai, Grc. 41N 24E 121
Settat, Mor. 33N 7W 128
Setúbal, Port. 39N 9W 120
Sevastopol', Ukr. 45N 34E 115
Severnaya Zemlya, Is., Russia 79N 100E 141
Sevilla, Spain 37N 6W 120
Seychelles, Ctry., Afr. 4S 55E 53
Sezela, S. Afr. 30S 30E 131
Sfax, Tun. 35N 11E 128
Shache (Yarkand), China 38N 77E 146
Shāhjahānpur, India 28N 80E 143
Shakhrisyabz, Uzb. 39N 68E 140
Shakhty, Russia 48N 40E 115
Shalqar, Kaz. 48N 60E 140
Shanghai, China 31N 121E 147
Shanshan, China 43N 90E 146
Shantou, China 23N 117E 147
Shaoguan, China 25N 114E 147
Shaoxing, China 30N 121E 147
Shaoyang, China 27N 112E 147
Sharon, Pa., U.S. 41N 80W 90
Shaunavon, Sk., Can. 50N 108W 72
Shawnee, Ok., U.S. 35N 97W 87
Sheboygan, Wi., U.S. 44N 88W 89
Sheffield, Eng., U.K. 53N 1W 117
Shenkursk, Russia 62N 43E 140
Shenyang, China 42N 123E 147
Sherbrooke, P.Q., Can. 45N 72W 73
Sheridan, Wy., U.S. 45N 107W 83
Sherman, Tx., U.S. 34N 97W 87
Shetland Is., Scot., U.K. 60N 2W 116
Shibām, Yemen 16N 49E 142
Shibīn al Kawm, Egypt 31N 31E 121
Shijiazhuang, China 38N 115E 147
Shikārpur, Pak. 28N 69E 143
Shikoku, I., Japan 33N 135E 147
Shillong, India 26N 92E 143
Shimonoseki, Japan 34N 131E 147
Shīrāz, Iran 30N 52E 142
Shivpuri, India 26N 78E 143
Shkoder, Alb. 42N 19E 121
Sholāpur, India 18N 76E 143
Shreveport, La., U.S. 32N 94W 95
Shuangliao, China 44N 123E 147
Shumen, Bul. 43N 27E 121
Shuqrah, Yemen 14N 46E 142
Shūshtar, Iran 32N 49E 142
Shuya, Russia 57N 41E 140
Shymkent, Kaz. 42N 70E 140
Siālkot, Pak. 33N 74E 143
Šiauliai, Lith. 56N 23E 116
Šibenik, Cro. 44N 16E 121
Sibiu, Rom. 46N 24E 121
Sibolga, Indon. 2N 99E 148
Sicily, I., Italy 37N 14E 117
Sidi bel Abbès, Alg. 35N 1W 128
Sidi Ifni, Mor. 29N 10W 128
Siena, Italy 43N 11E 117
Sierra Leone, Ctry., Afr. 9N 13W 128
Sierra Nevada, Mts., Ca., U.S. 38N 120W 84
Silifke, Tur. 36N 34E 121
Silistra, Bul. 44N 27E 121
Silver Spring, Md., U.S. 39N 77W 91
Simferopol', Ukr. 45N 34E 115
Simla, India 31N 77E 143
Singapore, Ctry., Asia 1N 104E 148
Sinop, Tur. 42N 35E 121
Sinŭiju, N. Kor. 40N 125E 147
Sioux City, Ia., U.S. 42N 96W 88
Sioux Falls, S.D., U.S. 44N 97W 88
Sioux Lookout, On., Can. 50N 92W 73
Sipiwesk, Mb., Can. 56N 97W 72
Siracusa, Italy 37N 15E 121
Sirājganj, Bngl. 25N 90E 143
Sisak, Cro. 45N 16E 121
Sittwe, Myan. 20N 93E 146
Sivas, Tur. 40N 37E 121
Skagerrak, Str., Den.-Nor. 57N 8E 116
Skelleftea, Swe. 65N 21E 116
Skikda, Alg. 37N 7E 128
Skopje, Mac. 42N 21E 121
Skovorodino, Russia 54N 124E 141
Slavgorod, Russia 53N 79E 140
Slavonski Brod, Cro. 45N 18E 121
Sligo, Ire. 54N 8W 116
Sliven, Bul. 43N 26E 121
Slobodskoy, Russia 59N 50E 140
Slovakia, Ctry., Eur. 48N 20E 117
Slovenia, Ctry., Eur. 46N 15E 120
Slupsk, Pol. 54N 17E 116
Smila, Ukr. 49N 32E 121
Smith, Ab., Can. 55N 114W 72
Smolensk, Russia 55N 32E 115
Snake, R., U.S. 45N 117W 82
Sochi, Russia 44N 40E 115
Sofia (Sofiya), Bul. 43N 23E 121
Söke, Tur. 38N 27E 121
Sokoto, Nig. 13N 5E 128
Solikamsk, Russia 60N 57E 115
Sol'-Iletsk, Russia 51N 55E 140
Solomon Islands, Ctry., Oc. 7S 160E 157
Somalia, Ctry., Afr. 3N 43E 131
Sombor, Yugo. 46N 19E 121
Somerville, Ma., U.S. 42N 71W 91
Songjiang, China 31N 121E 147
Songkhla, Thai. 7N 101E 148
Sopron, Hung. 48N 17E 117
Sortavala, Russia 62N 31E 140
Sosnogorsk, Russia 63N 54E 140
Souq-Ahras, Alg. 36N 8E 120
Souris, Mb., Can. 50N 100W 72
Sousse, Tun. 36N 11E 128
South Africa, Ctry., Afr. 28S 28E 130
South Bend, In., U.S. 42N 86W 90
South Carolina, State, U.S. 34N 81W 77
South China Sea, Asia 20N 114E 147
South Dakota, State, U.S. 44N 102W 76
Southern Alps, Mts., N.Z. 44S 169E 157
South Georgia, Dep., S.A. 54S 37W 52
Southhampton, Eng., U.K. 51N 1W 117
Southhampton, I., N.T., Can. 65N 85W 73
South I., N.Z. 43S 167E 157
South Orkney Islands, Is., S.A. 60S 45W 52
South Saskatchewan, R., Can. 50N 110W 72
South Shields, Eng., U.K. 55N 1W 116
Sovetsk (Tilsit), Russia 55N 22E 116
Sovetskaya Gavan', Russia 49N 140E 141
Spain, Ctry., Eur. 40N 4W 120
Spartanburg, S.C., U.S. 35N 82W 93
Spassk-Dal'niy, Russia 44N 133E 141
Split, Cro. 43N 16E 121
Spokane, Wa., U.S. 48N 117W 82
Spola, Ukr. 49N 32E 121
Springfield, Il., U.S. 40N 90W 90
Springfield, Ma., U.S. 42N 73W 91
Springfield, Mo., U.S. 37N 93W 87
Springfield, Oh., U.S. 40N 84W 90
Sredne-Kolymsk, Russia 68N 155E 141
Sri Lanka (Ceylon), Ctry., Asia 7N 79E 143
Srīnagar, India 34N 75E 143
Stamford, Ct., U.S. 41N 74W 91
Stanley, Falk. Is. 52S 58W 106
Stara Zagora, Bul. 42N 26E 121
Stargard Szczeciński, Pol. 53N 15E 116
Stavanger, Nor. 59N 6E 116
Stepn'ak, Kaz. 53N 71E 140
Sterling, Col. 41N 103W 86
Sterlitamak, Russia 54N 56E 115
Stettler, Ab., Can. 52N 113W 72
Steubenville, Oh., U.S. 40N 81W 90
Stewart, I., N.Z. 47S 168E 157
Stif, Alg. 36N 5E 128
Stockholm, Swe. 59N 18E 116
Stockton, Ca., U.S. 38N 121W 84
Stoke-on-Trent, Eng., U.K. 53N 2W 117
Stralsund, Ger. 54N 13E 116
Strasbourg, Fr. 49N 8E 117
Stratford, Ct., U.S. 41N 73W 91
Stratford, On., Can. 43N 81W 90
Strumica, Mac. 41N 23E 121
Stryy, Ukr. 49N 24E 121
Stuttgart, Ger. 49N 9E 117
Subic, Phil. 15N 120E 149
Subotica, Yugo. 46N 20E 121
Sucre, Bol. 19S 65W 104
Sudan, Ctry., Afr. 15N 29E 129
Sudbury, On., Can. 46N 81W 73
Sudetes, Mts., Czech Rep.-Pol. 51N 16E 117
Suez (As Suways), Egypt 30N 33E 129
Suez, G. of, Egypt 29N 33E 129
Suez Canal, Egypt 30N 32E 129
Suifenhe, China 45N 131E 147
Sukabumi, Indon. 7S 107E 148
Sukhumi, Geor. 43N 41E 115
Sukkur, Pak. 28N 69E 143
Sulina, Rom. 45N 30E 121
Sulu Sea, Malay.-Phil. 9N 119E 148
Sumatra (Sumatera), I., Indon. 2N 100E 148
Sumba, I., Indon. 10S 119E 148
Sunderland, Eng., U.K. 55N 1W 116
Sundsvall, Swe. 62N 19E 116
Sumy, Ukr. 51N 35E 115
Suntar, Russia 62N 118E 141
Superior, Wi., U.S. 47N 92W 89
Superior, L., Can.-U.S. 48N 88W 89
Şūr (Tyre), Leb. 33N 35E 121
Şūr, Oman 22N 59E 142
Surabaya, Indon. 7S 113E 148
Surakarta, Indon. 8S 111E 148
Surat, India 21N 73E 143
Surgut, Russia 61N 74E 140
Suriname, Ctry., S.A. 4N 56W 105
Surt, Libya 31N 17E 129
Susquehanna, R., U.S. 40N 76W 91
Suzhou, China 31N 121E 147
Svalbard, Is., Nor. 74N 20E 53
Sverdlovsk, see Yekaterinburg, Russia 57N 61E 115
Svobodnyy, Russia 51N 128E 141
Swansea, Wales, U.K. 52N 4W 117
Swaziland, Ctry., Afr. 27S 31E 130
Sweden, Ctry., Eur. 60N 14E 116
Sweetwater, Tx., U.S. 32N 100W 94
Switzerland, Ctry., Eur. 47N 8E 117
Sydney, Austl. 34S 151E 157
Syktyvkar, Russia 61N 50E 140
Synel'nykove, Ukr. 48N 36E 121
Syracuse, N.Y., U.S. 43N 76W 91
Syr Darya, R., Asia 46N 61E 140
Syria, Ctry., Asia 34N 38E 142
Syzran', Russia 53N 48E 115
Szczecin (Stettin), Pol. 53N 15E 116
Szczecinek, Pol. 54N 17E 116
Szeged, Hung. 46N 20E 117
Székesfehérvár, Hung. 47N 18E 117
Szolnok, Hung. 47N 20E 117
Szombathely, Hung. 47N 17E 117

T

Tabrīz, Iran 38N 46E 142
Tacheng, China 47N 83E 146
Tacloban, Phil. 11N 125E 149
Tacoma, Wa., U.S. 47N 122W 82
Tacuarembó, Ur. 32S 56W 106
Tadjoura, Dji. 12N 43E 142
Taegu, S. Kor. 36N 129E 147
Taganrog, Russia 47N 39E 115
Tagus, R., Port.-Spain 39N 8W 120